W9-CAB-980

HIMSELF!

ALSO BY EUGENE KENNEDY

The Genius of the Apostolate
(*with Paul F. D'Arcy*)

Fashion Me a People

Comfort My People

The People Are the Church

A Time for Love

The Catholic Priest in the United States:
  Psychological Investigations (*with Victor J. Heckler*)

What a Modern Catholic Believes about Sex

In the Spirit, in the Flesh

The New Sexuality: Myths, Fables, and Hang-ups

What a Modern Catholic Believes about Marriage

The Pain of Being Human

The Heart of Loving

Living with Loneliness

The Return to Man

Living with Everyday Problems

Believing

The Joy of Being Human

A Contemporary Meditation on Prayer

Human Rights and Psychological Research:
  A Debate on Psychology and Ethics (*Editor*)

A Sense of Life, a Sense of Sin

If You Really Knew Me, Would You Still Like Me?

St. Patrick's Day with Mayor Daley
  and Other Things Too Good to Miss

The Trouble Book

On Becoming a Counselor

Sexual Counseling

A Time for Being Human

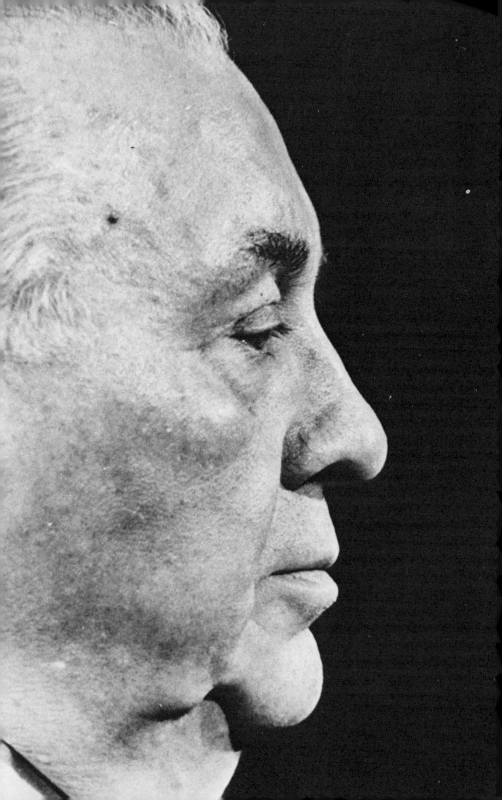

HIMSELF!

The Life and Times of Mayor Richard J. Daley

EUGENE KENNEDY

The Viking Press   New York

Copyright © Personal Consulting Services, Ltd., 1978
All rights reserved
First published in 1978 by The Viking Press
625 Madison Avenue, New York, N.Y. 10022
Published simultaneously in Canada by
Penguin Books Canada Limited

LIBRARY OF CONGRESS CATALOGING IN PUBLICATION DATA
Kennedy, Eugene C
Himself: the life and times of
Mayor Richard J. Daley.
Includes index.
1. Daley, Richard J., 1902–1976.
2. Chicago—Mayors—Biography.
3. Chicago—Politics and government—1950–   I. Title.
F548.52.D35K46   977.3'11'040924   [B]   77-28792
ISBN 0-670-37258-7

Printed in the United States of America
Set in CRT Times Roman

For Gertrude and Don
and
Isabel and Jim

Author's Note

The idea for this book came from Mrs. Jacqueline Onassis, whose encouragement and editorial advice at every stage of its development were consistently bright, perceptive, and marked with good humor. I am grateful as well to the hundreds of people who granted interviews or provided helpful records. My special thanks go to Dick Trezevant, who, as a friend and advisor, is in a class by himself.

Contents

Illustrations follow pages 42, 98, 148, and 208

Introduction

The afternoon was filled with the filtered light and strange quiet of the season's first heavy snow. It was falling just across Lake Michigan from Chicago while that city stood against the piercing winds that brewed the snow from the lake's moisture and carried it eastward. Driving back to Chicago on the day Richard Daley died was like passing through a great shifting curtain of dull light that would part and lift away as one passed the midpoint at the bottom of the lake. It provided mood enough in the silent anonymity it gave the world for thoughts about the mayor and his city.

The news media would predictably describe him as "the last of the big city bosses," and so, perhaps, he was. In that diffuse light of that late afternoon he seemed that and more, a chieftain who had known war and triumph and loss, an Irish leader, of course, but one who resembled every true chieftain who ever lived. What were chieftains like? And how, even for a clinical psychologist, could some approach be made to a better understanding of this man whose death had left Chicago in a sudden void of mourning? Psychology was good training for the task, and a writer's need to feel his way into other persons and situations would also help. The contract was already signed and the long haul of research lay still ahead. How much, I wondered, would it all be changed by his death? Would people talk less or talk more? Could Daley, as I had expected even when he was alive, be best overheard, could he be found in the effects and reactions which his presence had caused in other persons? This drive through the blurred world of snow was the beginning of a long journey of listening and study, of interviewing and reflecting, and of sorting out a thousand images and impressions.

He was, it seemed to me then, a true chieftain, with all the complexities of that designation. I would later find a description in a book on chieftains written by a British anthropologist:

> The ideal chiefly virtues which are looked for are those of generosity, fatherliness, hospitality and (much more ambivalently) strength. . . . The might of chieftainship, its greater strength than the strength of ordinary people, though it enables chiefs to bear the weight of so many social responsibilities, is more ambivalent in its moral value. Most proverbs and sayings that reflect this aspect of chieftainship have a cynical or else a menacing ring. "The word of a chief builds a *kraal*." (The chief's word is powerful and must be obeyed.) "The chief is a hornless cow" (*viz*, he is unpredictable and capricious). "The chief's arm has a long reach." "The chief does not put in the second blow, he is the killer." (A chief gets credit for and profit from what his subjects do.) Here we see reflected that ambivalent quality in all domination. (Ian Hamnett, *Chieftainship and Legitimacy* [London and Boston: Routledge & Kegan Paul, 1975], p. 88.)

Yes, there was something in this chieftainship thesis, for the idea was as Irish and as tough as the mayor himself. Yet it was more than that, because few public figures have been the objects of so much ambivalent feeling as Richard J. Daley. He had been invested by many observers with every vice and foible so that he floated on the slipstream of media consciousness as a bloated and ruthless big city boss, whose motives were never untainted and whose methods were at best accidentally honorable. On the other hand, he was close to being beloved in Chicago by the thousands of ordinary people who found in him a figure of identification, a man who knew how to speak to their stomachs and hearts directly. Yes, and even the bankers liked him almost as much as the bus riders and other common people. What would he be like as I tried to find out more about this political leader who pulled back from anyone who tried to write about him, who once grew impatient with a would-be biographer and closed the interview with the words, "What I know goes with me"? Well, now he was gone; was it all gone as well, or were there traces and signs, a trail that could still be followed, a personality that would coalesce from the interviews and research that remained to be done?

There was little doubt in my mind that chieftainship was the right metaphor. Chieftains have many things in common. All possess presence, something about them that makes others step back ever so slightly, a quality that invites association while it discourages intimacy. De Gaulle had been that kind of chieftain and had written about the importance of a natural leader's preserving an element of mystery, a core of the unknowable about him. And unknowability was characteristic of Daley, whose familiar face kept its secrets and guarded its processes of judgment from strangers.

True chieftains never leave any doubt about who is in charge. Their way of amassing and keeping power for themselves is one of the causes of ambivalent feelings toward them. They never seem uncertain about the nature of existence or about their role in exercising power. They are the only ones who can finally decide on even the slightest of matters; they hold tightly the power to dispense favors, promotions, or other largess; lasting chieftains never allow anyone even to seem to share power or authority with them. And they use their power against their foes surely, but also against friends if they forget for a moment who is in charge.

Such chieftains do not debate their positions endlessly; they live in the world of action, and they settle for what works in the human condition and neither long for nor seek perfect solutions. They trust their instincts about human nature and move swiftly. That is one of the other reasons that many of their associates experience admiration and fear or resentment toward them at the same time. They understand that the chieftain has made them, has given them their positions, and they are totally dependent on him, just as he is, in a sense, totally independent of them. The leader's power and strength attract them but also bind them closely and sometimes uncomfortably.

Real chieftains also stay in office; they keep getting re-elected; they know how to hold on to their power. Pseudo-chieftains arise on the political scene from time to time and then vanish, broken on the wheel of re-election, their lack of staying power finally revealed in their naiveté about exercising authority. They seem to lack the toughness or self-confidence needed to wield power effectively. "The chief," as the proverb goes, "does not put in the second blow." In an imperfect world he does what has to be done, forging compromises and less than ideal solutions constantly. Political romantics—how filled the woods of political exile are with these!—do not have the heart or the instincts for such gutty activities. But they are not chieftains.

So the metaphor seemed right for Richard Daley as the afternoon ceded its light and the veil of snow opened to a clear view of the steel mills at the southern edge of the city. Past these, at the rise of the Skyway Bridge, hung a great sign, one of hundreds like it at every gate to his city: WELCOME TO CHICAGO, RICHARD J. DALEY, MAYOR. Now it was a pressing invitation to try to understand this powerful and extraordinary man who had so little use for writers or for those who wished to know more about him. The months ahead would be spent in reading everything that had been written about the now dead mayor, in libraries and newspaper files, but more still in interviewing hundreds of people who knew or worked with Daley. Each incident or conversation I reported would have to be supported by at least two persons; each fact would have to be checked and checked again. There would be travel as well to all the places and backgrounds of Daley's life, for one would need the feel of such locations, whether it was Schaller's Pump in Bridgeport or the State House in Springfield. Daley would finally be found everywhere in the effects he had on others, in the way their existences had taken on a shape around his own dominating personality.

Daley's presence would perhaps be best felt at the next St. Patrick's Day parade, the first one at which Daley himself would not preside. The acting mayor, Michael Bilandic, looking uncomfortable in an outsized green fedora, joined the Irish consul and Daley's four sons in leading the marchers. But it was a day on which things did not hang together, and the precision that marked the parade when Daley lived seemed strangely missing. There were bands and floats and Irish music but, for the first time, the smell of marijuana drifted through the crowds of high school students lined up along the route. And there was shouting and drinking too, and beer bottles hurled into the gutter as the parade frayed and raveled at its edges. One sensed Daley in his very absence; one felt the intensity of the control which he had exercised over Chicago in the fact that it had been released, and that things were flapping loose everywhere. Yes, this was the city where Daley could still be felt in the suddenly empty places of his passage and his presence, in the fact that Chicago would never again feel the massive control it had known in his years in office. There was an unsettled feeling in the city and a hint of prophecy as well. Chicago would look the same and seem the same for years, perhaps for generations. And yet it was already different in the strange, melancholy, and unpredictable mood of a camp where anything could happen once the chieftain had died.

EUGENE KENNEDY

[1]

"I'm Coming in Now"

Monday, December 20, 1976. For Richard J. Daley, six times mayor of Chicago, boss of bosses, living the myth of Irish chieftains twice over in his soul, it was the last day. He would die in the final hours of autumn with the pale sun as far away from the city as it would ever get; and his wake, on the day of the year's least light, would begin in the first hour of winter.

There is a tension in the bridging of the seasons that outwits time, a sense of some journeys finishing and others about to start, of purposes being worked out beyond our reach in something as plain and vast as the midwestern sky. Such thoughts were not for Mayor Daley on that raw December high noon; at best they would register like the sound of distant traffic as he traveled, more the Gaelic warrior Cuchulain than the Irish poet, to the far South Side of Chicago for the dedication of a new gymnasium at Mann Park. For, according to legend, Cuchulain strapped himself to a tree in his last battle so that he could die standing up.

Daley had felt the enemy in his chest during the weekend, pain enough to arrange a Monday afternoon appointment with his doctor, whom he had seen only the previous Thursday. But his face, a mask of gravity for most emotions except for mirth and anger, revealed nothing, even to those closest to him during that morning. Control, tempered in the glowing furnaces of traditional Catholicism and political ascendancy, was not a small virtue. For the strength of self-possession, of impassiveness whether the cards were aces or deuces, was a source of power to him whether the news was good or bad, enabling him to choose his own moves against any foe: politician, newswriter—and even time itself.

Except for the pain in his chest, the morning had been a good one, almost a classic among the thousands in his mayoralty, which numbered now two years beyond the length of a generation. He had left his home on South Lowe Avenue, a street modest beyond telling with houses older than the century set no farther apart than the length of a child's cart. With his wife, Eleanor, he had driven off in his official limousine, the black 1973 Cadillac with the silver spotlights and the license plate, as sentimental as it suited him, 708-222, the number of votes cast for him in his first election in 1955. At 8:30 they arrived at the Bismarck Hotel, the gilded kind of hotel they used to build in the heart of big cities, where the Cook County Democratic Committee met, where Daley had waited out the election results six weeks before. In the Medill Room, the city department heads were waiting for their annual Christmas breakfast with the mayor, and this time as they gathered around the tables, where fresh eggnog had already been set out, they had a surprise. Colonel Jack Reilly, the mayor's chief of special events—a slender man with one black lens in his glasses and thatchy white hair, a man tougher than his frail, almost convalescent looks, a comrade over the years who could arrange parades, water festivals, and fireworks displays, a man to turn out crowds when crowds were needed—the colonel had thought of the right present for the man who, as he told his colleagues, "had everything." They would all contribute to purchase two round-trip tickets to Ireland for Daley and his wife, and they would announce the gift at the breakfast. There would be no surprise in this, of course. One courted lightning bolts with any attempt at surprise, for the mayor had not survived by allowing himself to be surprised on any occasion. Everything, even this gift of tickets, had to be cleared with Daley in advance. The room was filled with good feeling, with warmth against the cold; a hunter's breakfast was about to be set, and over the murmur of talk, Christmas carols and Irish airs drifted, played by a harpist from the Chicago Symphony. The crowd broke into applause as the Daleys entered and the mayor, at ease with Irish music and loyal friends, smiled broadly and greeted his aides. As he settled down to breakfast the harpist began to play "Danny Boy."

It was Daley's presence that held the room together, guaranteeing the lives and fortunes of everyone there and also projecting for them some sense of themselves, some awareness of purpose as well as security in life. Daley, like a tribal chief who would not surrender his spirit to the camera, was, in person, a presence that never came across on film; if there was a sense of power and vigilance about him, there was also a charm that was surprising and disarming. One felt that he was in command of his public self, that any doubts about his destiny had long since been disposed of, and that, with these behind him, he could move swiftly and surely across any stage. When he entered a room there was no hint of the simplest doubt that he was in charge. He was not unaware of his effect on others, not unreflective about the mystique of leadership and how much of it, like the reserves of any great energy supply, must be kept underground. He understood that about himself, that something of his secret, most protected self held these people in an agreeable and ambitious unity. They were there because he was there; outside the hall not one of them would have yielded a lifeboat seat to another—and that aggregate, multiplied down to the block level, was the source of Daley's ongoing power.

So he could walk quickly into the room with the lightness of a man who had given all the heavy packages to others. At seventy-four he moved well, looking more like a broad-chested old boxer than a paunchy Boss Tweed type. He wore a carefully tailored dark blue suit, a light blue shirt, and a striped tie.

But it was finally his face that commanded your attention. There was something larger and smoother and more alert about it than one expected, something pinker in his complexion, something darker in his hair, which he now wore more full at the back and sides. Yes, it was the face, with panes and slopes and outcroppings enough for a mountainside memorial, with one half of it taking away what the other half gave, that broke into the room's atmosphere like a sudden avalanche shattering the quiet of the valley's morning. So there could be the widest of smiles on one side of his face and the tempered slant of affected surprise on the other, one half twinkling in the sun and the other slightly clouded, softened in the shadows of reserve and caution; it was a splendid public face, bulging with ledges and crags that could merge into the merriest of smiles in one moment and go flat and somber and unrevealing in the next. The moods had long ago been mastered; they were instinctive by now.

An old associate, Fire Commissioner Robert Quinn, his face almost as battered as the misshapen helmet he still wore at fires, a septuagenarian like Daley who had, in 1959, caused mild panic in the city by turning on the air-raid sirens when the White Sox won the pennant, told the mayor how well he looked. Daley immediately spoke of the good Sunday he had enjoyed with his family, including all the grandchildren. Indeed, Daley on that particular Sunday had seemed to enjoy the private side of his life, the side where affection rivaled discipline, in a special way. A Christmas celebration had been held at his house that day, so that all the families of his children could be in their own homes on Christmas Day itself. There had even been a home mass, offered by an old friend, Father Gilbert Graham, and the mayor had helped prepare the informal altar and had read one of the scripture selections—words from St. Paul, "I have come to do your will, O Lord" — with emphasis and feeling. At the ritual's greeting of peace, a liturgical innovation that the traditional Daley had taken to strongly, there was a long pause while the mayor kissed all his children and grandchildren.

As Monday's breakfast drew to a close, Reilly announced to the Daleys that two tickets "await you at Aer Lingus for a trip to Ireland, where we know you're loved and which you love." The guests applauded and called for the mayor to speak. He turned to his wife, with whom he had been so engrossed at the breakfast—a waiter would recall that they talked "like young lovers"—and tried to get her to join him in rising, but finding her reluctant, he stood alone and offered an Irish wish. "From our home to your home we wish you one thing—good health, happiness, and a very Merry Christmas." In a few moments, a party that had gone well ended and the mayor, flanked by his sober-faced Chicago police bodyguards, strode through the biting wind to City Hall, in a block-sized building where soft lighting played on marble corridors and brass fixtures like those in a respectable old railroad station. The waiting elevator closed its doors and, as he had done every morning for almost half his adult life, Daley entered his office on the fifth floor.

It was then that he felt some discomfort, but at 2:00 P.M. he was scheduled to see Dr. Thomas J. Coogan, Jr., whose father had been the mayor's physician before him. Coogan had hospitalized the mayor in May 1974, when Daley had suffered a slight stroke which required an operation. Appointments had to be kept and, having cleared his desk of the paperwork of the day, he moved out of City Hall, head-of-state style, with policemen alerting other policemen over walkie-talkies, with the word that the Cadillac should be ready in a few moments. When Daley left the building, he walked across to the Civic Center Plaza, that stretch of openness in the center of the Loop where Picasso's celebrated birdlike steel structure stands and where, only ten days before, Daley, with the help of his youngest grandchildren, had lighted the city's Christmas tree. Now he wanted to look at the ice sculptures which the chefs from several of Chicago's hotels were putting on open-air display; it was another part of the public holiday that Daley loved to see presented for the people of what he always called "the great city of Chicago."

He climbed into the car and headed down the city's long

eastern leg, which reached south into the industrial area, pud-
dled by small lakes and shadowed by big factories, crossed by
the Calumet River and modern expressways, that opened at
the rim of the wide, flat fields on bands and clusters of neighborhoods, where the people who worked in the mills and believed in a decent and simple life lived. He was heading into
the Tenth Ward of Alderman Edward Vrdolyak, an ambitious
forty-year-old political leader in whose cold brown eyes Daley
may have seen something of his younger self. It was a quintes-
sential Daley trip, a journey to a man who delivered votes for
the Democrats, a comer in the party, a man with the moves and
smooth good looks of a dance instructor—a man to take care
of. It was also the kind of function that the mayor fully understood as the heart of meat-and-potatoes politics and essential,
therefore, to his own political strength and his pact of affection
with ordinary neighborhood people. Keeping in touch with
them had been a major feature of his success as mayor; spading
out earth at groundbreakings, sitting through chicken dinners,
going to wakes and funerals and dedications like this one:
They were as important as his meetings with bankers and business leaders and just as vital to his style of managing the city.

Mann Park lies in a section called Hegewisch, and it is made
up of small homes, some as old as those on the mayor's own
street, and others built on the diminishing vacant lots before
and after the Second World War. There is an open feeling to
the place; one runs into the McDonald's and the gas stations
only at the edge of the neighborhood, where the large avenues
cross each other. The park, set with a small lake, contains
playing fields, walking paths, and a large old brown stucco-
and-wood building (a not unpleasant air of the twenties about
it) to which a new gymnasium had recently been joined. It was
the kind of present an alderman liked to give to his constituents, the kind of exchange which seals indebtedness all
around, providing recreational opportunities for thousands of
people, most of them voters. It was, in other words, exactly the
occasion that summed up Daley's ordinary style and strength;

it was the kind of affair he had to go to but would not miss even if there were a choice; it was what he was in business for.

It was about 12:20 as the mayor's limousine pulled up to the new gym entrance. He had arrived, in fact, ahead of Vrdolyak. His bodyguards took his overcoat and Daley, smiling again, greeted those waiting to meet him, and let someone pin a carnation on his lapel. John Granich, a short, middle-aged attendant at the park, handed the mayor a program, saying with a smile, "You can't tell the players without a scorecard. You may even find some White Sox in there."

Daley laughed, shook the man's hand, and entered the gym, where metal folding chairs had been set up for the guests and for the 250 neighbors who had come for the occasion. Daley seemed relaxed as he looked around at the new building and chatted with the just-arrived Alderman Vrdolyak and with Edmund Kelly, the Democratic politician who headed the Chicago Park District, a man with the look of a savvy fighter who glances one way and throws his punch the other, a balding man as ambitious as Vrdolyak. How much of his life had Daley spent sitting between political competitors, rewarding each, balancing the tension between them to his own advantage?

The program was classic for a neighborhood gathering: the Grissom School band, the Hegewisch Raiders color guard team, and the Mann Park preschoolers, four-year-olds who began to sing Christmas songs without piano accompaniment. Only at the last minute had it been discovered that a piano could not fit through the new gym's doors. Daley turned sideways on his chair to see and hear the children better. Alderman Vrdolyak started to say something to Daley but the mayor raised his hand to hush him until the children were finished. Then came the speeches, brief and familiar, as indeed Daley's was; he had given it, in one version or another, in a hundred neighborhoods, in places like this hundreds of times; he would laugh good-naturedly with the local people about it. But it was the kind of speech they wanted to hear, the kind he loved to give. He thanked Kelly and Vrdolyak and said, in a speaking style that was flat and direct and filled with stubby Chicago intonations, "This building is dedicated to the people of this great community. They are making Chicago a better city, because when you have a good neighborhood, you have a good city, and this is a good neighborhood."

Santa Claus, played by park attendant Walter Lis, had given Daley a candy cane earlier, and now he approached him with a brand-new basketball. Those in charge of the ceremony had told Lis not to push the mayor about trying it out; the mayor did not like to be caught off guard with a public request which might be embarrassing. Lis was told to expect Daley to hand the ball on to Vrdolyak, so he approached the mayor, who was sitting on the aisle with his legs crossed, somewhat nervously. "Would Mayor Daley be so kind as to step up and get this basketball?"

The mayor smiled, rose, and took the ball. "Would you like to dunk one?" Lis asked, somewhat surprised that the mayor had held on to the ball.

"Sure," Daley said, stepping toward the basket. He hunched, pushed with his right hand, and the ball sailed through the hoop. He laughed and smiled at the applause and urged Vrdolyak and Kelly to try the same; they both missed and, good humor suffusing the hall, the mayor and his party turned and left for the last act, the sealing of the cornerstone for the field house. A leader of a local improvement association, Ed Borowski, announced that they were inserting a time capsule into the cornerstone and that it would include a set of "Daley for Mayor" buttons from 1955, 1959, 1963, 1967, 1971, and 1975. Vrdolyak added that they would make up a special button for "Daley in '79" and include that too.

As the crowd began to enjoy the hot dogs and soft drinks provided by the alderman, Vrdolyak asked the mayor, "Can you stay and have some fish at Phil Smidt's restaurant?"

"No," Daley replied, "I have a two o'clock appointment."

Then the mayor shook a few more hands, climbed into the limousine, and headed north against the stretch of cold white sky where, beyond the plumes of factory smoke, the skyline of downtown Chicago could be seen in the distance. It was 1:20 P.M.

The phone rang in Dr. Coogan's office. The receptionist, who had earlier been told by Dr. Coogan that the mayor would be making an unscheduled visit, picked up the receiver and heard a voice say, "Irene Fahey?"

"Yes," she answered, recognizing that the call was coming from an automobile phone.

The mayor's voice came on, "Irene, this is Mayor Daley. I'm coming in to see the doctor now."

"Yes, we're expecting you," Irene Fahey answered, and the call broke off.

At 1:45 the mayor's car pulled up to the side entrance of the 900 North Michigan building, to the canopied door on Delaware Street not more than a football field away from the 100-story Hancock Building and no more than that again from the new marble-faced 85-story Water Tower Place. Daley greeted the doorman, turned left, and entered an elevator whose inside door was painted a lacquer red. The gates opened on the second floor and Daley walked past a door displaying the legend "Gertrude Emelow Body Dynamics," toward the double-doored Suite 200 shared by Dr. Coogan and Dr. Robert H. Reid. Inside, Irene Fahey welcomed him; he seemed himself in every way and walked over to shake hands with some old friends, the Friedmans, who were sitting in the waiting room. While police officer Mike Marano, a husky, mustached bodyguard of twenty-seven, settled down to wait, Daley walked with receptionist Fahey to the examination room. He asked her how she was and told her softly that he had enjoyed his day with his family on Sunday. A new technician, who had never seen the mayor before, gave him a blue gown to replace the coat and shirt he would remove for the electrocardiogram that

Dr. Coogan had scheduled. Irene Fahey returned to her desk.

A few moments later Dr. Coogan, uncoiling the electrocardiogram paper, emerged and told the receptionist to call Dr. James Campbell at Presbyterian-St. Luke's Hospital to make arrangements to admit the mayor. Irene Fahey got one glimpse of the blue-gowned mayor walking back to the examining room as Dr. Campbell's secretary told her that Campbell was at a meeting. Irene, long accustomed to not mentioning the mayor on the phone unless specifically instructed to, waited to tell Dr. Coogan, who had gone back to explain to the mayor the need for hospitalization. The mayor said he would like to call his son, and Coogan left the room and returned to the reception area. The doctor then called personally and, having gotten through to Dr. Campbell, said he wanted him to make preparations for admitting the mayor. It was the same hospital to which Daley had been taken after his slight stroke of two and a half years before. Officer Marano stiffened in his chair.

Inside the examining room, the mayor sat in a chair and dialed the number of his son Michael, a lawyer in practice at 111 West Washington Street. Michael was talking on another line to lawyer James Collins in the I.B.M. building and interrupted this call to take the one from his father. He came back on the line to Collins, said, "My father's sick. I've got to go," and hung up. The elder Daley had told him briefly of the doctor's diagnosis, of the need for Michael to tell his mother, of the fact that he would be leaving for the hospital shortly. He put the phone back on the hook to await Dr. Coogan's return.

But something was happening to time in the dark and cold of that last day of fall, something was coming unstuck, something was getting away from him. It was as though the film of events were splintering in the projector and casting uncertain images before him. What was it that was condensed into this split second—was it hospitalization and recovery and rumors about his health all over again, was it a long recuperation, and learning to walk and work more slowly, was it the impact of these possibilities at some level deep within his unconscious?

He was strapped like the Irish warrior Cuchulain to the tree, but he would not go down in a heap to another man's will. He took one last breath and let go of it all. He slumped slightly forward in his chair as the film clattered on the floor and the screen went glaring white.

All that bodyguard Marano could see was that Dr. Coogan had moved swiftly down the hall to summon his associate, Dr. Reid, and had closed the door of the examining room. Marano jumped up and nervously asked Irene Fahey, "What's going on? They're running back and forth in there. There's something wrong!"

Irene, who would find a Christmas plant from Mayor and Mrs. Daley when she returned to her apartment later, went and listened at the door for a moment. "I don't hear a sound," she told Officer Marano, trying to reassure him.

Seconds later, Dr. Coogan emerged and said to the receptionist, "Call for an emergency squad!" and returned to the examining room.

Irene Fahey had just been reading about the new all-city emergency number, 911, and she dialed it immediately. A voice came on the line, asked for her name, and started to take down the details. She paused and went and asked Dr. Coogan if it was all right to tell them that it was for the mayor. As she told the emergency operator that it was for Mayor Daley, she could hear a quiver come into the man's voice.

Inside the examination room, Coogan and Reid had stretched the mayor out on the floor, and Coogan began to give him mouth-to-mouth resuscitation. In a few moments, two paramedic squads arrived, and they once again attached the electrocardiograph to Daley; the signals were transmitted automatically to Northwestern Memorial Hospital, where they would be monitored by Dr. James Matthews. The paramedics began closed-chest heart massage and a dextrose and water mixture was fed intravenously into the mayor's veins to keep them open. The activity was feverish in the tense, now crowded room.

Drugs aimed at starting the mayor's heartbeat were also administered: lidocaine and pronestyl. But there was no pulse; the face, the famous face was slack and ashen, and no spirit danced in the fixed pupils of Daley's open eyes. Dr. Matthews ordered the medics to begin defibrillation, the administration of electric shocks to the heart. The screen of the monitor reflected the jumbled waves of the shocks but leveled immediately afterwards into a straight line. Three times the shocks were given; three times the line flattened out. The doctors and medics exchanged glances and went back to their work. Other doctors were on their way from Northwestern; there was no sense moving the mayor, there was no time for that now.

In the confusion of the first few moments there was a report that Daley was to be taken to the Wesley Pavilion of Northwestern Hospital. Mrs. Daley and some of her children were driven there to await the mayor's arrival. In the offices of the *Chicago Sun-Times,* reports were phoned in that the mayor had been stricken while at lunch at the Tale of the Whale restaurant, which is located in the same building as the doctor's office. Someone else called: They were doing open-heart surgery on the mayor in a freight elevator. The news broke with equal confusion on the radio and spread rapidly across the city. Nobody quite knew the facts, but the mood matched the bitter, darkening afternoon. Mrs. Daley was driven from the hospital to the doctor's office, where she was brought into another room to wait while the efforts to revive her husband continued.

Father Timothy Lyne, rector of Holy Name Cathedral, left the rectory at about 2:15 P.M. to make his regular pastoral calls at Passavant Pavilion, also a part of Northwestern Hospital. Police Officer Patrick Dyra stopped the trim, gray-haired priest at the corner and said, "Father, there's some big politician they're going to take to the Wesley emergency room. Maybe you better stop by." Father Lyne quickened his pace and altered his route slightly to find out if he was needed.

As he approached the Wesley emergency room, he could see police cars and a number of ranking gold-braided officers in-

cluding the soft-spoken Assistant Deputy Commander Carl
Dobrich. "Just a minute, Father, I'll check on this," he said,
and he snapped on his walkie-talkie, listened for a moment,
and then said, "It's the mayor, at the 900 building. We'd better
take you there."

Father Lyne climbed into a squad car and was driven
through the blocked-off section of Michigan Avenue to the
doctor's office. When he arrived, Father Lyne knelt down
among the doctors to administer the last rites of the Catholic
Church by anointing the mayor's forehead; he knew instantly
that the mayor was beyond reviving even as the doctors renewed their efforts to do so.

Two doctors from Northwestern arrived, anesthesiologist
Barry Shapiro and thoracic surgeon John Sanders. The latter
inserted two tubes into the mayor's chest to relieve the pressure
that was building up in Daley's lungs and tissues as a result of
the resuscitation efforts. The electric shocks were tried again
and again and the medications were readministered. The line
on the machine remained flat. Sanders administered adrenaline directly into the mayor's heart; there was no reaction.
The work went on; the gathered family was told that medical
efforts were still being made. Mrs. Daley seemed lost in concern; she remained self-composed, like an Irishwoman await-
ing news of her husband at sea, as though she had long ago
marshaled the strength to face this moment which she knew
would one day come.

In Huguelet Place—more of a slanting alley hung with fire
escapes than a street—which runs through the block behind
the 900 building, the police had already erected barricades. At
the north end, on Walton Street, a cluster of newspaper, radio,
and television reporters had gathered. They could see the
loading dock tucked under an overhang of red brick and, although there had been no bulletins, they understood the silent,
symbolic language of what was happening. Paramedic Ambulance 42, a squat red and white Fire Department vehicle, was
backed up to the dock, and the attendants took some card-

board boxes they found there and began tearing them into flat sections which they used to screen the ambulance windows. It was a dumb show, done slowly and carefully, for there was no hurry now, a mute signal that the story had come to an end.

Upstairs the doctors, who had been joined by one of Daley's sons-in-law, Dr. Robert Vanecko, agreed that the situation was hopeless. The mayor was dead; he had been dead since the moment he hung up the phone and slumped in his chair. Dr. Coogan pronounced him so at 3:50 P.M. and went into the adjoining room to tell Mrs. Daley and the assembled children. The mayor's wife knew what he was going to say; her time for tears was not yet. She turned to her children, some of them sobbing, and said in a steady, clear voice, "Now we all have to kneel down and thank God for having this great man for forty years." She took out her rosary, knelt on the floor, and began to lead the traditional prayer. "The first sorrowful mystery," she announced, "the Agony in the Garden."

In the next room they brought a stretcher and laid the mayor, at last at peace from the fury of the efforts to save him, on it. Irene Fahey remembered that they had just bought a new blanket for the office and the attendants took it, unfolded it, and covered his body with it. The family finished their prayers and followed quietly as he was brought down the hall and back into the elevator and taken down to the basement of the building. He was carried across to the freight elevator and brought up once more to street level, to the dock where Ambulance 42 waited.

It was 4:15 P.M. A procession had been formed; it was being supervised by Central District Police Commander Paul McLaughlin—"Rosy" as they called him—the handsome, white-haired officer who had so often overseen security precautions for the mayor. He wore civilian clothes, with a shiny, star-shaped badge on the left collar of his overcoat, and looked solemn as he watched the squad cars, their blue mars lights blinking at the dusk, line up in front of the ambulance. He watched as the mayor's limousine, made ready for the family, pulled behind the ambulance. Then there was yet another car and finally more squad cars. Hordes of policemen, reporters, and onlookers stamped their feet in the cold as the procession readied itself. Over a walkie-talkie a voice could be heard. "No, it's just a question of whether they'll take him to Pres.-St. Luke's or right to the funeral home."

In a few moments the mayor's press secretary, Frank Sullivan, would come into the same alley and make the official announcement of the mayor's death. But everybody knew the truth now. The procession began to move, wrong-way on Walton up to Michigan Avenue, where the stretch of trees sparkled with tiny Christmas lights, and straight down it past all the great buildings and places into the falling night and back to Bridgeport, past the Daley bungalow, and to the neighborhood funeral home, McKeon's, directly across from the parish church.

would happen to their neighborhood now that the head of the clan lay dead, old men wiping their eyes and smiling a greeting through broken teeth, and women, mostly without makeup, their faces as direct and vulnerable as the streets and alleys of Bridgeport itself. They talked of Daley, the family man, of the Daleys as the first ones in the house when someone was sick or if someone died, of the man who—with his wife and children—was more than a mayor to them.

They came slowly past the mahogany coffin with the simple spray of roses across the closed lower section, and they gazed down on the man who had radiated so much life and power. He was dressed in blue suit, white shirt, and blue tie, and his hands clasped his rosary. He seemed greatly changed, gray in face and hair, quiet in a way no one could remember or imagine, for in life his immobile face had always held a thousand secrets and good stories, strategies undisclosed, and *his* move after *your* next one planned already. His spirit was indeed gone.

The rectory, connected by a series of intricate, old-fashioned passageways to the church, had become command post for the police as well as a haven for the Daley family. The pastor, a gentle amateur gardener whose brother Dan, of the Plumbers Council, organized each year's St. Patrick's Day parade, was speaking quietly to one of the police guards who were stationed throughout the hallways. "Phone, Father," called Shirley Connors, the attractive parish secretary, whose daughter had been Queen of the 1975 St. Patrick's Day parade.

"Yes," Father Lydon said in his quiet voice. "No, Father, I think it would be better if you didn't come for the mass. We're very crowded and there won't be much room."

He turned to a visitor. "You know, the mayor was always very helpful to me, very interested in the parish. Once, when I was just new here, he asked me how it was going. He seemed to sense that I was having some trouble. He grinned at me and said, 'Why don't you do what I do? Do your best and then the hell with them!' "

William Daley, one of the mayor's sons, a gentle, friendly young man with more than a hint of his father's features, came into Father Lydon's rooms looking for an open telephone.

"Use my private line," the pastor said, pointing toward a bookcase.

A few of the Daley grandchildren came in, drinking canned soda; they looked too young to comprehend the excitement that filled the old rectory. His family, prized by the mayor and brought out on every civic occasion, was subdued, still in shock, determined to follow the mother's decision to keep the funeral simple, to exclude the press and the other media, the intrusive reporters and photographers who had followed them all their lives, who had come to seem more the enemy than the Republicans. They would be kept out, kept at a distance from this personal time of grief. The funeral could have been held at the cathedral on the North Side. No, Mrs. Daley firmly decided, the hundred-year-old parish church where the mayor was baptized and married, the neighborhood where he lived his life, that would do. Even months later, the disappointment of some church officials could not be hidden. But she had had no second thoughts. Neither did she question her decision to have only one night of wake. She wanted the grandchildren to have a day between the funeral and Christmas Eve.

A bulky, late-middle-aged man with the look of a frustrated father-in-law in a situation comedy entered the room, also in search of a phone. He was coordinating security arrangements. "Has anybody got an aspirin?" he said, dialing a number. "What?" he said and paused. "Okay, we'll handle it." Then he hung up and turned toward a priest across the room. "Another goddamn swelled-head wants a police escort to get to the church."

Across the room, Father Lydon was hanging up from another call. "It's the Shannon Rovers," he said, referring to an Irish piping group. "They want to come with one piper piping."

"Say, Father," the security man said, taking the aspirin the priest had given him with a glass of water, "we're going to put up loudspeakers so the people outside can hear the mass tomorrow. But, Father, I've got one question: How can you keep people out of church on a cold day?"

In the church basement, the parish cook was feeding coffee and doughnuts to the policemen and firemen as they took their breaks from duty on the bitter-cold street. There were aldermen and old friends there as well, neighbors and political associates who knew their way around the parish church which had been so much a part of their lives. Joseph Power, former law partner of the mayor, whose Irish face seemed dulled by a film of shock, a man who had not been retained on the bench by the voters in the November election but who had a new political appointment with the Park District, was talking softly about Daley and about his way of dealing with others. "He wouldn't let you know what he wanted; he didn't try to force you. He wanted others to come up with proposals and he'd keep drawing them out of them. And sometimes he'd be looking sideways so you thought he wasn't listening. And then he'd say, 'Did you think of this?' and most of the time we hadn't."

Nearby, an old man with watery eyes and yellowed white hair that had been matted down by his winter hat was talking to anyone who would listen. "I knew Dick Daley as a boy. Yes, I remember him as manager of the Hamburg Club athletic team. Great lad. Say, did I tell you I'm twenty-one years retired from the Fire Department and that I hold the world's record for free-throw baskets?"

In the back of the basement a contingent of men and women began to assemble, members of the Eleventh Ward Democratic organization, the local club, just two blocks away, and they would ascend the stairs and pay their tributes together. Each wore a black, silklike emblem pinned to the lapel, lettered with the inscription *In Memoriam.*

"All right now," a man in a homburg hat and a camel's hair coat was saying. "Are we ready now? Where's Marge? Has anybody seen Marge?"

At the back of the hall the police, once again under Commander McLaughlin's steady gaze, the archetypal look of a traffic officer hearing out an improbable excuse, were devising a plan to route the mourners from the street through the basement in order to warm them up on their way to the upper church. "Now, just a minute," McLaughlin was saying, "let's get this straight . . ."

Back in the rectory it was almost supper time and the pressure had grown more intense. A young plainclothesman with a handlebar mustache, for all the world a young gun in Dodge City, was obviously distraught. "Just let any reporters try to get in that church tomorrow. We've got enough trouble already. Carter's coming, and Rockefeller, and Teddy Kennedy. Colonel Reilly's sending out the special invitations—all of them okayed by the family—and nobody gets in without one."

He spoke so vehemently that those near him pulled back just a bit. "Now," Father Lydon said gently, "I must go over the list of the priests who are coming. I think I gave the wrong list to the Secret Service."

Dan Lydon, the pastor's huskier brother, had arrived and was waiting to consult with the priest. "I'm bringing a busload of plumbers in shortly," he said, "and I think we'll come through the basement to the north door."

"Okay," his priest brother replied. "You knock when you get there and I'll let you through."

The young security man was still talking of plans and counterplans on the other side of the room. "Look, there won't be much room, probably no room for the public. So you get the people from the Eleventh Ward club into the basement beforehand, and we'll let them up from the inside when we get all the officials in."

Two blocks away stood Schaller's Pump, a Bridgeport bar and restaurant that had been a landmark, largely unrestored, for generations, since the latter days of the Irish immigrations to the area to work the canal and stockyards and to become firemen and priests and politicians. Schaller's was crowded, its long bar jammed with people who had been through the line and who now wanted a drink and some dinner and some talk. A television crew had been there earlier to capture what they thought would be the mood of an Irish wake. But while it was noisy enough, it was less than boisterous. Indeed, an edge of drabness, something slightly dank, the atmosphere and odor of some species of repression seemed to fill the air as much as the cigar smoke did.

The waitresses, with the look of colleens, hurried about their business, edging through the crowds, and at one end of the bar three men in business suits a cut above those typical of the neighborhood were standing and drinking.

"We've been here since noon," said the tallest, a man with the Irish look of someone who observes more than he discloses. Indeed, his gravity fit his profession, for he was an undertaker who had left the neighborhoods like Bridgeport behind to take care of the Irish who had prospered in various professions and businesses and had moved to suburban affluence on the far South Side. He was there with two companions who were in the same business; they had, in fact, provided the coffin for the mayor.

"Yes," said one of them, a shorter man with the slightly intimidated look of a husband who knows his wife wonders where he is. "We had a call from McKeon's last night. They had nothing of this quality in stock, so we had to get busy right away—"

"Yes," his companion interjected, "we had this wonderful African mahogany, three inches thick. Nothing else like it in Chicago—"

"We had the girls at the factory up at six this morning to get it ready."

"We had to sew the lining properly and see that it was all set," his companion added.

"Yes, and when it was all prepared, when we were about to get it off to McKeon's about eight this morning, all the girls in the shop wanted to come down and touch it. They all wanted to touch the coffin we made for the mayor."

At a table sat Jimmy Breslin, columnist for the New York *Daily News,* the burly, tousle-haired Irishman who had come to cover the funeral, and who sensed something of his own Queens neighborhood in the Bridgeport area. He looked sad as only the street-wise and melancholy Irish can.

"We could be in a bar in Belfast," Breslin said, gesturing with his arm at the crowded room, in which the slightest feeling of people under invisible siege could be detected. "Look at these faces," Breslin kept saying, as though he would rather be drunk on them than on whiskey any day. Not all of them were Irish. Many were Middle European. After all, Bridgeport had a street named Lithuanica not far from Emerald Avenue. But it was the Irish look, open-faced and seemingly innocent of eye, that predominated. At some tables mothers and daughters sat together, the mothers in middle age, their beauty beginning to break up under the pounding surf of a hard life, but the daughters—was it a time for such magic?—were their image, with the unlined fairness their mothers must have had twenty-five years before.

Soon Breslin was recognized, and some of these mothers and daughters asked him for his autograph. Jimmy returned to the mood of the room and to some thoughts about Daley. "He understood jobs as the key, jobs as the number-one thing for people, the number-one thing for a city. Not many American politicians understand that. I wonder if this marks the end of the great Irish domination of politics."

On his way out Breslin stopped to greet Circuit Court Clerk Morgan Finley, another Bridgeport native who had risen to political power under Daley. Next to him sat a Slavic-looking judge who said to Breslin, "If you write about this spell my name right. It's W-O-S-I-K."

Leaving Schaller's, you could see the church clearly against the night. It was illumined by searchlights from a huge fire truck and, white and bell-towered, it looked like the Alamo. The pounding sounds of generators could be heard, and television cables and other communication lines were strung across the street. The crowds still pressed against the wooden barricades, each emblazoned with the words "Police Line. Do Not Cross." It had grown colder and the Salvation Army had set up a truck to serve coffee. Smudgepots had been placed along the line of the mourners to generate some small warmth; they seemed like torches from another time stretched along in the darkness, their flames billowing in the wind and making a haunting sound, a hollow flapping of great tongues of fire against the darkness. High above the church, yes, directly above it, a single star shone in the sky of winter's first night.

Inside the church, the Shannon Rovers, wearing their tartan kilts and sashes, had just assembled to join the line of mourners. They were led by Tommy Ryan, another classic blue-eyed Irishman, and they had piped every year at the St. Patrick's Day festivities, usually leading the parade and playing both at the church and at the evening banquet. But they had left their bagpipes outside tonight and moved to a slow drum roll through the church, whose own lights seemed feeble after the sun had set. Slowly, they passed the coffin, and Tommy Ryan stopped to speak to Mrs. Daley. "Men may come and men may go," he said softly, "but the name of Richard J. Daley will go on forever."

"Tommy, he loved you," Mrs. Daley said, and, after they had all filed past, she called them back and asked them to return with their bagpipes to play one last air. And so they re-entered the church and marched down the cleared aisle, piping the "Garry Owen," the mayor's very favorite tune, a melody rousing enough for battle, the regimental music, in fact, of George Custer's Seventh Cavalry. And so the shadowed church was filled for a few moments with an Irish battle hymn. The pipers in the night had made a last sign, a sentiment that was saved from self-indulgence by the discipline of the cadenced march, a sentiment that touched but did not break the mood of control, of grief contained, that held until near dawn when the last of 100,000 mourners had passed through the church.

The morning of the funeral was as bitter as the evening before and the wind blew even more strongly. In the eastern sky there were only high, thin clouds that had been turned pastel pink, subdued as the canvas of an Impressionist painter, by the rising sun. The whole city was quiet as Vice-President Rockefeller and President-elect Carter arrived. Inside the church, their Secret Service agents were in a subtle competition to gain the first aisle place of honor for one or the other. It finally went to Rockefeller, who was representing President Ford, but not without a bit of preparatory stress. Judges and aldermen and old cronies, all those who had the black-edged invitations, were admitted. And there were mayors, and bankers, Jesse Jackson and other religious leaders, and Ann Landers. Senator George McGovern arrived ("Hell of a nice thing for him to do," a Daley aide whispered), along with Senator Edward Kennedy, both of them without hats or overcoats.

The clergy formed in procession. There was a handful of visiting bishops who, along with the Cardinal Archbishop of Chicago, would preside. And here the elves and the leprechauns, held so long in sway by more solemn Irish spirits, asserted themselves. As the procession was about to move, an aide to the cardinal glanced at a bishop who was wearing an unusual outfit, a papal-like white cassock, a scarlet sash and biretta— hardly regulation episcopal tailoring. The aide recognized the dark-haired, heavyset man as a character with no small fame in the city of Chicago. He was no Roman Catholic prelate; he was, in fact, thought to be a pretender, a man who claimed ordination in some old Catholic sect which had broken from the Vatican a hundred years before. But he had also been a chef at a famous Chicago restaurant and had been accused of maneuvers that gave off the faint odor of confidence games. The aide, fearing that the man might pull something during the ceremony, checked with Commander McLaughlin. "I might have to put on a cassock myself," McLaughlin retorted, "just to watch him closely."

And so the procession began, as the choir intoned the first hymn, "O God, Our Help in Ages Past." The cardinal and the other priests and bishops, and even the dubious prelate with the mixed vestments, headed into the church. (The last was finally seated directly opposite Cardinal Cody in the sanctuary and was unaware in his gestures of apparent piety that Commander McLaughlin was keeping a hard blue eye on him.)

The Mass of the Resurrection was offered in white vestments, a rite changed from the grimmest black by the Vatican Council reforms, and the hymns were marked with strength and hope. The Daleys sat together, hardly glancing in the direction of any of the distinguished guests. The important ones had all kissed Mrs. Daley, of course, but now they were as quiet as forest animals hearing the hunter's tread in the church where Daley had received his First Communion before the First World War, and where now the mass he so believed in was to be offered for his eternal rest.

But rest, eternal or otherwise, seemed a strange reward for the man who had been so energetic; no, the idea of stillness, the quiet of the grave, did not seem right at all. It would take some getting used to. On the other hand, as the service proceeded, as Father Graham omitted a eulogy—"It wasn't [the mayor's] style"—and spoke only briefly of Daley's power to love, Daley seemed very dead, dead in the hush between prayers that was broken only by the coughs or footscrapings of the mourners, dead as a collapsed star is dead although still a dense force that leaves an immense void of melancholy in its wake, dead as a king from whose hands slip the power and the glory instantly, dead as only a powerful political leader can be.

The time for communion came, and Senator Kennedy had to scramble over Rockefeller and Carter in order to get out of the narrow pew to receive the sacrament. It was a maneuver as familiar to lifelong Catholics as the sign of the Cross; there was a small, homely fittingness to it. Communion was distributed even in the bitter cold outside the church. The reception of the host—head back, tongue out—is a lifelong activity for Catholics, an intimate part of Catholic culture, something that binds Catholics together no matter what antagonisms they might suffer with noxious clerics or stuffy church administrators, food for all, a precious common sign and a symbol as good as we were likely to get for the mayor who prided himself on being one of the people, "an ordinary fellow," as he used to say with a twinkle, "from the stockyards." A violinist played the "Ave Maria" as the mourners received the host, many of them weeping openly.

The service was ended in just over an hour with the last prayers uttered by the cardinal in his slightly nasal accent over the closed coffin, covered now with the four-star flag of the city.

> Father, hear our prayer: Welcome our brother into the heavenly Jerusalem, the lasting city of peace and unity. Help us to comfort one another with the assurance of our faith until we meet again in Christ to be with you and with our brother for ever. We ask this through Christ Our Lord.

From the crowd came a rolling "Amen." The pallbearers, most of them bodyguards or former bodyguards—their expressions not much different from those they wore when they searched the crowds around him during his life—carried the coffin—as soldiers might once have carried their leader on a shield—out and down the steep front steps and into the waiting hearse. Huge crowds had waited in the cold for this moment, even as they would line the streets on the way to Holy Sepulchre Cemetery on the Southwest Side, where Daley's mother and father lay buried.

"They won't actually bury him today," an onlooker was explaining. "They don't do that in Chicago. They take you to a big chapel in the cemetery, and they say the prayers in there rather than at the graveside. It's easier on the family that way."

In a few minutes the limousines had unsnarled themselves on the narrow streets, where the traffic lights continued to blink red and green above the forming procession. The gold and white draping on the front of the church whipped savagely in the raw wind as the cortège started off, heading in its first turn down Lowe Avenue for a brief pause by the Daley home. Then, with police helicopters whining overhead and trumpeting like emergency vehicles, it made its way under the now graying skies toward the cemetery.

It was to be a private service, reserved for the family only, but the news media had charted the route and the television cameras were waiting near the cemetery to record the procession's arrival. Someone gave a false signal and the cameras began to televise an earlier funeral, not the mayor's. The announcers broadcast their descriptions, in the voices of golf-course reporters, over the airwaves.

But, meanwhile, all along the route the ordinary people waved as the Daley cortège came into view. It was delayed by a freight train on an open crossing at 111th Street. Those in the car with Cardinal Cody suggested that they take another route to the entrance on 115th Street. When they arrived, a tall state trooper blocked the way. "But this is Cardinal Cody," an aide said.

"I don't care who he is. Nobody gets in this gate today."

A priest got out of the car and spoke quietly to the policeman. "You don't understand. Cardinal Cody owns this cemetery."

"I don't care," the officer replied.

"Look," said the priest, shivering in the cold, "get on your walkie-talkie and tell your boss that Cardinal Cody is here and wants to get into his cemetery."

The officer snapped on his unit and delivered the message. There was a slight pause while he listened to the response. "Yessir," he replied emphatically, "I already let him in."

And so the cars all finally arrived at a great brown canvas tent, large enough for Bedouin royalty. The mayor had kept his options open again. He would be buried directly in the ground in that simple, final Catholic ceremony that faces the reality of fresh earth. It was all over in a few minutes, the last prayers said by the cardinal and Father Graham. Bishop Cletus O'Donnell of Madison, Wisconsin, read the Twenty-third Psalm and the last holy water was sprinkled. The mayor, with a president and politicians, yes, and a phony prelate too, with captains and minor kings all around—but mostly the common people lining the way—had been laid to rest.

The next morning was raw and cold. Heavy clouds massed in the southern sky and a rainbow arched out of them over the edge of the lake. In Bridgeport the streets were quiet. Nobody was out although it was almost eight o'clock. A police car was still parked in front of the Daley home on South Lowe, where the flag, like all the others in the city, was at half-mast. At Union and 37th the blue barriers had all been removed from the street and papers scuffed and tumbled in the strong breeze. The center white and gold drapes on the church had blown loose and hung like flags of surrender about the middle door. Schaller's Tap was closed, and nobody seemed to be out on Halsted Street at all. Up past the offices of Daley and Daley Insurance, the Ramova Theater, set in the middle of the storefronts the way movie houses were in the thirties, had a last tribute on its marquee:

"R.J. Daley, We Will Miss You."

Underneath it read "Coming December 31: *Shout at the Devil.*"

[3]

Our Lady of the Lake

Richard J. Daley, more trim than fat, more handsome in a dark-browed Irish way than not, a dandy in blue suits even in high school, was, above all else, a good boy. He was, to the day he died, in fact, what his parents expected him to be: dutiful, religious, hard-working, and self-controlled, a man who understood that success and power were finally delivered to those who took their codes of loyalty and discipline seriously. For if ambition could not be mentioned too loudly, could not even be named in the recesses of one's psyche, then it could best be pursued through virtue itself, plain and old-fashioned as Bridgeport, the town within the city where Daley grew up just four miles south of Chicago's City Hall. If there was a lock on the public Daley, it was forged there on the streets he never left, in the relationships and traditions of its Irish, Catholic, and Democratic people. At the end of his life he was no Citizen Kane, breathing his longing for his lost childhood in any word like "Rosebud." That would have seemed humorous, if not incomprehensible, to him. Daley never separated himself from his past, never said good-bye to any of it, kept it like a chieftain's treasure in a mailed fist, holding it with a mixture of possessiveness and tenderness. For these qualities blend in something close to sentimentality, so that Daley, the self-perceived dutiful son carrying out his pledges to them still in his

school, became finally a mood of existence rather than just a set of practiced responses, an outlook, by turns melancholy and joyous, about life and its contradictions, a sense about men and women and the inevitability of sin, an expectation of and a search for perfection and at the same time an acceptance, operational rather than theoretical, of a great jagged flaw arching across the face of things, an awareness of angels and demons, a sense of an invisible world of grace that lay like a cleansing mist over the grimy city.

There can be no discovery of the real Richard Daley without an appreciation of the anchoring effect of the Church, which, as a conjuror of the ambivalence of the spirit, could close one eye, cold and chipped as an old marble, and open another that was warm and full of light, offering forgiveness through confession for those who wanted to put their sins behind them. The Catholic Church may have manufactured guilt, but it also knows how to process it so that it does not clog the soul like the phlegm in a sick man's lungs; no, sin and evil may be everywhere, but they can be acknowledged and dealt with in the sacramental system, which, like the tapers of pilgrims, softens the craggy arches and gives warmth to the stones of an old church.

The Irish in Bridgeport were already yielding their dominance in the population as Daley was preparing to enter high school. Lawler Avenue, in the fine kind of political move that would later rechristen Crawford Avenue "Pulaski," was renamed "Lithuanica"; it was no great thing to change the street signs as long as you gave away no real political power in the process. Such instructive gestures were not lost on young Daley, who was fascinated in his own quiet way by the Irish politicians who controlled the Eleventh Ward. The affinity of the Irish for political maneuver was not unconnected with their experience of Catholicism, the faith that bound them together in an ancient mystique of relationship that could be easily recognized but not so easily named, the religion for which they had been persecuted in Ireland and for which they had suffered discrimination from the lords of American Waspdom; how like the bloody English they seemed. The same predilections and skills that led the brightest Irish sons to assume political control of the Catholic Church in America served their brothers and cousins well as they moved forward in seizing control of its cities and their municipal services. The fact that the Irish, who lived with the poor, could speak English, made them natural representatives of all minorities in dealing with City Hall. There was also a taste almost for power in itself, which, by whatever name they chose to give it, they vigorously exercised with identical features of loyalty, discipline, and a sense of Divine compliance, if not of indebtedness to them for their labors.

Everywhere the young Daley looked on the streets of his upbringing, he could observe the energies of Catholic politicians and priests working for the good of "their own." It had been the priests who had marched for the rights of their people in the time of the Stockyard dispute; it was Father William Dorney, a local pastor, who had worked out a settlement, the same Father Dorney who had persuaded the saloonkeepers of the area to remain closed until after Sunday mass. And it was the priest's opposite number in the Democratic organization, the precinct captain, who ministered to the needs of the people in his own political version of pastoral service. It was not a totally solemn business; power warmed the heart but so did a good laugh, a contented smile at holding on to power through outwitting a stuffy Republican establishment. There was a mixture of fun and triumph in keeping the faith and maintaining the government against the cold and haughty stares of the self-righteous do-gooders and the sour-faced moralists of America's Puritan empire.

Something everlastingly boyish survived in the Irish Catholic Democrats' social and political ascendancy, something outrageous in rubbing the establishment's nose in the waste products of its defeats, something like truants turning cartwheels under their classroom windows, or a willingness to wink at a

Notre Dame foul against Southern Methodist. Some force of mischief compounded with malice and virtue emerged as a clear pattern in the grain of the culture.

Daley's father, Mike, was a business agent in the Sheet Metal Workers union, a wiry man who always wore a derby, a quiet man who taught his son the lessons of taciturnity and shrewd observance, a second-generation Irishman who, because he had only one child and a job, usually had some extra money. He would live to see his son elected mayor of Chicago; not only did he give advice to young Richard, but he was at least in part the architect of Daley's controlled style, of the impassiveness which invited every man's interpretation of his thoughts but yielded their truth to no one; besides that, who could hold anything against you if only you knew your own plans? The future mayor grew up in a house that was not boisterous, in an atmosphere of order and quiet contentment, in just the place to learn your lessons, do your chores, and receive the approval that a good boy deserved.

His mother, Lillian Dunne Daley, was thirty, and eight years older than her husband, when Daley was born. She was, by most accounts, and from Daley's own recollections, a bright, aggressive, and active person, a leader who marched for women's rights, taking her son with her on occasion, a woman with a sense of humor who would tell young Richard that on St. Patrick's Day she had to go down to City Hall to have her "behind painted green." No shrinking shamrock, then, and the possessor of a practical sense of getting things done. Who can doubt that she, with the one son of her life to care for, lavished attention and concern on him, and taught him lessons about how to accomplish one's aims that he would recall profitably later on?

On one occasion that Daley would remember merrily decades later, a new priest was assigned to the local parish, a shy young man who wanted to start a Bingo game but who could not bring himself to introduce it. Mrs. Daley gave him some advice about raising the question at the next meeting of the ladies' group. He did so, diffidently and tentatively, saying in an unsure voice that he hoped to begin Bingo in the parish. At this, Mrs. Daley cried out, "And we all do, too," and began applauding, infecting the other women with enough enthusiasm to carry the motion as if by acclaim.

Such lessons in practical politics, such good-humored stories about how to get what you want out of others, were daily fare for the quiet, good boy who so loved his mother, and who would never really transcend his early relationship with her. Some accounts tell us that she was shy and quiet, but this does not jibe with the view, as filled with truth as a brief glimpse through a partially opened door, of Lillian Dunne Daley as a dominant activist with well-developed political instincts and plenty of time to spend with her growing boy. Even in later life, he never lived more than a block away from her, and seldom gave a talk in which he did not quote something she had told him; it is impossible to doubt that much of Daley's presence and most of his intuitions about the cloudy depths of persuadable human beings were formed by her.

Being good, following his religion, making something of himself with the help of the right friends: These were only some of the lessons he absorbed from her forceful personality, one last echo of which we catch just before her death in 1946. Daley had won the nomination for Cook County sheriff, and he went with a friend to tell his mother about it. She would not live to suffer his election defeat, but she remained sure of her expectations and her judgments. This would not do, no, this was not her idea of what her son should be seeking.

"I didn't raise my son to be a policeman," she said flatly.

Perhaps although Daley lost the race, he saved his later career in that bittersweet moment of realization that he had brought the wrong prize home, for what good son could have made the right choice and displeased his mother at the same time?

But Lillian Dunne Daley can best be sensed in Richard J. Daley himself. One can understand that she played an important role in developing the marked obsessive tendencies in her only son, for she was the mother of all expectation as well as our lady of final approval, the gifted person who dressed him well and looked for propriety and goodness from him.

We must see the growing Daley against the background of the Catholic culture which also had no small hand in forming his obsessive style. Everything, after all, was not unsullied virtue, even in Bridgeport, where street gangs like Ragen's Colts were well known. Goodness had to be pursued diligently, and it was the reward of those who listened obediently to mother and to Holy Mother Church. Catholicism kneaded promises of heaven with great batches of guilt, demanding and controlling by using its power to open the gates of paradise or the pits of hell for all its believers. One avoided guilt by avoiding what was forbidden; one needed the approval of this vast earthly and heavenly array, and it could be had if one chose the path of dutifulness and care, if one made sure by doing things twice over and respecting authority, if one closed off the energies of rebellion inside oneself. The obsessive is caught between two impulses, the one to rebel against repression, and the other to comply in order to gain approval. Richard J. Daley shaped a life and a style on this conflict, the inner simmerings of which could be observed throughout his lifetime.

But one must not judge obsessive features in personality too harshly. Daley and generations of other Irish Catholics have clearly displayed these tendencies, but they have also capitalized on them, integrating them into their own purposes. This readiness to prove the self anew, this dependency that piles up anger around stifled rebellion were linked to the authority systems of that age which, in both Church and state, were still functioning well. There was something outrageous about the neighboring Catholic pastor who circulated in the streets at curfew time with two large and menacing dogs, looking for youths who were out too late, something outrageous, yes, and yet here was at least a personality, however stolid, to contend with, a man against whom to measure oneself, and a code of belief and behavior that could not be ignored. There may have been rebellion in the loud laughter of recollection at such things later on, but it is hard to believe that permissive neutrality, or the lack of any convictions at all, has been any better for people. Discipline and loyalty were natural parts of Bridgeport life; they were essential to the family, the Church, and the Democratic party.

At the De La Salle Institute, the high school which Daley entered in 1916, there were more uncompromising demands to be met. The Christian Brothers, wearing long black gowns with stiff little white collars under their chins, expected good behavior and hard work in the stone building, grim as the courthouse of a hanging judge, which they had opened in 1889 at the corner of 35th and Wabash, just a good walk for the energetic young Daley from his Bridgeport home. The brothers, many of them Irish, brought scholarliness, determination, and a large measure of political understanding to this venture.

They were still telling good stories about the founder, Brother Adjutor, when Daley began the three-year commercial course that would prepare him in shorthand, typing, and bookkeeping, as well as in the more conventional subjects like geometry and religion. Brother Adjutor, who looked not unlike Daley in his mature years, was a mover and shaker, a builder with a mind filled with schemes and maneuvers for the success of his school. He sometimes dressed like Jesse James when calling on prospective benefactors, telling them that he did not want to hold them up, but that he did expect a donation. Yes, Brother Adjutor was a model of clout in a cassock, a meat eater unafraid of vegetarian bankers, a Catholic proud of the faith and determined, despite fights with local pastors and occasional disastrous fund-raising schemes (such as turning the school into a hotel during the 1893 Columbian Exposition), to build an institution to educate the Catholics on Chicago's South Side, which stretched down and away from the lake like protoplasm on a slide.

And so they came and in great numbers, boys from near and

beyond the stockyards, boys who took the streetcars from as far south as Calumet City, boys some of whom would, like Daley, become successful in Chicago. De La Salle would count four mayors among its alumni and countless judges, commissioners, and assorted politicians. It was an environment of disciplined learning and religious instruction, an extension of the values that predominated in the neighborhoods from which the students came. De La Salle emphasized winning; the school paper was even named *Victory,* and it is clear that the students were pressed to give their best in pursuit of virtue and success.

Daley maintained close ties with the Institute all his life; his record was not, in fact, a famous one scholastically, but he had been prompt and cooperative, a handball player at noon recess, the quiet, good boy with a deep voice and a way of listening and noting everything that went on around him. Daley would raise funds for the school in later years, just as he would have the brothers work for his election; it was all part of the Catholic culture, all of a piece, with the abiding mixture of irritation and affection that so many Catholics developed for their Church and its schools, for the army of demanding priests and religious brothers and sisters who seemed such an intimate part of their growing up. If Daley would later call the De La Salle principal to assemble the school band hastily for a Democratic memorial service, he would also send out a city engineer to make sure that the Illinois Institute of Technology, a northern neighbor of De La Salle, did not take away all the brothers' land in its expansion program. Daley stopped the land acquisition of this institute with instructions that enough land be left north of the school "to build a football field for the brothers." It was all part of the ambivalent relationship that marked Catholics and their membership in their Church, for being a Catholic remains something that people never quite get over.

It was not exactly an "old boys" network, or ivy league fellowship. No, all that seemed like dry sherry and old money, desiccated rectitude in paneled rooms, righteousness and reform and lofty ideals of public service exchanged in airless

rooms by men in three-piece suits. There was something row-
dier in the aspirations of immigrant Catholics, for they understood Original Sin and had an optimism about heaven even as
they had a sadness about life; they wanted power and influence
as the prizes of their deliverance from their oppressed state,
and they could be as reckless and driving as Irish warlords in
pursuing these goals. Their aims, intermingled with so much
Catholic experience and symbolization, were finally impossible
to sort out satisfactorily. It was close to a holy cause, this march
toward power, this justification of one's own beliefs and, thus,
the advancement of one's own people. It was the air that Daley
breathed, the ethic of the neighborhood that never changed.

One can sense the mood of life for the young Irish Catholics
from places like Bridgeport in the recollections of those who
attended high school with Daley. Most of them seem to have
aged, like the old men with rheumy eyes who sit each morning
on park benches, men long gone from their original neighborhoods, men strangely unlike Daley, for time has had its way
with them. They recall Daley as the quiet chum, "always with
the rest of us, always neat, always a gentleman, but how did we
know he would be mayor someday?" And they can tell you of
the way the cattle were marched through the nearby streets to
the stockyards and the great clouds of dust and the smells that
hung over the area; they can tell you too of the simple life of
the day with what they remember as contentment in the modest cottages.

"My father," said one old man, a city employee for close to
fifty years, "was a common laborer, bright, don't you know,
but uneducated. He couldn't read his name if it was on a neon
sign. But he educated himself, especially when the radios came
in. That was the kind of life we had. We went to dances at the
athletic clubs, at the Wallace's at Thirty-seventh Street, and at
'Our Flag' at Forty-seventh and Halsted. And everybody loved
boxing. Why, there were boxing gloves in every yard, good,
clean exercise."

And they can tell you of the coming of the First World War
and how, as high school students along with Richard Daley,

they went and drilled on Saturdays at the White Sox ball park, and of how, too young to serve themselves, they were proud of the De La Salle graduates who were overseas, like Captain Martin Kennelly, who would precede Daley as mayor. But Daley they always recall as the proper, friendly young man who dressed better than they did.

"The best," another old man would say, waving his hand as though to make the old days reappear. "Daley was the best." And the school, one asks, how was that? "The best," he says again in exactly the same tone of satisfied recollection.

"The Christian Brothers?"

"The best," he says, smiling now, perhaps as another hint about the Irish in Bridgeport, who recall only what they want and in small measure.

One can feel something of the quiet, observant Daley in them to this day. They watch you and say little, because you have come from somewhere else, and who can say what the purpose of your questions might be. It is a natural caution, a resistance to undue inquiry, a determination, fired to great strength in the open hearth of a highly disciplined life, to shield their souls from strangers. It was something Daley understood well, one part of the culture he had absorbed early and which he used at will in dealing with almost everyone who ever asked him a personal question.

Bridgeport was also the setting for political activity, not only through the local Democratic ward organization, but through the Hamburg Athletic Association, which Daley joined at this time. Located in a somewhat rambling and anonymous-looking building at 37th and Emerald, the club provided some athletic facilities and social rooms in which the young men of the area, like those of every similar section of every other American city, could talk sports and politics. Daley would later become president of the club and serve in that position for fifteen years. Early on he became a manager and coach of the athletic teams. One observer felt that the future mayor's talents could easily be seen in the way he handled the players, devised his game plans, and saw to all the details with great thoroughness.

He was practicing the lessons he had been learning so quietly at home, at school, and in the neighborhood.

Politics was constantly in the smoky air of the Hamburg Club; one of its presidents, Tommy Doyle, won an aldermanic seat in 1914, and in 1918 he went to Congress in the same election that sent Joe McDonough, the five-foot-three-inch, three-hundred-pound Villanova football hero to the Chicago City Council. In 1923 McDonough, who frequently ate a whole chicken as he presided at his favorite tavern hangout at 47th and Wentworth, would appoint Daley his ward secretary and make him a clerk in the City Council, but right now he was the most powerful man in the ward, the heroic figure given to epic excess, the man who would have a thousand cars in his funeral procession when he died at forty-five. He was the mentor young Daley observed quietly, the patron he would draw close to through diligent work as a footsoldier and later as a precinct captain in the local Democratic ward.

Daley worked for a while at the stockyards after his graduation from De La Salle in 1919, and there is the legend of his being a cowboy who herded the cattle up the ramps in the early morning and worked in the office in the afternoon. It is easier to envision the obsessive young man moving rapidly into the office job, even though the cowboy story was used in mayoral campaigns with some effectiveness.

Daley was not afraid of hard work; indeed, later in his life, he was forever working at manual chores, especially at his summer home in Michigan, where he was industrious and neat in cultivating gardens, chopping wood, repairing the roof, or doing other odd jobs with great energy. But if his mother had raised him to be more than a policeman, one can be sure that she did not settle for his working among the lowing herds when he could be doing sums in a clean shirt and pressed suit inside the office.

The dutifulness and punctuality, the rapid gait and erect posture, the good manners and the careful work: These are the features of the young man watching silently for the right chance and making no mistakes in the meantime. Daley was

Left: Like many other Catholic men who succeeded in business, politics, or municipal service, Richard J. Daley had been an altar boy. Such men looked back on the activity as a special bond of relationship, and the phrase "We were altar boys together" identified a knowing camaraderie about their Catholic culture. (*Chicago Daily News*)

Below: Richard J. Daley, as carefully groomed and tailored as he would be all his days, pictured as a member of the legislature. His first election would find him succeeding a venerable Republican, David E. Shanahan. Daley moved to the Democratic side of the House on his first day there. (*Chicago Daily News*)

The Daley home at 3536 Lowe Avenue, the street on which Daley lived his entire life. The house, which was built along classic thirties "bungalow" lines, remained a citadel that few ever entered, as closed to press and public—and even to most other politicians—as a home could be. (*Chicago Sun-Times*/Quinn)

Opposite below: Morris B. Sachs wept on the shoulder of Martin H. Kennelly, mayor since 1947, who had just lost the 1955 primary election to Richard Daley. Sachs, a highly popular clothier in Chicago, had run on Kennelly's ticket. Daley, recognizing Sachs's vote-getting ability, soon dried his tears by transferring him to Daley's own ticket, which went on to win the mayoralty election on April 5. (AP photos by *Chicago Sun-Times* photographer Larry Nocerino)

Below: Daley, who seldom made such histrionic gestures, as the champ, the newly victorious mayor-elect on Election Night, 1955. His great ambition achieved, Daley would speak softly of his desire to "embrace mercy and walk humbly with my God." (*Chicago Sun-Times*)

Left: The sweet moment of inauguration having arrived, Daley accepts a mildly enthusiastic handshake from outgoing Mayor Martin Kennelly. Mrs. Daley sits smiling just in front of them. Daley would surprise those gathered in the City Council chamber by giving an address that indicated clearly that he alone would be the executive in Chicago. (UPI)

Below: On Easter Sunday, 1956, Mayor and Mrs. Daley walked to church with their children. From the left, they are Richard, Eleanor, John, William, Patricia, and Michael. (*Chicago Sun-Times*/Quinn)

not wasting his time carousing, not when there were things to learn and duties to be carried out. The young man was a model, the delight of his approving parents. It is impossible to place him in an active position in the race riots of 1919, although a number of commentators have pictured him in the pose of the brick-throwing thug. Daley may have been ready to defend himself, and he was as good as the next fellow at name-calling, but he was not the man to look for a fight, not when there were other ways to handle events and people. He may have been a forceful young man, but he was not the kind to spoil his good looks or his freshly pressed suit, no, not the kind to disobey his mother's advice about making and keeping friends, not likely to be physically violent when he had spent so many years mastering his impulses and learning to control any rages he may have felt with an expression that gave away nothing of his genuine inner emotions. Daley the obsessive was not Daley the impulsive brawler, and it is Daley as the former who emerges out of Bridgeport, well dressed and on time.

The obsessive features of Daley's personality served him well as a clerk, an organizer, a man who, throughout his life, was interested in the smallest of details and the most remote entries in budget statements. The Daley who for most of a decade attended night school getting his college and law degrees, the man who then went home and studied while his friends went dancing, this was a man with no slight obsessive twinges; this, in fact, was a man obsessed with his destiny, laying each paving block carefully so that his road to success would bear the weight of his ambition.

There was a sweetness to be savored by Daley in each move forward, in each acquisition that he swiftly tucked into the sack of treasures that was never emptied. There was energy in the prizes, nourishment for him in every bit of knowledge he acquired, in each sweetmeat of political manipulation, in every tasty affirmation of his goodness that came back to him, like shimmering radar blips, from the widening universe of his dutiful achievement. He seemed to know exactly what he wanted with the stubborn conviction of an unlettered holy man, and he never asked for more. Did the ambition to be mayor come with work in the City Council, or did it rise when he was a precinct captain? He never said when, but he came to want the job of mayor with a determination that accepted the waiting, indeed, grew strong on its discipline, for it made the eventual achievement of the office even sweeter.

If that seems simple, Daley was himself complex. He had the power to control the anger of his tempered rebellion; wrath was splendid fuel for the revenge he would seek, in partnership with Joseph P. Kennedy, against all the foreign and domestic persecutors of the Irish Catholics; yes, the White House would do for one of "his own people." He would need all his obsessive attention to detail to maintain the Chicago Democratic organization, and there would be more than a few moments when his anger in exercising party discipline and punishing political enemies would seem as justified as that of an avenging angel. Some experts on the obsessive style note that the driven person "must keep his conflicting emotions and indeed all emotion, as secret as possible. . . . This leads to one of his most characteristic defense mechanisms: emotional isolation." (MacKinnon and Michels, *The Psychiatric Interview*, Philadelphia, W. B. Saunders, 1974).

But, listen, and hear Daley described by the same authors, who write that "possessiveness and the need to save everything relate to the fear of separation from any loved object as well as the defiant aspects of the power struggle." Or again, that in his efforts at emotional isolation, the obsessive only appears to be engaged with you. "He can whisper, mumble, or speak in such a way that the interviewer will have difficulty hearing what is said. . . . The obsessive is a master at concealing his inattentiveness." This side of Daley would frequently be seen in the long years that stretched before him, along with his rage and his bull strength, all of it bound twice in on itself until the hoops of control all shattered at once in his last breath.

What became the calming center of gravity for this extraordinary man who pitted himself for so long and so successfully against the shame and humiliation that were the enemies of his culture? His wife, yes, surely, and his family, guarded by him as fiercely as the watchman guards the city gate. Yet, these all seem subsumed in the first and greatest love of his life, Chicago herself. We read, concerning obsessives, of the "original omnipotent partnership . . . of the infant and his mother, who seemed to be all-knowing, all-powerful, and all-providing. He continually seeks to re-establish such a partnership. . . . This alliance does not have to be with an individual, but can be with a system of thought, a religion, a scientific doctrine." And, of course, with a city.

For Richard Daley everything that was precious, everything that could be counted on—mother, neighborhood, wife, family, religion, everything from which he resisted separation—was symbolized in Chicago, the mother of power and spoils and not a bride to wear white, as much a whore as any big city, but for Daley she was always pure. For him she was Our Lady of the Lake, and he would never stop building shrines and lighting candles for her. Daley served her with the heart of a knight, for in her company and in their reciprocal fidelity, he could keep it all—mother, bride, and daughter—in a mystical union in which all his deepest longings for power and love and approval could be met every day.

[4]

Nobody Walks
through Life Alone

We pause now at the edge of Richard J. Daley's early political career for we must make passage across a desert with only an occasional oasis; in the flowered shadows we will hear tales of the famous and the infamous and of treasures buried here and there and of the secret springs that run deep under the sands.

But it is a fact that must be faced: Politics on any level can be as extreme in its dullness as in its raw energy and excitement. The successful politician, the man whose life will be politics, must have an uncommon taste for the routine of organizational and governmental existence. It has been observed that only a naive and inexperienced man like Dwight Eisenhower could have termed his Presidential campaign a "moral crusade." The seasoned politician, the man whose clothes have the permanent odor of cigar smoke, views politics as a business, of deals proposed and deals arranged on a pragmatic rather than a moral basis, with no more room there for a do-gooder than there is on the floor of a stock exchange.

Local and state politicians are fundamentally bureaucrats. That may be why it is so difficult to be interested in what they are doing. And to read about them, as a traveler might in a newspaper from another city, is to invoke the gods of fatigue. So it is with the cast of characters who will now appear, because, despite their antics, they are masters of the routine, some rogues and some, like the young Daley, with an ideal of service mixed in with their ambition. In the main, they are involved in doing the same things over and over in order to preserve their control and their power. That is only one of the ways in which they grow as tough and callused as old beasts at the edge of a watering hole. The man who ends up with the largest share of power often possesses the greatest attention to detail and the greatest patience in living in a world of paper, meetings, and small, homely services to constituents, the whole of it tied together by male bonding of a chauvinistic sort. To know the complete political bureaucrat is to know a special species of killer.

To understand the man Richard J. Daley, one must appreciate the steady apprenticeship of his political career and how his fascination with and achievement of power were linked at every step with his capacity for bureaucratic activity, for discovering sustaining delight in balance sheets, patronage lists, the dusty inner springs and levers of legislation, and the endless round of social engagements—weddings, wakes, and funerals—dutifully kept. His great political power was built on his own personal power to live the minor city and state politician's life and to wait, with hardly an expression on his face, but with all the patience of the hardened bureaucrat-beast, for the moment to strike.

So the individuals, many forgotten and others dead or retired, who stand in the wings of our narrative must be appreciated for what they are—bureaucrats of a highly specialized and toughened nature who are much the same from one city hall and statehouse to another. Daley, of course, grew to be the toughest bureaucrat in the forest.

This is not to deny the colorful side of political life nor to ignore the army of characters, far more interesting even than the fictional entourage of "Ditto" and "Knocko" and the others in Skeffington's organization in *The Last Hurrah*. Such men have always been present in Chicago, men with nicknames like

"Hinky Dink," "Bathhouse John," and "Short Pencil," braces of "Big Jim"s and "Big Ed"s, and even "The Figure Four," the nickname of minor Democratic politician Jim Denver, who gained the title from crossing a leg cut off above the ankle over his good one as he leaned on his crutch to speak. Their language was also colorful, perhaps more colorful than their long afternoons of conniving about deals and splits and "Lacey's bit," which signified what fell from the table after a division of political loot.

But we shall let them speak for themselves as they appear. The heart of our wanderings, however, even when we are in the company of the most engaging of rogues, remains the wilderness of bureaucracy, which has always been the promised land to politicians.

What did Richard Daley overhear as he made his way through the familiar streets of Bridgeport, what themes could he make out in the tone poem of its decent workaday existence, filled with the rumble of wagons and the whine and screech of streetcars, the measured chuff of locomotives and the lowing of the herds headed for the stockyard hooks and vats? What was it if not the breathing of the city, hot and bloody as that of a jungle animal sated from the kill? Daley was like a young hunter with a feeling for his quarry, who knows it is there even though he has not yet seen it, who knows, indeed, that the hunt is right for him, and that his natural gifts—the patience to wait out the prey into the quiet evening if need be, and the keen eyes, blue and unblinking even as the trigger is squeezed—were uncommon and would only be diminished by being overadvertised. Halfway across the world, Lenin was discovering that power was scattered in the streets of St. Petersburg waiting to be picked up; Daley, the tracker rather than the theorist, was intuitively picking it up in the streets of Chicago.

The young graduate of the De La Salle business course was absorbing from the Bridgeport air a wisdom about the energies and forces that moved men and events, and about the politics, as plain and as powerful as the street life itself, that made the city run. If it was not all noble in style and execution, it could be made so under the banner of higher purposes and ideals of public service with which only the most mean-spirited critics could argue. And, if blooded rivers thundered through the closed-off part of his soul, their rush could not be heard on the surface where even the winches of self-control were soundless, where silence was a shroud for his intentions or motives. This young man, who listened so carefully and responded so dutifully—who was sober and chaste besides—was a good recruit for the local Democratic club. He would not dismantle it or tear it apart. No, he had other plans, even though he had not unrolled them completely even for himself; he would wait, like the hunter in the glade, because the quarry, whose shape he could only sense in the stirring of the reeds, was power, and he intended to have it all for himself.

Daley was, in fact, making a synthesis of the varied aspects of his political education. His quiet ways were almost courtly—he displayed old-fashioned gallantry to women all his life. He stood up in stiff and respectful attention to greet anybody in uniform—military, clergy, policemen and firemen. These traits marked him as a gentleman just as his neatly pressed clothes did. He did not demand much of others, but he did not miss much, and if, in the recollection of many, he seemed the unexceptional bureaucrat, the manager of the Hamburg athletic teams who brought his books to practice, he was not inattentive to anything that could be gleaned from his commitment, as solemn in his pledge to the Democratic party as he had been at his First Communion.

In the framework of his culture, he was proceeding as many another proper young man would; the Irish had mastered the diligence and restraint involved in getting jobs, going to night school, and staying unmarried until an apprenticeship for adult life had been served. Young Daley, working the books at the stockyard commission house of Dolan and Ludeman and Company, living with the security and sweet aromas of home cooking, became a worker for the local Democratic club, moving within a few years to the rank of precinct captain, absorbing, without changing the expression on his not unhandsome face, every nuance of block-by-block organization and every fact of life, from the simple concern of neighborhood families for each other in times of trouble to the squandering of abilities by so many of the sweet-singing and heavy-drinking Irish. He learned the politics of the human condition without passing a parson's judgment, without revealing to anyone what he felt very clearly. He could watch and learn from it all with a compassion for sin and failure in others, and with a sympathy for a practical political process built on the way people were rather than on the way they might be, while he imposed the most rigid discipline on his own life and behavior.

Young Daley was circumspect and had every appearance of modesty as well as loyalty; one lesson he had learned early was to pose no threat to a political patron, to give him no reason to think you are smarter than he or that you are plotting behind his back.

The first law of political survival and ascendancy was loyalty, a pragmatic response fashioned into a reflex, a free-standing devotion that needed no principles for support. Other young men, like William Lynch, five years younger than Daley, a short, sharp-featured Bridgeporter as feisty as a James Cagney character, seemed too impulsive and outspoken to be as trustworthy as Daley. Lynch would in time become Daley's closest confidant, a law partner, and finally a federal judge. He was a bachelor Irishman, a designer of ruthless and effective strategies in politics and government, the cozy dealer of Daley's later administrations who would have his own lonely nightmare of drink near the end. But now, in the twenties, with Warren G. Harding in the White House and Big Bill Thompson, a foraging bear of a man, in City Hall, all the young men of Bridgeport who would rise like stars around Daley the sun-god, some early and some late, some in themselves and some in their children, all of them were growing up together.

Daley watched the alliance which McDonough had made with Anton J. Cermak, a Bohemian and a non-Catholic, a councilman from the Lawndale section of the city who was the sworn enemy of the Irish politicians who ruled the Democratic organization and who consistently thwarted him and his enormous ambition. Against all blood oaths and sentimental Gaelic ballads, McDonough, who recognized Cermak's control over important franchises concerning the public utilities and the transit lines, made his pact of allegiance, an act filled with lessons for the observant Daley. There were Irish, after all, who had moved uptown and taken on airs along with their lace curtains, the "bicycle Irish," as they were termed by the Bridgeporters, whose ridicule was as rich and dark as Guinness stout, "the bicycle Irish who made your ass sore," the Irish who had wandered far from their immigrant neighborhoods and who looked back at those who lived and worked near the stockyards as "pigshit Irish." There may be no bitterness more deadly and unforgiving than that which separates such classes of Irish, and Daley felt he was not betraying his own in becoming part of the Cermak faction. Indeed, he was to apply the lessons he learned from Cermak to his own later career. They were hard and brutal and they allowed no exceptions, for their intent was to consolidate all the political power of the party and of the office of the mayor in one man.

Cermak had the look of a shrewd shopkeeper who had no time for solicitors for charitable causes, a man who would wear his butcher's apron to the dinner table and pore over the account books during the meal, a boss who knew that vigilance, attention to detail, and the sour vapors of paranoia were the staples of a political survivor. "Pushcart Tony" the Irish leaders, Roger Sullivan, George Brennan, and John Powers, called him. So Cermak, in the first flash of the insight through which he would later strengthen the Democratic organization as a coalition of ethnics and thus give birth to a thousand balanced tickets, aligned himself with the German aldermen, Paddy Bauler and Charles Weber, both of them as harsh and remorseless as avenging Junkers. Cermak still fumed at the Irish, especially after he was rebuffed in his efforts to be slated to run against Mayor Thompson in 1923. These slating sessions, bloody as a stockyard run, would become increasingly fascinating to young Daley, for it was here that the power of the Democratic party in Cook County was concentrated; it was in gatherings such as this one in December 1922 at the downtown Sherman Hotel, in which Cermak was turned aside and an Irish reform candidate, William Dever, was selected, that the prizes lay. On the way out of the slating the furious Cermak muttered, "I will fuck those Irish someday!"

So Cermak was a man to watch and a man from whom to learn, but Dever was the man headed for City Hall in 1923, and so was Daley, summoned by McDonough for a job as clerk in the City Council and for the first of more than a half a century of municipal paychecks. Daley, of course, had learned about paychecks while working back in the Eleventh Ward doling out the patronage jobs which were controlled by McDonough. He was learning the business of politics with the concentration of a medical student who has laid bare the deepest entrail and the last flap of anatomical revelation in a dissected animal; with equal thoroughness and care young Daley could lay out in his mind the streets and houses of Bridgeport, the interlacing of families and clans, and each job and its salary and prestige and its guarantee of political footwork and votes. It was something he never forgot.

The job at City Hall was nothing if not inglorious. The City Council was composed of a roistering bunch of political rulers and pretenders, most of them up from the streets, with little education and a polish as unbuffed and dull as that of the spittoons that sloshed with their bile and tobacco juice. Young Daley, eager to please and excited by the atmosphere, served as secretary to four aldermen, typing their letters and running their errands and taking no notice of the dice game that went on almost every day in the anteroom. These were men who had developed a taste for the sporting life, for betting on the horses and going to the fights, for good beef and the best of Prohibition liquors and wines, for time off for the Kentucky Derby in Louisville and for the World Series wherever it was played. Such was the life led by McDonough, who found that, wherever he was, he could depend on Richard Daley to take care of his business back in Chicago for him.

Cermak was president of the County Board, a position which gave him great power in Cook County and which made McDonough's—and Daley's—job secure. In later years, Daley would grow prickly at any reminders about his menial duties, flaring up when the old days were mentioned by William Clark, son of Alderman John Clark, for whom Daley had worked at that time. These were not years or associations free of conflict for Daley, not times to talk about later on, not the relationships with which he identified comfortably in the controlled retrospect of the great years of his power.

It was more comfortable to remember the hard work and the determination that sent him back to school. He enrolled at De-Paul University, a Catholic school run by the Vincentian Fathers that was housed in a building on Jackson Boulevard, just a few blocks from City Hall. Every night Daley attended classes from six until eight and went home to eat dinner and study and wait for dawn and the cycle to begin again. It was at once the dream of Horatio Alger and the nightmare that broke the seams of night for the pyramid builders.

Something of the exceptional man was here made plain—his consuming diligence, his intelligence, the reciprocal devotion of his home life, the willingness to wait through more than a decade to make up the prerequisites that were missing from his commercial high school course and to achieve a bachelor's degree and then a law degree. Add, as well, his religious devotion, for there were few mornings on which he missed mass; and count in his newly achieved presidency of the Hamburg Athletic Association, which gave him yet another test of managing men as well as an athletic outlet—how many priests had urged just such a balance for the pure of heart?—and we can

see the young Daley more clearly, virtuous by every judgment
of his training and education, a man who had already separated out the elements of his life as surely as the Constitu-
tion built a wall between Church and State.

There was a public life in which one might have to make
friends with the friends of the mammon of iniquity, for power
was not delivered at a distance from them; but one could stand
back from the smoking pits of lust and greed. And there was a
private life, filled with the self-assuring pursuit of each brightly
lit Christian virtue. A raw and awesome power emanated from
the young man, all the more impressive because the engines of
its origin were sunk deep beneath a surface that was calm and
sober and twinkling and merry by turn. Even then he had it all,
everything he would need later on, and he knew, as chieftains
finally realize, that he could count on his own strength, because
he had tested it endlessly; yes, he could count on himself, he
would have to count on himself for the long wait, like a leader
in the hills who knows that impulsive raids at the wrong time
do not deliver the city to you, and that, in some mysterious
way, he would work out his destiny. In later years, especially
after savory triumphs, Daley would quote his mother as saying, "No man walks through life alone; he must have many
friends." But, in a way, young Richard Daley did begin his
walk alone and, beyond his family, gave acquaintanceship to
many, but the intimacy of friendship to hardly anyone.

The twenties were then a period of preparation and obser-
vation for him, a decade when his full schedule left little time
for following the stories of Al Capone or letting himself speculate too much on the apparent alliances between so many people in government and the beer-running mobs. For Daley there
was no pause to examine Cermak, McDonough, or any of the
rest of them too closely. He had mastered a style of knowing
everything and not judging it, of living with a conscience
which focused on his private life. He glanced away, like a
blushing matron, from the activities of corrupt politicians.

It was also the decade in which he would fall in love for the first and last time. He was introduced to Eleanor Guilfoyle, then nineteen and a secretary at the Martin-Senour Paint Company. She was a beautiful young woman from Throop Street in the adjoining neighborhood of Canaryville, a woman of wit and strength from a large family; she was as Catholic and Irish as Daley himself. He took her to a dance at St. Bridget's Hall that evening and embarked on a courtship that was biblical in mood and length. Young Daley had to finish school before he could marry this woman, fair and remarkable in her own right, who waited out the seven years until their wedding in 1936. He would court her on her front porch, giving a visiting cousin a quarter to leave them alone, or, dressed in his best clothes and wearing a straw hat, he would take her to picnics and church socials; sometimes she would meet him after his evening classes at DePaul, and they would go to the Auditorium Theater and sit in the highest tier of seats to listen to concerts together. She was strong enough to ride with him all the way, sole keeper of his inner heart and all his secrets.

In 1930, Cermak, who had become head of the Cook County Democratic Committee when Brennan died two years earlier, slated the faithful Joe McDonough for county treasurer and, in the local Democratic sweep of that year, the former athlete, now ballooned to over three hundred pounds, was elected. He moved across to the county side of the huge downtown building which also housed City Hall. Daley, twenty-eight, on the home stretch of his hard-bought education, pleasantly in love, and filled with information about people and events and civic procedures, went along as his secretary.

These were low days for the depressed nation but high ones for McDonough, who spent as little time at the office as possible; indeed, McDonough once explained that he was so besieged by those seeking favors that he stayed away from his office in order to get his work done. These were the days when he traveled in the grand style to which politicians with extra sources of income had become accustomed. One reporter recalls being with McDonough in a speakeasy when the latter removed a crisp one-hundred-dollar bill from his wallet, placed it on the bar, and nudged it deftly toward the young man with hoarse instructions to buy himself some drinks and to keep the change. This was McDonough, the antic practical joker, eating and drinking his way toward an early death, the moon-faced benefactor who depended on Daley to run the county treasury for him. Young Daley was entirely reliable; it mattered little to him that McDonough got the credit for work that he was actually doing. He was, after all, in the counting house itself, mastering the intricacies of finance and budgets, of the funds for and sources of patronage, of the sweetest secrets about the maneuvers and processes in the jangling till of power.

At the same time, the federal agents were catching up with Capone on income tax charges, and Big Bill Thompson (who had returned to office as mayor in 1927) virtually barricaded himself in the Sherman Hotel, staying out of City Hall for an entire year while a police lieutenant cooked for him. As scandals and charges blew about him like papers on a windy Chicago day, Anton Cermak was consolidating the Chicago political organization which would make him the next mayor. If Daley needed a blueprint for solidifying his own organization a generation later, it was to be found in the design Cermak was working out with a thoroughgoing ruthlessness that took nothing for granted and let no man or force cast even an accidental shadow across his path to absolute control of the city government and the Cook County Democratic party.

There is a spell on the narrative now, a cloud of misadventure and the gathering of the brooding birds of fate; it is a dream in which the inheritance of powerful spirits seems transmitted on the dark wind of death; it is Chicago made host to furies, and its streets and boulevards made the setting for an interlude, not grand enough to be tragic, and yet broken out of time, like events that happen off-stage in a Shakespearean play, mean events of politics and war about which we hear the characters speaking but of which we know nothing more.

At the hollow center is the figure of Cermak, king of the hill, who, in a trade-off of destinies, contracted amoebic dysentery because of sewage that seeped into the water lines of the South Michigan Avenue hotel in which he lived. This was the same Cermak who had worked so diligently to construct a drainage canal to provide Chicagoans with pure water. Cermak went to Florida to recuperate in Paddy Bauler's winter home and, although he was not enamoured of the President-elect, Franklin D. Roosevelt, the mayor had to attend a reception for him in order to settle arrangements for federal patronage for Chicago with Roosevelt's campaign manager, Jim Farley. The reluctant Cermak went to Bayfront Park in Miami and, as he stepped toward the open car in which the next President was sitting, a young man named Giuseppe Zangara opened fire with a revolver. A bullet pierced Cermak's lung and lodged in a vertebra; he fell forward into Roosevelt's arms and was transported to a local hospital. A Chicago reporter, John Dienhart, provided Cermak with legendary words, "I'm glad it was me instead of you," an ennobling phrase for a tough politician who died hard after nineteen days of suffering.

If Roosevelt was spared, Cermak was enshrined with a funeral that was so large it had to be held in the Chicago Stadium. While twenty thousand attended these rites and fifty thousand more braved the bitter cold to journey to the burial in the Bohemian National Cemetery, the followers of the dead Cermak, dead as only a political leader can be, wept for themselves in the night of their abandonment.

The way was clear for the Irish to retake City Hall and Joe McDonough, stricken and restive in the unaccustomed mood of mourning, went to Paddy Bauler's speakeasy on North Avenue to drink away the sting of sorrow, to take a swing at another customer and fall heavily into the old-fashioned stove in the middle of the floor. Richard Daley, model of control even when demons seemed to infest the night, kept his own counsel; whatever he felt, he lived by the Irish adage that a shut mouth never did any harm and, besides that, he had learned long ago to wait and not to make unnecessary enemies in the meantime.

[5]

Where Do You Want to Sit?

The fates had not yet exhausted their influence on affairs; there would be deaths and resurrections before the main chance would rise weightlessly out of the void and drift in Richard Daley's direction. One must not suppose, however, that the future mayor was either simply passive or lucky. Daley was, in fact, preparing himself for the realization of the dream he had first had years before, that glorious vision, bright as a parade float, of serving the city he loved as mayor. He worked hard, mastering each job thoroughly, presenting himself to the public as a servant eminently worthy of their tax dollars and their gratitude. Doing his best and skipping no details, not even in the last long paragraph of a legal document, remaining pleasant as well as polite—these are the memories of Daley as administrative assistant to County Treasurer McDonough. He was not the product of blind destiny, but he nourished a sense of practical far-reaching purpose and made himself ready.

When the Irish, who had been despised by Cermak, retook City Hall, they were not out for vengeance. Party Chairman Patrick Nash, earnest and bespectacled, with the shrewd glance of a man good at sizing up men, horses, or real estate, wanted no fights among the Democrats—they did that better than almost anything else—and he chose Edward J. Kelly, chief of the

Chicago Sanitary District, as the new mayor. Nash and his brother were in the sewer business; he knew how to work with Kelly. The Kelly-Nash organization was to make political history of its own; indeed, Kelly, a lordly looking Irishman, handsome in a heavyset way, a native of Bridgeport who had prospered in his responsibilities for Sanitary District contracts, was to serve for fourteen years. After leaving office he would die, as Daley later would, in his doctor's office, a man forgotten in many ways, a political great from whom old friends drifted away at lunches, an embarrassed former leader who, without change in a hotel men's room, would not even be recognized by the attendant. But all that was in the future, as indeed, were the relatively wide open years of his reign; now he was moving into City Hall, and both he and Nash wanted peace among the party regulars. Everybody would be cut in on the spoils and the patronage, and if this enraged some of the Irish who hated Cermak—men like County Board President Dan Ryan and the somewhat patrician John Duffy—it made room in the inner circles for the Cermak loyalists, the twins of vulgarity, saloon keeper Paddy Bauler and Alderman Charley Weber. And, of course, Daley stayed in the treasury office with McDonough.

Daley missed none of the transition period tactics and, according to political commentator Len O'Connor, it was in observing Kelly's relationship with the new Democratic President—getting federal funds to give Chicago teachers their first paycheck in half a year—that the future mayor began to appreciate the wisdom of good relationships between a big city and the national government. Daley's focus was always on the city and on what would be of help to it; his world was always Chicago and Cook County. He hardly ever really cared who won the Presidency or the governorship; none of that mattered when offices in Cook County were at stake. That was the seat of power, that was the kingdom and the glory of his longing. In his later years as mayor, Daley would refuse even old friends and causes to which he had previously given his support, if they held dances or dinners outside the city limits; he became a distraught lover when others spurned the city as, for example, when George Halas announced in 1975 that he would move his Chicago Bears football team to the suburb of Arlington Heights. Daley denounced the idea at a news conference and, with the proprietary sense that he could give or withhold the city's good name, he declared that if the Bears moved they would have to be known as the Arlington Heights Bears, for he would deny them the blessing of Chicago.

Now, however, Daley's love of Eleanor and the city were, despite their intensity, disciplined and restrained. In the spring of 1934, Daley had law school behind him; he could at last look forward to marriage in the not-too-distant future. What he could not foresee was that his patron, the hulking Joe McDonough, breathing heavily but still only forty-five years of age, would collapse and die of pneumonia on April 25. Young Daley was one of the pallbearers at the requiem mass at the Church of the Nativity of Our Lord in Bridgeport—how many pols he would carry out of church in the years ahead!—and he went in the thousand-car procession to the cemetery. A fellow pallbearer, Hugh "Babe" Connelly, was made the committeeman for the Eleventh Ward, and Tommy Doyle, the Bridgeporter in the House of Representatives in Washington, was recalled to take McDonough's place on the Chicago City Council. Doyle, who had also been a heavy drinker, came home with lung trouble and a year later he also died. Was Daley wise enough to know that each of these changes brought him closer to an opportunity for one of these offices himself? If so, he was shrewd and patient enough (always pleasant on the outside) to wait for the timing of history rather than to try to force it prematurely. Meanwhile, Connelly added the aldermanic seat to his duties as committeeman; Daley liked Babe well enough—he was, after all, Daley's sponsor now—but Daley would watch him carefully and would finally unseat him for good in 1947.

Meanwhile, Daley continued in the treasurer's office, working for a time under Pat Nash's nephew, criminal lawyer

Thomas Nash, whose good looks had not yet been ravaged by cancer of the jaw; he had defended a number of mob figures, including Scalese and Anselmi, the pair of hoods who had shot down Dion O'Bannion in his flower shop across the street from the Holy Name Cathedral. It was said that Capone himself later killed them both with a baseball bat.

"Had they paid you?" a friend asked Nash.

"Yeah, they paid," he replied.

Naiveté about the facts of life was not a qualification for public service in Chicago. Tom Nash and Daley would have major differences in later years—Nash would try to thwart Daley's accession to the party chairmanship in the fifties—but for now they worked together.

The wonder is the way in which Daley, as determined as the young Napoleon to get power for himself, managed to stand among the scoundrels and thieves who were everywhere in city government and still keep aloof from them. He entered the slaughterhouse every day, but he ducked the spraying blood and had little time—no time, in fact—for carousing; he looked as neat at the end of the day as he did at the beginning. He went to mass and said his prayers, but he missed no lesson about human frailty. He could learn from that, too, learn the weaknesses of a generation and more of fellow workers and refine his instinctive reactions to others—those reliable indicators that were essential and invaluable parts of the one person he knew he could rely on: himself. He had a feeling for the amount of pressure people could take, for the soft spots and the open gates of their souls, a sense of what motivated men in close encounters, in the last minutes in which they had to choose the truths by which they would finally live—or at least vote.

Daley was untouched by, but not unknowing about, the raucous side of life in Chicago, about the city that the stately-looking Kelly proclaimed as a "liberal" place. The city was the center, for example, of the famed horse-betting parlors, decorated like lounges, with armed guards at the doors, in which colorful descriptions of the races at tracks across the country were announced from information that was fed across lines leased from the American Telephone and Telegraph Company. Such "handbooks," as they were called, were found in the big downtown hotels; one flourished in the very hotel in which the Democratic party had its headquarters. Smaller betting operations were all over the city, and protection money was dumped like confetti across the town. Prostitution, strip joints: everything that went with a profitable liberal interpretation of "liberal"—that was Kelly's Chicago. Kelly was able to live with it all in the familiar style of Irish Catholic politicians who went to mass, led lives of personal fidelity, and were not scandalized by an imperfect world. It was a heyday for good times and con games, for working the city for what it was worth, for letting it turn into an angel in rags on the lakefront.

The corruption, the smell of an unclean city sleeping off a drunk, revolted Daley, who recognized the way things were and led no crusades, but who had another vision of the city's possibilities, as a place of progress and jobs and neighborhoods like Bridgeport where people cared for each other, as a place where money might still be made by politicians, but where the shame and stench of indulgence would be lifted away. Yes, Bridgeport was still a haven of values and also the home of Mayor Kelly, not a bad sign for an able young man from South Lowe Avenue. Kelly would, however, leave Bridgeport for a fine home near the University of Chicago, forsaking the old ward for the rewards of upward political mobility.

Bridgeport is a symbol, one we have observed before, a grid of old-fashioned streets and ideals, of neighborliness and church-going, of municipal workers, multiplied by patronage wildly beyond the proportion due the number of voting Democrats, life plain and simple and, in the mood of its very air, repressed. It was, for Daley, with parents and wife waiting for him on the same avenue, filled with grace and comfort, a pure place after a day among the grabbers and takers downtown, a place to come home to where he could be certain of stability after the flights and alarms of the day. Daley and Eleanor had been married in June 1936, three years after his graduation from law school. With some extra money borrowed from Daley's father they took a train trip to the West Coast, and their first child, Patricia, was born in the following year. The family grew rapidly over the next several years, with two more daughters, Mary Carol and Eleanor, being born before the four sons, Richard M., Michael, John, and William.

To work toward the day of his own power, Daley needed all the control he could gather. He had to walk among the vandals and to go along with their corruption without condemning it openly, without, indeed, allowing himself to inspect or pass judgment on it, to accept it, finally, as the way of things, the grease without which the cogs could not turn. All of this required the constant exercise of the strongest psychological defenses, the denial and repression characteristic of obsessive Catholicism, the very defenses that could be restored and reinforced in Bridgeport. So it was not only the small town friendliness, the parish church two blocks in one direction and Schaller's Pump two blocks in another, it was not just these conveniences, it was that they were always there and that they were always the same, it was that people talked little about their private woes or difficult choices, that time itself had a stop here where he could feel personally approved; it was here that the self beyond moral reproach could be affirmed and the privacy of the sacred things, family and faith, could be preserved. He had to keep his two worlds separate, and Richard Daley did it for a lifetime with muscular resolution.

And yet he almost jumped at the opportunity that came suddenly in the fall of 1936 when State Representative David E. Shanahan, aged seventy-five, a man from the neighborhood who had been in Springfield continuously since 1894, took to his bed and died just two weeks before the biennial elections. Here was yet another incident that seemed managed by spirits, by the angel of merriment as well as the angel of death. Shanahan, in a wonderfully smoothed golden statue, made even softer in the filtered light of the Capitol dome in Springfield, still looks mildly puzzled about it all as he stands in a swallow-tail coat, his gavel in hand on a draped pillar, staring across at Stephen Douglas. For Shanahan was a Republican and, as he lay dying, he summoned a priest and married his secretary, Helen Troesch, a forty-one-year-old woman with the look of a schoolteacher, who had worked with him for twenty years. Just such a story would set the neighbors clucking in an area that needed a good dose of gossip to relieve the boredom of its virtue now and then. The story was to get better later on when Shanahan's will was read, and his new bride inherited some $850,000, a bequest that was quickly challenged in court by the representative's two cousins, Mary and Margaret Flynn, who felt that the estate should go to them. It did not.

But while the ward was enjoying the whole story, Daley was busy organizing a write-in campaign so that he could succeed on—of all strange and slippery places—the *Republican* ticket to his first elective office. Now was the time for the organization to produce for him, and his knowledge of its charts and secrets was no small advantage in the few days that remained before the election. Daley did not let the Republican standard, almost as bad as an orange sash on St. Patrick's Day, bother him. That could be remedied later. Right now, single-minded-ness and concentration, two aspects of his self-mastery, counted for everything, because his election would give him an office of his own and, incidentally, would further demonstrate his abilities to the Democratic chiefs downtown. He left nothing to chance, not now, not after all the waiting and the intervention of fate; no, this was the run for the roses. When the returns came in, Richard Daley, halfway through his thirty-fifth year, and almost halfway through his life, was elected state representative by 8,539 write-in votes.

The holidays of Christmas and New Year's were sweet indeed for Richard Daley. He had pleased his mother and father and his young wife; he had pleased the Democratic organization, and, in the deepest chambers of his heart, he had pleased himself mightily. He would, however, "walk humbly with his God," as he grew fond of whispering after the great election victories in the years ahead. He would make the trip down to Springfield, through the flat black farmland, past the granaries and storage bins, past the melancholy farm machinery that waited for the release of spring, and arrive in the state capital just ninety-nine years after another young lawyer, Abraham Lincoln.

He was hardly Lincolnesque in appearance; he was more like the Capitol, slightly out of proportion, compact and grave looking. It was January 6, 1937, when he made his way through the neighborhoods of old houses, as comfortable in their way as those in Bridgeport, and to the Capitol, that great leaden-domed hive in which the politicians, either by instinct or out of fear that they might miss somebody important, greet friends and absolute strangers with equal warmth. Daley moved swiftly into this building of frosted light globes and filigreed archways, of paneled wood and no sharp angles, of darkened and cracking frescoes of Illinois heroes (Grant taking command at Cairo), and up three floors to the House of Representatives, where he, a Democrat to the depths, presented himself under Republican colors. He glanced around the squat room and its sweeping semicircle of desks split by three aisles, and he watched the old politicians gathering for the new session, the opponents who fought in the chamber in almost ritual fashion, like animals that do not really want to kill each other in combat.

He was obliged by the circumstances of his election to spend his first morning on the Republican side of the House beneath a pool-table-sized portrait of Lincoln. In the afternoon, a Democratic representative from Chicago, twenty-nine-year-old Benjamin Adamowski, the son of an alderman, and a figure who would challenge Daley in many ways in the future (including running against him for mayor in 1963), a man with dark brows and an ambition as strong as but less controlled than Daley's, offered a resolution to allow the new representa-

tive to sit with his fellow Democrats. The Republican leader
rose and pointed at Daley, who sat expressionless before him.

"I don't care about the resolution," the Republican said. "I
want to know where Representative Daley wants to sit. Where
do you want to sit, Representative Daley?"

Beyond the Speaker's well, on the wall above the Democratic section, hung a portrait to match Lincoln's; it was of Stephen Douglas, the "Little Giant," and he stood with his finger
pointing down, as if he were giving a direction to the new representative. Daley, his black hair slicked back, stood and
pointed toward the Democrats, saying softly, "There."

"Then," the annoyed Republican leader responded, "go on
over there, because we don't want you over here."

Springfield, Illinois, in the thirties had not yet become the
fully developed Lincoln shrine that it is now. Lincoln's Tomb,
the deep sunk sepulcher that, according to some cynics, was the
only thing around that was secure against further rifling, lay at
the edge of town, and one could see the house he had lived in,
as well as the old Capitol, lifted out of proportion by the addition of a third story. Down away from the center of the city,
where the new railroad station stood hard by the St.
Nicholas Hotel, one could see the houselike depot from which
Lincoln made his last talk to his neighbors before leaving for
Washington.

Young Representative Daley was interested in history, interested in walking through the drab old city with its stage-set
buildings, and the sounds of merriment, music, and loud voices
that drifted out of the bars and hotels, although these had no
attraction for him. A brisk walk in the night on the slightly un-
dulating streets of the old capital, that was recreation for the
young representative, a walk around past the State Supreme
Court Building and by the Governor's Mansion, which was set
next to, of all things, the house of a poet, the spacious white
clapboard home of Vachel Lindsay.

If Daley had not read any of Lindsay's work, he had picked

up a phrase of Lincoln's that he would keep in his office when he was mayor of Chicago: "I believe that a man should be proud of the city in which he lives, and that he should so live that his city will be proud that he lives in it." It was simple and direct, the kind of unadorned language in which Daley himself would try to compress his deepest sentiments about Chicago all his days. But emotion clogged the passages of conviction, and his words often broke or stubbed painfully against each other. Daley's private feelings were like the pressures in a congested boiler, for they had to be controlled, at least until he was safely back in Bridgeport, where Irish singing, patriotic assemblages, and family reunions gave him a personal freedom to laugh and cry and sometimes rage. But this side of Daley was intensely personal and not for many men to see. In Springfield he was a public figure, the man who walked a lot and talked but a little, the man waiting for the next opening in his move toward power through public service.

The waters of divination stirred again in early 1938 when death visited Patrick J. Carroll, a state senator whose district included the Eleventh Ward. Daley immediately made himself available as a candidate in the February 1 election to fill the vacancy and was able to move across the State House as a bona fide Democrat to the Senate chamber, where the Republicans had a three-to-one edge in membership.

Daley would serve two four-year terms in the Senate, finally becoming its minority leader, as well as the man Mayor Edward Kelly of Chicago expected to represent the interests of the city in the state capital. In the Senate, a plainer room than the House, with open corridor galleries on the sides and two-story-high windows, Daley worked with men whose faces would swim in and out of his consciousness for the rest of his life, men like the fierce Adamowski, and Thomas Keane, whose father was a legislator before him, a pouch-faced Irishman with a taste for riches and art, a man who would at times be against Daley, who, in a nose-to-nose staring contest, would develop a relationship with him in which Keane would have seized the mayoralty if Daley had glanced aside for a split second. Tom Keane and Daley would come to an understanding in the manner of professional athletes with equally respectable skills, and the wavy-haired Keane, even more publicly pious than Daley himself, would become chairman of the City Council Finance Committee and prosper mightily. Years later, he told writer Mike Royko, "Daley wanted power and I wanted money; we both got what we wanted."

Then there was Abraham Lincoln Marovitz, trim and athletic as a former boxer, an ally and supporter of Daley's throughout his long career, an able and friendly man who would remain a bachelor and who would swear Daley in for each of his terms as mayor; Abe Marovitz, the old criminal lawyer who would come to be an intimate of show business people like Joe E. Lewis and Frank Sinatra; Talmudic Abe sitting on the federal bench in Chicago and recalling the years in which he and Daley drank buttermilk in the Springfield hotels while their fellow legislators were turning their livers to stone on harder stuff; Abe Marovitz, who would live to hear Daley reject his advice near the end of his life. But that story had hardly begun as they walked the city streets at night and talked about the current bills, before Daley went back to his room to call home and to study carefully all the business that would be considered in the Senate the next day.

Then there was Vito Marzullo, from the West Side of Chicago, an Italian immigrant with no education to speak of, who would become an alderman and deliver his ward to Daley with lopsided margins in election after election; Marzullo, of the finely wrought political judgment ("I'm not right all the time, just ninety-nine times out of a hundred"). Marzullo, who looked like a man who had made considerably more money in the pizza business than he expected, forthright and direct, proud of the efficiency of his political organization, already deeply respected Daley, who, in his soft-voiced way, would approach him for a vote on the most personal of terms: "Do it for me, Vito. Will you do it for my sake? Otherwise you'll make me look bad."

Recalling such incidents in the hour after Daley's death, Marzullo, tears welling up behind his aviator glasses, would say, "It was like the hand of God on my shoulder. Any legislation he asked us to support was always screened and double-screened. And I would say 'Dick, I do it for you—not for your boss.' "

Daley developed a reputation as an energetic and effective senator. In the April following his switch to the Senate, the Legislative Voters League noted that Daley "has made rather an astounding record for a new member." The new senator had not, of course, left Chicago behind; by virtue of the death of Michael O'Connor (yet another Irishman—their ghosts were all about him now) he had been appointed, in December of 1936, chief deputy county controller by County Clerk Michael J. Flynn, whom Daley would succeed on his death thirteen years later.

But now Daley was in Springfield and in possession of the combination of the very bank vault of the City of Chicago; he was paid for his work as controller, but the secondary gains in information about the distribution of patronage in the Democratic party, about the finest-drawn details of who was on what payroll and for what reason—a man's payroll assignment not necessarily having any relationship to whatever duties he actually performed—this was the knowledge that was power indeed, information to be stored away and used at the right time. It was like being let loose with a camera in the War Room of General Headquarters; it was both the place to stand and the lever Archimedes wanted in order to move the world. Daley never lost his eye for the map of connections of a municipal payroll, as intertwined as the conduits for all the lines and pipes beneath the city itself. Years later, he could study it and find who was doing what for whom; he could recognize the special meanings and the extraordinary arrangements; where there was fat and where there was bone, as he once did when he observed that payroll checks were still being issued to a laborer who had been dead for three months.

"Well, you know, he was an awful drinker," an aide from

the Eleventh Ward explained, "and we were thinking of the wife and kids."

"No," Daley said, "this has got to stop. Pay her one more month and that's all."

So Daley was on two payrolls and was becoming well known as incorruptible in Springfield; a fellow senator, "Botchy" Connor, from Chicago's North Side, complained of him, "You can't give that guy a nickel; that's how honest he is!" The young senator understood that ultimate power in Chicago was not delivered with cash in white legal envelopes; it would come through mastering the organizational diagrams, through amassing information, the fissionable material of politics, on all the people with whom you worked, through favors done and the development of the species of friendship that is two parts ingratiation to three parts of cunning. His plan was to understand all the plans and to make his way quietly but surely to the front of the line.

Some politicians liked to display their influence, liked to get recognition for their ability to wangle a favor for a client, just as there were many who felt that the best homes, cars, and clothes were the signs of their success. This was never Daley's style, partly because he was secure in his own sense of the world, and partly because his political sense warned him that making a show of oneself almost always made somebody else unhappy, that doing too much to settle someone else's problems was almost sure to leave one side antagonized by defeat and the other irritated by the consequent indebtedness; and because leaving Bridgeport, where he was the biggest man on the block and just one of the neighbors at the same time, leaving behind that clot of homely blocks in which his spirit found both its strength and its ease was an unthinkable price to pay just to buy a finer home or to seem to have risen in the social order.

So Senator Daley was a minimalist in words and deeds; as science seeks the simplest explanation, so his brand of politics sought the simplest gesture with the fewest implications. It was a style which required a discipline whose every joint and ligament he had kept in perfect condition so that his responses seemed effortless; indeed, they had a certain taciturn grace. This applied in all his relationships at every level, to political associates, and even to friends. In 1936, for example, he took some old friends, William Lynch and Peter Fazio, whose law firm he had almost joined, to a political picnic with another lawyer who had been associated with them, James Cullen. Lynch, impulsive and aggressive, a man ready to be crossed, drove Cullen home from the picnic grounds in his car. Soon he roared past Fazio and Daley, who were riding together. "There goes that wild Irishman," Daley said to Fazio.

In a few minutes, they caught up with Lynch, who had been pulled over to the side of the road by a motorcycle cop.

"Let's watch," Daley said, stopping the car several hundred feet away. "Lynch is going to lose his temper."

They could both see Lynch waving one finger and shouting at the policeman, who promptly ordered Lynch and Cullen to follow him to the station house.

"Let's follow," Daley said, "and see if we can help our friends."

When Daley and Fazio arrived, Lynch and Cullen were in the lockup. Daley, following the minimalist route, said to the desk officer, "My name is Daley and this is Pete Fazio. Is there anything we can do to help our friend, who has apparently said something wrong?"

The officer said that no bail had been set and that if Daley could get Lynch to apologize, everything could be worked out. Daley and Fazio spoke to Lynch, who agreed to make amends. Recalling the episode later, Peter Fazio says that Lynch, a bachelor, knew that Fazio and Daley had young wives waiting for them at home, so he broke off his apology and berated the policeman again. Lynch and Cullen were thrown back into their cell. Fazio turned to Daley. "Why don't you tell them who you are, that you're a state representative?"

Daley replied, "We're going to get them out one way, the proper way. We have to be patient."

In a little while, the captain came in, recognized Daley,

asked, "Why didn't you tell them who you are?" and proceeded to get Lynch and Cullen out.

It was 1:00 A.M. when Daley got home, but he had followed his principles exactly. He had stayed with his friends, realizing that sooner or later the situation would work itself out, and he had refrained from using his influence. He was indebted to no one, had antagonized no one, and had betrayed no annoyance. His mother would have been proud of him, for there was no hint of a fix; he had bet on nothing but the weight that events themselves acquire when you let them float through time. It was a strategy, mostly intuitive, that he would often use in the long zigzag path of deals and arrangements that stretched before him.

So Daley did not have to say much on the floor of the Senate; he was so well prepared, his late night study of the pending legislation was so thorough, that his actions were merely the final outcroppings of carefully prepared maneuvers, of ground gone over and gone over once again so that most difficulties had been anticipated and the answers already prepared. It was remarkable how much could be done and how little needed to be said when one was well prepared. It was the same with power; its rewards could be gained without actually using it, without bringing it out into the open, without wasting or diminishing it. In fact, the more measured its use, the more awesome it grew. People would confess or compromise or tell you far more than they should if you listened carefully, without giving anything away, if you had the power to begin with, and if you were sure of yourself and prepared to use power, swiftly and without an examination of conscience, when the time came. Being hesitant was the most fatal of moves; it did nothing but make you vulnerable; it showed your hand to the enemy.

In Springfield, Daley met the downstate Republican courthouse politicians, the hard-eyed assayers of beans and wheat, who were suspicious of big-city Catholics, the men who represented the farming interests, farmers themselves many of them, so that the deceased House Speaker Shanahan was accustomed to adjourn proceedings by announcing, "Let's unhitch."

Young Daley needed all his patience and self-control to deal with these descendants, these second cousins almost, of those who had persecuted his own people in Ireland and in this country. He had to forward the interests of the cities and win the approval of the rural legislators at the same time. His experience in government gave him a clear view of what was needed for financially sound operations. On May 10, 1939, he offered what was then a provocative proposal: He wanted a 2 percent tax leveled on income in order to spare the poor the burden of an increased sales tax. The bill did not pass—Illinois would not have an income tax until thirty years later—but it was a clear illustration of his practical governmental mind at work. He also urged the University of Illinois to establish junior colleges in Chicago, and he pioneered in developing lunch programs for schools and welfare centers.

After the Second World War started, he was interested in legislation to benefit servicemen, and he sponsored leaves of absence for civil service employees who entered the military service. (Because of his large family and the fact that he was almost forty years old when the war started, Daley did not volunteer for service himself.) He fought for the poor, both to lower the sales tax and to prevent home evictions. These were issues about which he had feelings as well as political intuitions; there was passion in Daley's efforts to prepare adequate housing for the returning veterans in 1945 and, in the same year, there was even greater feeling in his investigation of people like Ainslee E. Horney, a Chicagoan who owned the violently anti-Semitic *Hoosier Press*. Warning that the American form of government was seriously menaced by persons who disseminated misinformation "calculated to create hatred of racial and religious minorities," Daley summoned Horney to a hearing in Springfield and, in a rare burst of public emotion, he announced, while serving the subpoena to Horney, "And you'd better come." Perhaps it is not surprising to find Chicago political columnist Milburn P. Akers (even though he misspelled his name as "Daly") writing in 1945 that the senator "is probably the best exhibit of the hard-working, decent, honest organization politician that the Kelly machine can produce."

One fascinating insight into the personality of young Senator Daley, however, can be found in the letter which he wrote to Abe Marovitz on December 1, 1943. Marovitz had left the Senate in 1943 to join the Marines, having said in a prophetic speech that he would return to see Dick Daley become the mayor of Chicago. Daley was to look after his interests in Springfield, to serve as his counsel in keeping his seat from being appropriated by some Republican move. Daley sat in his recently built bungalow on South Lowe Avenue, placed a number of sheets of General Assembly stationery on the desk before him, and in brown ink, with level lines and Palmer penmanship flourishes that would have delighted his grammar school teacher, began a personal letter of explanation to his friend.

December 1, 1943

My Dear Abe:
    Glad to receive your letter and especially happy to hear you are feeling fine.
    Clyde Lee, the Senator from Mt. Vernon, was sworn into the Marines yesterday.
    Of course, you know John Parish is a Lieutenant in the Navy.

But pause now, and you can hear Daley in action, careful, thorough, and listening carefully, sidling up to an associate who would soon tell him what he wanted to know.

    Recently I met the Committeeman from the 24th Ward, and he commenced the conversation by talking about the vacancies in the State Senate. I listened to ascertain what vacancies he had in mind. Of course, the Smith and Gunning vacancies are recognized automatically by law. Elrod said he was with you 100% but some of the leaders in the party were inquiring about the vacancy created by your action. He was overzealous to impress me of his love)or you and his pledge that you should have the office when you returned. Altho my Gaelic blood was inwardly running high I bantered to ascertain who the leaders were so I could map out my procedure. He mentioned Joe Gill and Al Horan. I then proceeded to remove the thought of vacancy in your district by telling Elrod that I had prepared a long legal opinion on the question and my view was supported by legal opinions of the Illinois Supreme Court. When I showed Elrod the language of the court decisions and the definition of a military office, he was convinced there is no vacancy in the Senate for the 19th District. As a final blow I said this is a matter which is entirely and solely in the hands of the Governor. He is not amenable to Mandamus and in my opinion public policy would rebel if the Governor would call an election for any man in the Service. I reiterated the case of Sen. Droste where the Governor refused to call an election, despite the fact that Droste had accepted a commission, until after Droste resigned. Abe, as your legal representative and counsellor, don't let anyone talk you into resigning and don't accept a commission.

After conferring with Elrod I contacted Joe Gill and Al Horan and virtually repeated the information I gave Elrod.

Unquestionably Governor Green will do nothing about your position because any action he would contemplate (other than the one we want him to pursue) would be unsustained and unsupported by legal opinions, reasoning or legal precedent and would be contrary to public policy. In addition his promise to you, and my retention as your lawyer clinches the matter. Don't worry, I shall be in there watching and pitching for any development. Also I would suggest that you and me keep this problem absolutely confidential. If you should mention it to someone our plans might go astray. I also straightened out John Dreiske, who wrote the attached letter in the Mugwump.

Nick Hubbard is contemplating running on the Republican ticket. What a speech the Gentlemen from the 9th and 19th Districts in the Senate could make on this action.

Bill Vicers, Representative Powell and Knauf were in Chicago yesterday. They said we are unorganized downstate and it behooves us to start early in organizational preliminaries down there [sic] way.

Many unexplainable moves are taking place in local democracy. Your friend the coroner is still Sheriff and according to the local press the leaders are looking for a businessman, instead of a politician. If only men would remember that politics is the greatest profession in the world because it is the service of one man to his fellowmen. Martin Kennelly has refused the appointment as sheriff, and the scouts are searching for other prospects in the business world.

Tom Byrne, the old sage of the Southside and a member of the Sanitary District is dead and will be buried Saturday.

Mike Flynn conveys his warm sentiments and regards. Although things have been a little tough for Mike, he is emerging smiling and O.K.

Babe Connelly and all the boys from the Hamburg A.A. wish you well and say Hello.

Lieut. Bill Lynch is doing remarkably well and is now a Senior Lieut. I was his guest at the disastrous Notre-Dame–Great Lakes Game.

Ed Hughes is still sick and there is no indication as to what he will do next year. Rumors are rife that the States Attorney will be the candidate for Governor.

A fight is looming on the Republican horizon in Illinois—the importance of which is unpredictable at present.

The Monsignor—Tom Nash is battling vigorously for John Duffy for Sheriff.

Well Abe if I don't stop I will write a book.

Give your Mother and Bernice, if she is there, the warm and personal regards of the Daleys.

Luck and Good Wishes from my Dad, Mother, Wife, Patricia, Mary, Eleanor, Richard, Michael and your pal

Dick

It is all that a letter should be, right to the point, after a few preliminaries, just way the sisters taught that it should be done. It has heft, a respectable weight like that of a well-oiled and loaded .45. It is a classic illustration of Daley's style, careful and exact, drawing the others out, and then producing overwhelming and twice-confirmed evidence to refute them. It is a letter to set a friend's mind at ease, and yet it is not without caution. Divulging any of this carefully planned strategy might imperil it; there was no need to say anything because everything was taken care of. It is a model letter into which Senator Daley throws some news and some gossip, some political tidbits, and no small measure of sweetness, the best wishes of a friend who has senatorial affairs under control, sincere good wishes that even the stiffness of the letter cannot muffle.

[6]

A Pact with the Spirits

The immediate postwar years were not days of glory for Richard J. Daley. It was a time for the conjunction of inhospitable forces and unkind stars, for cold winds and the ice-water shock of political defeat and of grim insight into political reality, a time for the warrior who sensed he was a chief to draw his robes about him and to stare unblinking into the campfire. To look one way or the other, to catch the wrong eye across the flickering light, might pledge an allegiance that could lead to complete disaster. The Democratic camp was divided and bitter, and powerful men, leaning on their varied shields, studied each other for signs of weakness.

The weakness was generally thought to reside in Ed Kelly, then in his seventies and blamed by many for the poor showing of the Democrats in 1946. He had asked Senator Daley to give up his seat in Springfield and to run for sheriff of Cook County, a job of spoils and plunder in which many another man had grown rich.

It was a flattering offer but, as it turned out, it was also an invitation to a lynching. Daley would speak later of the experience and of what he learned from it. He was being thrown to the wolves as part of Kelly's payment of a political debt to Chicago's meat-packing industry. Its leaders wanted Daley defeated in retaliation for the stand he had taken against them and for the Office of Price Administration during World War II.

Daley did not understand what had happened until he began his campaign. The support he expected from the Cook County Democratic organization was not there; the halls and meeting places were empty of the party workers and precinct captains whose help he needed to win. He knew he had been sacrificed and, bitter as was his loss to unknown Elmer Michael Walsh, it was an experience from which much could still be learned. The defeat—the only election loss of his career—reminded him of how power, in the form the Democratic organization, could crush a man. He would never allow himself to become that vulnerable again.

His ambition now budded not just once but twice: It would never do to become only the mayor; he must also take over the party machinery as Democratic chairman. He decided that the only way to protect himself from power was to take it all for himself—that would be his plan, never admitted or spoken aloud, for a man did better without publicity when he was bent on stealing the whole kingdom.

The experience not only spared Daley from what many considered a lucrative dead end and sharpened his instincts, but it also gave him reason to pull back from the imminent slaughter of Boss Ed Kelly. In the meantime, he went off with his friends Lynch and Marovitz for a consolation trip to New Orleans.

John Duffy, from the prosperous suburb of Beverly, and a member of what Jack Arvey, chairman of the all-powerful Democratic Central Committee, called the "Turkey Irish," was head of the City Council Finance Committee, and he was also making plans. He wanted to take all the power and glory of Chicago for himself and his chief ally, Tom Nash, the criminal lawyer who was Democratic committeeman of the Nineteenth Ward. James McDermott, a tough honest man who looked as though he had passed through a season of hard drinking—but, in fact, had not—was part of their camp as well and would carry the flag in later fights with Daley.

They wanted Kelly out. Although he was still popular with the people, he was a rider shaky in the saddle, a leader gone for increasing stays in Palm Beach to treat his colitis. Duffy would pressure Colonel Arvey to dump Kelly at the slating in December 1946 and then, later on, he would force Arvey out of power as well. Daley, still in his appointive job in the controller's office, was not to be drawn into either defending Kelly, to whom he had been indebted, or allying himself prematurely with Duffy. He would be forty-five in May; he had a large family now, and large ambitions. He kept staring straight ahead, keeping his anger and his frustration—and his plans—to himself.

So they talked it over—could Kelly make it again? And what were the real reasons that the death sentence had to be passed on the man who had said on one occasion, "You run the organization or the organization will run you"? Kelly and Chicago had developed scandalous reputations; the city was wide open, the schools were in trouble, there was measurable discontent. One thing the bureaucrat-politician can do is count, especially votes, and—ghost of the worst prejudice smoldering beneath the blandest rationalization—there was also concern that the voters, fearful of Negroes flooding their neighborhoods, would go against Kelly because he had taken a stand for open occupancy laws. Arvey thought Roosevelt had influenced Kelly in this regard and, although he liked Kelly, he had to make a hard, unsentimental, political decision. It was difficult. One committeeman told Arvey that Kelly would lose by 250,000 votes; the same committeeman told Kelly he would win by that margin. He explained, "I wasn't going to be the one to tell him he was dead."

Arvey asked an associate to make some phone calls about Kelly's popularity. The aide took the phone book and, at random, picked out three Irish names on the North, South, and West sides of the city. Introducing himself as a representative of the "Universal Radio Survey," he asked the respondents about their favorite programs and then added, "Would you vote for Mayor Edward Kelly in a contest against someone else?"

Each one answered in similar fashion: "I did before but never again."

"Why?"

"He's too good to the niggers."

When apprised of the results of this sampling, Arvey, thinking of all the other problems with Kelly, shook his head. "I've heard enough," he said and decided to break the news personally to the elderly mayor.

Kelly took the blow face-on; sudden death in politics was not something about which he was ignorant. He adjusted his glasses, smiled the smallest of smiles, and said, "When two horses go to the post, it's a different thing."

So while the Democrats shifted about for a presentable candidate, Daley considered his own situation. He wasn't in on the bloodletting, and he was also out of the councils of local party power. He was strong in the Eleventh Ward and he had a job downtown, but he needed something more if he was to take advantage of a political situation whose implications he could read as clearly as an old fisherman reads the skies and tides. The party was coming apart; the time for moving swiftly was at hand. Hugh Connelly was still the committeeman, still, in fact, the alderman from Daley's ward. Big Hugh, the baby-faced saloon keeper, had not been feeling well; Daley, more by instinct than by calculation, whetted his sword and prepared for a mercy killing.

It would be said in later years that just as no one killed like Capone, no one killed like Daley either. And he began with his old mentor Babe Connelly by slating an opponent, Stanley Nowakowski, to replace him as alderman. He finished the job publicly on October 23, 1947, when the precinct captains of the Eleventh Ward gathered in St. John's School at 30th and Lowe to vote the Babe out and put Richard Daley in as committeeman. Connelly made a statement to the papers that his health simply would not permit him to run again. Daley looked grave—it was his all-purpose look and it fit at funerals, convocations, Bar Mitzvahs, and events that bordered on being public hangings—but he had managed to gain a seat and a vote in the Cook County Democratic Committee. He was secure and in a favorable position to increase his power and authority in the fragmenting Democratic scene. Daley's father, Mike, had consoled him after his election loss the year before: "The Lord never closes a door that he doesn't open a window." And, indeed, Committeeman Daley, a keen watcher for the slightest crack at any window, could smile inwardly at the marvels of providence.

The battle lines in local Democratic politics had already been clearly drawn. Duffy of the South Side would wait for the 1948 election campaign before he moved to oust Colonel Arvey in order to move ahead with his own plans for controlling the party. In that year, however, in that long championship season in which it was generally felt that incumbent President Harry Truman would have little chance against the Republican candidacy of the clean, self-righteous wax dummy, Thomas E. Dewey, in that year in which so many wise elders and brash pundits would be confounded, Colonel Arvey put together what was described (for once not generously) as a blue-ribbon ticket.

For the United States Senate, he slated Paul Douglas, liberal City Council member, professor, and returned Marine veteran; for the governorship, he slated the man who would become the hero of every naive liberal's political dreams, Adlai Stevenson. Few observers have ever credited the Chicago Democratic organization for discovering and supporting these household gods of political idealists, but, in fact, without the machine, the liberals would never have had them to revere. It is also worth noting, as we pass once more through that bannered and band-filled campaign, that both Douglas and Stevenson maintained great respect for Richard J. Daley, who delivered his ward so handsomely for them on Election Day.

So Illinois suddenly had a senator and a governor struck in a noble mold; Colonel Arvey, thought to be on the way to exile, was hailed instead as a political genius. Indeed, the Democratic organization in Chicago had served Harry Truman's cause very well; Congressman William Dawson, the Emperor Jones of the Second and Third wards, the peg-legged black leader who had been converted from Republicanism by Mayor Ed Kelly, delivered a massive vote that gave the state to the Democrats. Duffy, caught off guard by the unexpected victory of his own party, would have to wait, would have to nourish his spoiled ambitions in that special sullenness, in that avenging melancholy of the Irish that leads to more complex plans for later opportunities. But the Gaelic spirits would finally hold nothing for Duffy but the sound of things that almost happen.

Stevenson understood Daley's ability and appointed him a member of his state cabinet as revenue director. No two men could have been more opposite in background, and yet Stevenson, innocent as a boy who never surrendered his mother's first stories about how the world turns, needed a man with the reputation and ability of Daley. It was not just political reward that prompted the appointment. Stevenson, the almost indifferent candidate who on Election Night had asked a reporter as he headed for dinner, "Oh, is it going well?"; Stevenson, who had yet to yearn almost painfully for the Presidency, did not act on accepted party principles and allowed many holdover officials to retain their positions.

Daley, now a more thickset and solid figure, warned the new governor that these people would betray him, as indeed they did, but the patrician Stevenson, who approached political reality with the caution and insecurity of a man in evening dress whose office is in the middle of a greasy and sparking foundry, only learned this the hard way. So Daley, who would bear a major responsibility over the next year in helping Stevenson run the state government, took the oath of his new office in the presence of his wife and seven children. He made a brief statement in very serious tones: "There will be no sinecures in the Department of Revenue as long as I am director. And, of this I assure you, there will be no tax-fixing."

It will always remain difficult for those who prefer the image of Daley as the political hack, the well-tailored carnivore, to recognize him as the highly conscientious and energetic man who immediately mastered the details of every job. And yet, this was clearly the Daley of the Stevenson years, a man compiling a good record and always learning more in the process, a bright and vigilant political leader who stood at the second tier in all the political photographs of the period, the man just a step back, no, half a step, close enough for Arvey and Stevenson to feel his breath on their necks, but it was not that vintage exhalation of older pols which, hot and fouled as a dragon's, pumped the whiffs and odors of large meals, liquors, and cigars into every room of their gathering. Daley's tastes were not for alcohol and tobacco; he was not the Thomas Nast caricature; he was, rather, the monk who kept the monastery accounts and understood who bought and sold everything from the hymnals to the fresh bread; the monk who, never late for choir, stood as if in meditation not a shadow away from the abbot.

The abbot Daley wanted to succeed was Martin H. Kennelly, up from Bridgeport the hard way, a mild and handsome-looking businessman who had succeeded Ed Kelly as mayor of Chicago. Kennelly, a bachelor who had moved far away from the Eleventh Ward to an apartment on Lake Shore Drive, was not an organization man; he did not understand the arrangements and favors that a city's chief executive had to grant in order to keep everyone at least mildly contented. He would not negotiate in the ordinary political coin—he would not even see that the policemen in his security detail were gradually promoted—and so he was never the true master of the city.

The City Council's fifty aldermen enjoyed enormous power, not only in administering city affairs—they presented the budget to Kennelly rather than the other way around—but most of them prospered through their own outside law firms or insurance agencies as well as through the routine grafting that went with purchase orders, building variances, and a hundred other permits for everything from driveways to parking places. The late forties were fat years and Kennelly, with the righteousness of a fundamentally weak and indecisive man, felt he was doing well by not cooperating with the machine. "I'm keeping them out of jail," he would say as he turned his attention to tightening civil service regulations, the very drawstrings that would choke the life out of any political organization which depended on patronage.

Daley could see City Hall from his office in the State of Illinois building, the office in which he had hung a picture of Governor Stevenson that was inscribed, "To Dick Daley, God love him!" If Daley said little, it was not that he lacked plans or convictions. And it was Chicago, the Chicago of his dreams, though it reeked of so many disfiguring and unappetizing scandals, the city and its Democratic organization which he would gradually take over.

In March of 1950, Michael Flynn, county clerk, having patched up his relationship with a younger woman in the eyes of the Catholic Church on his deathbed, closed his twinkling eyes for the last time. Daley gladly accepted the appointment to fill out his unexpired term and was ready to run on his own in the November election. He could not have been more different from Flynn, a tire dealer who had made his way into the Democratic inner circles through his early support of Ed Kelly. Flynn was a horse fancier who promoted illegal cockfights on the far South Side, a prosperous Irishman who took a kickback from all the workers in his department to whom he gave overtime work, an old-fashioned politico in spades who lived undisturbed by the inevitabilities of its darker aspects. There had, for example, been considerable trouble in his ward over horse parlors, the "handbooks" that flourished throughout the city. At the time of Pat Nash's wake, Mayor Ed Kelly went to the funeral home, only to find Flynn sitting in a swing on the porch. "You're pretty hot, Mike," the mayor said, referring to the violence in Flynn's ward.

"Ah," replied Flynn, "There's nawthin' to that, nawthin a-tall." That there had been at least one murder didn't faze Mike.

Flynn, now prayed over mid the austere melodies of the Latin Requiem Mass and carried by yet another team of solemn-faced politician pallbearers to the cold consecrated ground, was soon but a memory; and Daley, closing in on his forty-ninth birthday, moved quickly to take complete and efficient charge of the office which was responsible for records, licenses, elections—and which was also a rich storehouse of patronage jobs. Daley liked the work and, in his fashion, modernized operations and cut costs, even as he settled into a stronghold of local Democratic power.

A reporter who had covered city government for twenty years met Daley at this time and recognized something different about him. Most officeholders, their eyes on the next rung up the ladder of power, had always seemed content to allow the existing staff to run the departments. It was not so with Daley. Even before he ran for the office on his own, he involved himself completely, according to this observer, in understanding the governmental operations of the county clerk. "I decided," the reporter said, "that this was the kind of a man who really understood city government, and that I'd hitch my wagon to his star."

1950 smelled good to the whole Democratic organization until, the fates twisting sharply, a Democratic senator, Estes Kefauver, came to town with his Committee to Investigate Organized Crime in Interstate Commerce. The hearings, part of Kefauver's plan to attract attention to his own Presidential aspirations, finally brought disaster to the Democratic ticket in November, woe to Colonel Arvey, who had enjoyed only two years of being a political genius, and woe as well to his enemy, John Duffy, who lost his bid to become president of the Cook County Board of Commissioners; woe of a biblical texture, woe like that seeded into a city like a plague, woe to everyone but Richard J. Daley, who was elected county clerk by 147,000 votes.

It is difficult to imagine that the spirits, flowing through the crack of the midcentury, were without influence in everything that happened from the first momemt of conjecture among the Democratic leaders about whether the chief investigator for the state's attorney's office, Daniel "Tubbo" Gilbert (who would soon be known as the World's Richest Cop) should give testimony or not. Tubbo was not, in fact, fat; he had led the good life and found plenty of time for the golf that kept him in excellent physical condition. But Captain Gilbert's name was associated with a number of shady activities, bookmaking for one. What should be done, in view of the fact that Gilbert had been slated by Arvey as the Democratic candidate for sheriff of Cook County?

The Democratic leaders gathered at the Hotel Morrison. The local newspapers were raising questions about Gilbert. Suppose, someone suggested, that Gilbert volunteered to testify before the Committee in secret? A vote was taken and the ayes had it; meanwhile Alderman Arthur Elrod would work out a deal with the Committee. Gilbert would be questioned lightly in return for his cooperation; he would, in the words of Elrod, "get a pass."

But Gilbert discovered that no pass was forthcoming once he got into the hearing and was questioned by counsel Rudolph Halley. Captain Gilbert, who had declared a taxable income of $45,000 in his last return, and who held stocks and bonds worth more than $300,000, explained that he had wagered on events and combinations of events, on baseball and football, on the market, on fights and elections.

"I have," he said, in the manner of a man who has suddenly found the logical explanation for things, which explanation, once delivered, will allow him to go home, "I have been a gambler at heart all my life."

It was as American as apple pie; yes, it was all that simple until Halley asked, "This gambling you do—that is not legal gambling, is it?"

One can hear the pause, the silence in which the baited hook sank into Tubbo's jaw, before, disconcerted, half out of the water and a goner for sure, he replied, "Well, no. No, it is not legal. No."

"They threw the book at me," he reported back to his friends at the Morrison Hotel later in the day.

But the testimony was secret and, save for another Irishman, reporter Ray Brennan of the *Chicago Sun-Times*, it might have remained that way until after the election. Brennan, however, went to the printers, represented himself as an aide of Kefauver's Committee, and secured a set of proofs of the testimony. He hurried back to his desk and went to work on a story that would explode in front page headlines just five days before the election. The furies broke loose on the city. Even the machine could not redeem Gilbert's airy explanations with enough votes to elect the Democratic slate. Illinois Senator Scott Lucas, President Truman's majority leader on Capitol Hill, was carried down by the force of the public's rejection of Arvey's slate. A Republican, a former congressman from Pekin, Illinois, Everett McKinley Dirksen, became the Republican senator from Illinois.

When the storm had passed, the camp was almost empty except for Richard J. Daley, a leader become more sure of his pact with the keening spirits, and a man who understood that a new period in his life had begun.

[7]

The Tip of the Sword

There is a legend that in old Gaelic society a mother would give her son his first solid food on the very tip of his father's sword, a symbol of her wish that he should find death only in battle.

After Colonel Jack Arvey's hasty departure from the chairmanship of the Cook County Central Committee in 1950, Chicago's Celts, this ancient vision rising in their dreams, had at each other with a vengeance. Everything was at stake now and, like bands of warriors looking for the best footing for battle, the Irish of the Fourteenth Ward arrayed themselves against Daley's clans from the Eleventh Ward. Garfield Boulevard ran like a river of new affluence through the Fourteenth; it was the neighborhood to which the Irish who had made it moved first, and its alderman, Clarence Wagner, half Irish—"the best half," he would say, cocking his strong chin and fixing you with his slightly skewed eyes—and Superior Court Judge James McDermott were paired as the allies of the Nineteenth Ward's John Duffy and Thomas Nash. Daley, who became first vice-chairman of the Democratic Committee when Arvey was replaced by an "acting" chairman (the sixty-six-year-old Joseph Gill, who would ride out the 1952 Presidential election and then step down) viewed this chairmanship as his next step toward complete power.

Wagner was in a strong position. He was chairman of the City Council Finance Committee and, because of Kennelly's hesitancy, practically ran the city itself. Kennelly, called "Snow White" by many of the local Democratic regulars, was under a political death sentence, one that would be final and swift and unseasoned by mercy after he completed his second term in 1955. He had alienated Congressman William Dawson, deliverer of the huge black vote, by allowing the police to raid the policy operations, whose wheels and numbers were, according to Dawson, "a way of life" for his constituents. Dawson, a spellbinder who usually ended talks to his people with a piously phrased farewell, "Walk along, little children, and don't get weary 'cause there's a big camp meeting at the end of the road," was in no sweet mood when he threatened to withdraw his support for Kennelly's second term in 1951. He had returned from Washington to harangue the mayor at a secret meeting like a preacher passing judgment. Stomping around the room on his wooden leg, Dawson yelled, "Who do you think you are? I bring in the votes. I elect *you. You* are not needed, but the votes are needed. I deliver the votes to you, but you won't talk to *me?*" Kennelly never knew that the Democratic leaders (among them Daley) had concluded, after the meeting, that his second term would be his last.

So two flags of power—those of the mayor's office and of the party chairmanship—hung as prizes in the wind. But both sides had to wait out the disastrous Democratic year of 1952, the season in which Stevenson thought that he really could win against Eisenhower. Duffy, a florist as well as a politician, a man of urbanity who talked out of the side of his mouth, regrouped his forces. He had ceded his City Council leadership to Wagner when he made his fated run for the County Board presidency in 1950. Now the strategy, as simple and complicated as seizing a castle and the king too, was to have Wagner step down as committeeman of the Fourteenth Ward in favor of McDermott, who would then resign as judge; McDermott would thus place himself in a favored position to be elected Democratic chairman in 1953. In 1955 either Wagner or Duffy himself would make the race for City Hall. Daley knew all this, of course, and it took every bit of his self-control to remain calm and to keep his promised supporters in line, as he waited for the meeting, scheduled for July 8, 1953, at which Gill would resign as chairman and, according to his sheaf of plans, he would succeed.

And so the politicians gathered at the Morrison Hotel, fifty committeemen from the wards and thirty from the townships of Cook County. An armistice would be signed in a few days in Korea, but another battle was about to be mounted here as Joseph Gill, now sixty-eight, pounded the gavel to call the meeting to order. Gill would announce his retirement and, in one of the most arduous and yet durable of political traditions, he would hear speeches of praise from the committeemen; then he would solicit nominations for his successor. Daley expected to return to Bridgeport with the flag of the chairmanship in his hand.

But Clarence Wagner rose to speak smoothly; he argued for a delay on such a serious matter and proposed that the vote for the new chairman be postponed until July 21, and his motion carried. Even though Daley remained confident of his ultimate victory, he was stunned by the action and was clearly upset when he returned to his county clerk's office to find a reporter waiting to interview him as new chairman. "If you're not the chairman," the reporter said to the flush-faced Daley, "who is?"

"Nobody," Daley replied tersely. "Joe Gill is still 'acting.' "

According to Len O'Connor, Daley explained, "Clarence stopped it. Gill calls for a motion to nominate me and Clarence gets up and says, 'Now, wait a minute. Let's not be hasty.' And there was a big argument and we didn't get to vote."

Daley went on to explain Duffy's plan of getting the post for Judge McDermott. "He'll quit as judge. Clarence will quit as committeeman of the Fourteenth and Jim will take that. Then he can be chairman."

It was, Daley agreed, Duffy's plan to take over all of Chicago. Later, Daley would say that the opposition never had enough votes to defeat him, but on that July afternoon he was clearly frustrated; he would have to wait behind his own Gaelic mask, wait them out and face them, in fierce battle, if need be, two weeks later.

But the wind suddenly died down; it was a strange interlude, like the quiet of a summer afternoon when dread lies on the trees and fields and the towering clouds may deliver a gentle rain or a murderous storm. There was no hint, however, of the forces that were gathering already in the oppressive mood of this summer interim, no signal that in a mean place near Nagurski's Corner, Minnesota, everything would be settled in an instant.

Clarence Wagner had gone with State Senator Donald O'Brien and their sons for a fishing trip to Lake of the Woods, Ontario. Wagner was driving his official Cadillac at about 7:00 A.M. on July 10 when, for reasons no one knows, the car swerved off the blacktop road near Nagurski's Corner, lifted off the ground for thirty feet, sank back into the road's shoulder, and, for a terrifying few seconds, dug along the erupting turf, then slammed into an embankment and arched over onto its roof, its wheels still spinning in the clouds of dust. Inside, Clarence Wagner lay dead beside the battered but surviving O'Brien and their sons.

Back in Chicago a newspaper reporter was putting a question to Thomas Nash, chief plotter along with Duffy of the delayed vote on the chairmanship. How would Wagner react, the writer wanted to know, to the idea that he give up his ward committeeman's job so that Judge McDermott could have it? Nash, feeling a new confidence about the turn of Chicago politics, answered, "He would be willing and happy to do so."

But Wagner lay dead, and the dreams of Nash, Duffy, and McDermott were smashed as well. There was a grand wake for Wagner, of course, the kind of wake a man gets when he dies with lots of friends as survivors, and his house was almost sick with the smell of funeral sprays in the July heat. It was not, however, an event that lacked a pinch of mystery and a measure of irony. It had fallen to the strong and honest McDermott to break the news of Wagner's death to his wife; it was also his task to open Wagner's safe-deposit boxes and to make other arrangements as soon as possible. He was amazed at the amount of cash that he found—over $400,000 according to some estimates—and some of the other aldermen were quick to lay claim to it. Wagner still lay in his own living room, the mass cards and the spiritual memberships in various religious orders piling up beside the visitors' book that had been signed by every Democratic officeholder and hanger-on in the city, but he was surely dead, and no amount of sentiment ever blocks a politician's clear intuition that debts should be cleared before the casket is closed for the last time.

Alderman Harry Sain of the Twenty-seventh Ward on the city's West Side came to see Judge McDermott on behalf of a number of his friends. "Jim," he said, "there was an envelope Clarence was holding for us and I come over to get it."

The judge, no man to be cowed by anyone, admitted nothing.

Sain went on. "There was an envelope with a hundred grand and it's our money and the boys want I should get it."

McDermott remained impassive, asking whether Sain could identify the envelope—if there was one—or if he had a signed agreement from Wagner.

Sain, growing irritated and expecting some form of aldermanic honor to be present in McDermott, pressed his case, even though he had no proof of ownership. McDermott is reported to have turned him away—is there a cruder way to break a wardheeler's heart?—saying that whatever money there was belonged to Wagner's widow and children.

Years later, Alderman Paddy Bauler would rage about the loss to writer Len O'Connor, "So Clarence has this envelope and then he gets kilt and that son of a bitch McDermott won't give back our money. . . . It was one of them franchise renewals, the phone company or the gas people or somebody. Listen, you think we should do things for them people for nothin'? Holy Cry, you don't think they expect to get it for nothin', do you? What's fair is fair, you know."

But all that was far in the future. Now Daley, hiding his ambivalence beneath the gravest of looks, attended the wake, the funeral, and the special convocation of the City Council where speaker after speaker paid tribute to Wagner, whose desk was draped in black. Mayor Kennelly wept twice during the ceremony. "Why shouldn't he?" an observer asked later. "Wagner did all his work for him."

McDermott kept up a brave front for a few days, saying of Daley's allies, "I know that they have the shiv out for me but I think it looks pretty good for us."

But it did not look good at all. They could not hold any of Wagner's friends together for their own cause, and Daley's principal supporters, Joe Gill and Albert Horan, held municipal court jobs that controlled patronage. On July 20, the precinct captains were to elect McDermott committeeman of the Fourteenth Ward but the judge withdrew his name that afternoon. The last of the enemies had thrown down his spear.

Richard J. Daley was elected county chairman the next morning.

[8]

Entering the Kingdom

Seek ye first the political kingdom and all
things shall be added unto you.
— Kwame Nkrumah

Martin Kennelly, a few months past his sixty-seventh birthday
and unaware that the hanging judges of the Democratic Committee had already passed sentence on him, studied the telegram he had just received. It was from the Central Committee
and it requested him to appear before it on December 15, 1954,
during the hearings that would decide the party's candidate for
mayor in 1955. The telegram was an insult; he had announced
for re-election already and had opened his campaign headquarters at 7 South Dearborn Street on December 1. He had
received no word at all from party chairman Daley after he
declared for his third term. Such silence was ominous and
frosty, eloquent in its own way, because the void tingled with
the controlled power of Richard Daley, who, on the verge of
claiming the nomination for himself, projected sullen and
paralyzing waves of displeasure without the slightest twitch or
blink, without moistening his lips or moving his head. He
sometimes spoke, of course, in a tone as straight as his face, as
when he was asked if he would accept Kennelly's invitation to
visit his headquarters. "I promised to take my kids to see Santa
Claus that day," he replied. Another reporter asked Daley who
the Democratic mayoralty candidate would be. Daley's irritation, indeed, his own eagerness to run for the job could be

measured only in an indirect way. His lips were pursed as he spoke softly, like the most innocent of witnesses about to enter the antechamber of judgment, saying everything by saying hardly anything, compacting menace and power into a small movement, like the rippling muscles on the back of a crouching lion. "I have been asked," Daley said slowly, "just whom the Democratic party will endorse. Obviously, I cannot answer that question because I do not know."

Kennelly did not know how to respond to what amounted to a summons to his own execution. "The hell with them," an aide suggested. "Call them over here and then throw them all out. You don't have to go to them like that."

Kennelly's personal lawyer thought otherwise, and the mayor decided that he would have to present himself to the committee, stacked with Daley supporters, just like some unproven hopeful. Kennelly was about to undergo classic Daley treatment, the complete, nothing-unthought-of, no base-untouched purge; the party chairman had waited too long to make any major mistakes at this moment.

And Kennelly was basically unsure of himself, a virtuous man who was hesitant about a wide variety of things, a man who was always asking his assistants whether he should go here or there, whether he should do this or that. When a speechwriter prepared a text which included the phrase "massive retaliation" in it, Kennelly called the *Chicago Tribune* to see if it sounded acceptable. Poor Martin Kennelly! He seemed so genuinely innocent about all the things going on in the world around him. Having posed for some publicity pictures with trumpeter Louis Armstrong one week, he was scheduled to be photographed with former football star Jim Thorpe the next. "He's not another one of those colored fellows, is he?" Kennelly asked his incredulous staff.

Kennelly had been rocked by the Kefauver Committee visit and by later revelations about the criminal activities of his chief of uniformed patrolmen, Captain Raymond P. Gibbons, but he had recovered and, in fact, enjoyed a certain popularity with the citizens of Chicago. His real crimes, in addition to crossing Congressman Dawson on the policy wheels, lay in his unwillingness to work with the Democratic organization. The capital offense, however, centered on the highly respectable Stephen Hurley's work with the Civil Service Commission, which had pried as many as 12,000 jobs off the patronage lists. This was attacking the vitals of the organization, for the whole structure of effective service in return for votes depended on controlling the livelihood of party workers. So Kennelly, the dangerous do-gooder who thought he was championing clean government, was, in effect, a threat to his own party. "Fartin' Martin," the vulgar Paddy Bauler growled. A man who would be more understanding and cooperative was needed, and Richard Daley, county clerk and party chairman, as quiet until now as the hangman himself, was ready to step forward and take over.

As party leader in Cook County, Daley had listened for more than a year to all the complaints about Kennelly. He listened, of course, without changing expression; he was as careful as a man has ever been not to give callers the impression that he sided either with them or against them. He listened, with the calmness of a veteran wiretapper who has passed beyond emotional reaction to his work, but no person could quote him or make a claim on him. Daley knew what he wanted to accomplish; he had overcome the Nash-Duffy-McDermott troika, and the shiniest apple on the tree of his ambition was almost within reach. But he needed to get into the public eye; he needed some public prominence, even though he would trust finally in the organization's capacity to turn out votes more effectively than media exposure could.

Daley disliked the media intensely; he disliked most reporters, and he never changed his mind or his heart about them. In the fall of 1954, however, he would make some appearances for, on the surface of things, he was running for county clerk again and was opposed by John Hoellen, a perpetually harried-looking man who would run vainly against him for mayor almost twenty years later. Hoellen had appeared on a local television show, "City Desk," and had made some charges against Daley and his handling of election returns, a responsibility he shared as county clerk with the Board of Elections. Daley accepted an invitation to appear on the same show, to be interviewed by a group of Chicago political correspondents.

This was perhaps the first time the public at large had been exposed to his style, powerful and mysterious as a garbled telegram from headquarters, although it would become comfortably familiar in the decades ahead. It was a style easily disparaged, the style of a warrior who was quick to resent false charges and even quicker to get at the nearest enemy's throat; the whole of it blended in a cracked cauldron of run-on sentences, mispronunciations, and a sense of loss and injury that would fit into a plea for Dreyfus, the style of an angry man who, having held himself in control for so long, had forgotten the combination on the locks of his own speech. And yet the speaker could not be underestimated, even though his gaffes would attain a classic status over the years. What he meant was always more important than what he said and, if the tone of this first sample would be heard many times in his career, so too would the force beneath it be felt, the running-straight-on, javelin-in-hand attack of a roused leader whose mode of assault, primal in intensity, contained the blunt core of his message and his identity.

Charles Cleveland, political editor of the *Chicago Daily News*, began the questioning by saying, "There has been a lot of speculation that you may run for mayor. In the event that Mayor Kennelly decided not to run next spring, what guarantee will we have that, if you're elected county clerk, you won't serve a few months and then run for mayor?"

Daley's response was modal, as he rushed past the question toward the issue, the attacks by Hoellen that had eaten at his soul like acid.

"Mr. Cleveland," Daley answered, "before I answer that question, I'd like to go into some statements that were made

The classic set piece of a Daley campaign—the torchlight parade (actually railroad fuses were used) complete with bands, banners, and marchers of every age and station. This is a picture of Daley's home-base Eleventh Ward Regular Democratic Organization moving through the streets of Bridgeport in 1959, a year in which Daley scored an enormous victory. (*Chicago Sun-Times*/Palmer)

Left: Before he became known as a kingmaker in national politics, Daley was busy making judges in Chicago, the traditional right of a political patron. There is no doubt about who is central in the distribution of power in this picture. Wearing glasses in the background is Colonel Jack Arvey, who had been chairman of the Cook County Central Democratic Committee before Daley. At the right is Judge Abraham Lincoln Marovitz, who had served with Daley in the Illinois legislature and, as he left for the Marines in 1943, predicted that Daley would one day be mayor of Chicago. (Murphy Photography, Inc.)

Above: Daley whispers to Congressman William Dawson, the powerful black Democratic leader who played a major role in Daley's acquisition and preservation of total political power in Chicago. Dawson delivered his wards with large Democratic majorities on every Election Day.

Above: Daley and Adlai E. Stevenson at the Democratic National Convention at Chicago's International Amphitheater in 1956. Daley supported Stevenson's nomination for another run for the Presidency while he worked hard to secure the Vice-Presidential nomination for Massachusetts Senator John F. Kennedy. Thrilled to have the Democrats meeting in his city and almost in his own neighborhood, Daley said afterward, "If Sam Rayburn [the convention chairman] had recognized the right people, Jack Kennedy would have been nominated." (*Chicago Sun-Times*/Zack)

Left: A high point of the year during which Daley hit his stride as mayor. In the summer of 1959, Daley, surrounded by his family, welcomed Queen Elizabeth and Prince Philip to his city. (Murphy Photography, Inc.)

Daley escorts Mrs. Eleanor Roosevelt at a 1959 dinner. In the next year she would pressure him intensely during the Los Angeles Democratic Convention to switch his support from John F. Kennedy to Adlai Stevenson. Daley had committed Illinois to Kennedy after Stevenson had told him he would not run. Still, the arguments of Mrs. Roosevelt, whom Daley revered, subjected the mayor to great emotional stress. (Roosevelt University)

Daley greets Adlai Stevenson and Former President Harry Truman at a dinner in the late fifties. Always an admirer of Truman's decisiveness and total loyalty to the Democratic party, the mayor also thought highly of Stevenson. A mutual respect existed between Daley and Stevenson, almost as though each longed for the qualities that the other possessed. (UPI)

President Kennedy joined the mayor at a Chicago banquet on "John F. Kennedy Day" early in his administration. Daley admired Kennedy not only as an individual but also as a symbol of the arrival of the Irish Catholic in WASP-dominated American society. (AP)

two weeks ago on this very program." Now his voice began to rise. "The man that was on that program made a most reckless, unwarranted, vicious, and malicious statement . . ."

He then denounced his opponent without naming him, a technique Daley used all his life. Then, his righteous indignation beginning to blaze, Daley ran head-on into a key mispronunciation, something that would also be an abiding characteristic of his public statements: "A man running for a public office to make such a statement without consulting the *statue* of Illinois and the laws of Illinois, gentlemen, it's ridiculous."

Daley's next move was also indicative of a later style of rhetoric. Having distracted his listeners as well as the interviewer, he promptly denounced the potential evils of the medium itself. "Mr. Ray," he began, addressing the program's moderator in the tones of a confessor about to lecture on the occasions of sin, "it points out to me a very serious problem in this new mechanism of television. And that is when statements can go out over the air wholly and totally inaccurate and untrue and can be verified by anyone who will reach for a statue [*sic*] of Illinois and tell the people the truth. I say it's about time that we start tellin' people on these various programs and we candidates the truth . . ."

There was hardly a pause for breath, as there would not be in hundreds of similar periodic sentences he would construct over the years; he accelerated, like an angry carpenter who grabs whatever boards are handy—short, long, or splintered— and hammers them rapidly into something that can serve as a wall, ". . . and I think when a man appears on a program like this and attempts to tell you four men or this large listenin' audience of the city of Chicago and the county of Cook bareface, inaccurate, malicious, reckless, and unwarranted statements, then it's about time some steps be taken to correct it. Surely you wouldn't want to deprive me of the right to correct the good people of Chicago and Cook County and tell them the truth, that you know as well as I do is the truth, would you?"

Charles Cleveland turned again to the question of whether

Daley, presuming he were re-elected county clerk in November, might serve only a few months and then run for mayor in the spring. Daley replied in subdued tones, "Well, Charlie, that question is highly problematically and loaded, as you know. . . . You would think, then, that they should not elect me as county clerk? Is that your interpretation?"

Cleveland responded, "If you're going to run for mayor, a few months later, I think not."

Daley shot back, "I think I'm a candidate, Charlie, and you know it, for county clerk."

"Will you," Cleveland asked directly, "serve out four years as clerk, or will you—"

But Daley was not to be pinned down. "The question you asked, Mr. Cleveland, has too many contingencies and too many possibilities for any intelligent man to answer at the present time."

Political commentator Len O'Connor broke in. "Then you will not say that you will not be a candidate for mayor next year?"

Daley had not missed the point of broken field running in his years of coaching the Hamburg teams. "I am not discussing the mayoralty of a candidate, and I appeared on this program as a candidate for county clerk."

John Dreiske of the *Chicago Sun-Times* then put this question: "Your opponent, Mr. Hoellen, points out that, besides being county clerk, you are county chairman of the Democratic party. Do you feel you can serve all the citizens properly, without divided interest?"

Daley drew immediately on the deep wells of his righteous indignation. "Mr. Dreiske, I would say to you, that's an attackt [*sic*] on my integrity, and no one has ever attacked my integrity as long as I have been in public office."

"He did," Dreiske shot back.

"Sure he did," Daley quickly responded, "because of his remarks in the early part, which I tried to refute and which you all agree was inaccurate. . . . The unwarranted and reckless attack on the county chairman is what? . . . I took the chairmanship of the party, and you people know that I did, to try to do something with the Democratic party, to improve it, and I think we did when we come with the candidates we did here in 1954, some of the finest candidates ever presented to any public at any time, any place, anywhere."

The grammar could always be faulted, but the energy and the message could never be misunderstood. Nor would wise people ever suppose that the man who spoke in paragraphs that resembled train wrecks was anything but shrewd and intelligent. He would never master the art of conventional public speaking, despite lessons and practice over the years—he would even acknowledge publicly just a few weeks before he died that few people mixed up the English language the way he did—but it can also be said that no one ever failed to grasp his meaning.

Daley was re-elected county clerk in the November elections. Among those re-elected with him was County Assessor Frank Keenan, a powerful man with whom Daley would have to struggle within a few months. But now Daley's attention could be turned to the ousting of Martin Kennelly, the mayor whom the county chairman had purposely not involved in the just completed campaign. Daley would not even invite the mayor to the traditional precinct captains' luncheon, the pre-election gathering of the almost 3500 foot soldiers who organized the city right down to the level of the individual householder. Kennelly went right ahead with his own plans, telling reporters that he would beat the organization in the way that Governor Henry Horner had in 1938.

Daley was moving quietly because he wanted to underplay the dumping of Kennelly to avoid a bad reaction in Chicago's business community. The outcome was assured anyway, and why not wait until as close to the holidays as possible so that the developments would be swallowed up in other news and concerns?

Kennelly, however, had already declared, as had Daley's former crony from Springfield, Benjamin Adamowski, who described himself as an independent Democratic candidate. The newspapers speculated about Daley's chances of being slated even as they printed daily reminders of the dwindling number of shopping days before Christmas.

It was December 15 and Kennelly walked from City Hall to the Morrison Hotel to present himself to the slate-making committee. He knew that five days earlier one of the men he would have to face, Barnet Hodes, law partner of Colonel Arvey, had announced the formation of a "Go Forward Chicago Committee" for Richard J. Daley. Daley himself had been asked whether he would make any statement to the slating committee. "Yes," he said softly, "if asked to make one." He went on to say, "I am sure the committee will pick the type of candidates we had on the county blue-ribbon ticket in 1954."

A reporter asked him if the Democrats did not have blue-ribbon city candidates in 1947 and 1951, the years of Kennelly's campaigns. Daley spoke slowly, "I wouldn't say yes and I wouldn't say no," and returned to his Morrison Hotel offices.

Martin Kennelly entered a room in which fifteen members of the slate-making committee were seated around a large table. There was no greeting, no praise for his work, just silence as aged Joseph Gill, the chairman, looked expectantly toward the mayor. Kennelly could see Richard Daley seated on a couch near the wall in the back as he began to read a statement he had brought with him. "You are all familiar with my record as mayor since April of 1947. I am proud of my administration. Our many achievements reflect credit on the Democratic party."

There was hardly a cough or a shuffle of papers in the few minutes it took Kennelly to finish reading. He looked up. "Are there any questions?"

The silence, by now an awesome force, pressed its own message against the old mayor. No one stirred, no slate-maker spoke, and Daley seemed lost in thought as he gazed straight at Kennelly. The mayor pulled back his chair and left. He had been in the room just three minutes and fifty-six seconds.

Back at City Hall he would speak of his irritation to his aides. He was particularly upset that Daley had sat in on the hearing, and that his old friend P. J. "Parky" Cullerton had said nothing on his behalf. To newspaper reporters Kennelly said simply, "They seemed glad to see me. I read the statement and they asked me no questions. I said good-bye and walked out."

Back at the Morrison, other reporters asked Daley why he had attended the session. "My office as chairman is next door to the room where the committee is meetin'," he replied. "I pop in now and then."

Would Daley be a candidate?

"That," Daley replied with his famous innocence, "is up to the committee."

At City Hall, Kennelly was attacking the slate-makers more vigorously, claiming that they were interested only in bossism while he was interested in Chicago. He complained that they had not been willing to give him as much time as Roger Bannister needed to break the four-minute-mile barrier the previous summer. "Oh," Joe Gill said to a reporter later in the day, "we gave him a lot more time than four minutes."

It mattered little because the next day heavier artillery moved into position as the slate-makers continued what they characterized as serious deliberations. On December 16, steel union official Joseph Germano attacked Kennelly as a man who "disregarded the Democratic philosophy," not consulting widely enough with "political, labor, religious and educational leaders in arriving at decisions." On the seventeenth, Kennelly was strongly criticized by a spokesman for the United Electrical Workers Union. His downfall was being orchestrated slowly in the waning days of the year. On the eighteenth, Kennelly announced that Assessor Frank Keenan, a blood enemy of Daley's, would manage the "Greater Chicago Committee for the Re-election of Mayor Kennelly." Keenan, a tough professional who would spend time in jail later on for income tax evasion, was ready for a hard fight. He disliked Daley and felt that he could swing support away from him. "A lot of committeemen would like to be with Kennelly," he announced, "if they had their own free choice."

On that same day, Richard Daley sat in with the slatemakers in their final two-hour, closed-door session. It was a Saturday and carols filled the air, and Santa Claus figures stood at every street corner in the Loop. The last weekend before the holidays was at hand; the time had come for the decision. Joe Gill announced it, making it sound as though anguished soul-searching had actually gone into the final recommendations. "Since last Tuesday," he said, "this committee has been in constant session, finding it necessary to have a night session yesterday." He cited the pure-hearted motives and diligent work that had gone into their examination of the many fine men who had presented themselves. "It is the unanimous conclusion of the committee that Richard J. Daley will unite the people of Chicago, conduct a vigorous, courageous, and aggressive campaign, and give to Chicago a positive program for municipal betterment."

While Frank Keenan was describing Kennelly's primary campaign as a "crusade," reporters were crowding around the newly anointed Daley, the chairman who was now another giant step closer to the office he had longed for so ardently. What, the journalists wanted to know, was his reaction to being recommended by the slate-makers?

"It's a great honor," Daley answered, "and I never dreamed it could happen to me." He paused and said that he would have to think it over and talk about it with his family; yes, that was the thing he would have to do, for this was no small decision to make. He would reveal his decision on Monday afternoon.

Daley knew that a tough primary race, complicated by the presence of Adamowski, lay before him, but the dream that had never left him was now within reach. He would stretch it out a few more days, keeping the papers interested in him rather than in the others, commanding lengthy space in the Sunday editions, and then the headlines once more on Monday. It was a solemn moment, a time for the final plighting of his troth with Chicago, the love of his life. He prepared a statement to read on Monday afternoon, December 20. Daley would hardly ever depart from its themes; he would, in fact, use the phrases ten times over, and multiply that ten times more, in the years ahead.

> Although I have not sought this honor, [he began with a completely straight face] there is no greater distinction in the world to me than to be the mayor of the city in which I have spent all my life.
> In all my years of public service I have tried to live up to the guidance and example received from my good mother and dad. In all the words that have been written about me in the daily press, I am proud that not a single one has criticized my conduct in public or private life.
> In the task you have assigned to me, I shall always try to do justly, to embrace mercy, and to walk humbly with my God.

Daley would never forget, however, that on that very day when the recommendations of the slate-makers went to the fifty ward committeemen for their formal approval, there was one vote cast against him, that of Frank Keenan. Daley had been humble and almost as pious as a novice responding to a noble vocation, but something of the warrior flashed when he was asked why Kennelly had to be replaced.

"He has failed," Daley said simply.

How had he failed, the reporters wanted to know.

There was more than a hint of the unforgiving chieftain, of the leader who had no weakness for misplaced mercy. "In every way," Daley said and, ignoring further shouted questions, he turned his back and walked away.

[9]

The Kid from the Stockyards

I'm a kid from the stockyards and I say
I'll stand with you!
—Richard J. Daley, February 14, 1955

"They'd like to get back in control," said the silver-haired Martin Kennelly, warming to the self-righteous themes of the primary campaign he had decided to fight against Richard J. Daley. Was he dumped, the reporters wanted to know, because he had been trying to shut down gambling operations in the city?

"I think that's one of the considerations," Kennelly replied, and then added, referring to the Democratic organization, "They don't like real civil service, the city purchasing system, or taking and keeping politics out of the schools."

Such ideas would dominate Kennelly's efforts to hold on to the job of mayor of Chicago; he had cast himself as the hero in a Frank Capra movie about political corruption, and he felt that if he could reach enough voters who distrusted the organization, he could deny Daley the prize he had been seeking for so long. In his own eyes, Kennelly was an aged but honorable knight, the leader who had been ousted because of his honesty and independence. He was the good guy, a trifle naive but untouchable, an innocent among the corrupted, the last noble warrior trying to prevent the city's reverting to the status of a wide-open prairie town. Kennelly fancied the role, and his campaign manager, Frank Keenan, would make him play it like an old matinee idol on his last tour.

A few blocks away, Richard J. Daley said very little. It had never been his style to respond to such political attacks; silence had its merits, because it provided a man with a sheltered space in which he could make his own plans. So he said nothing while the newspapers carried the statements about Kennelly's campaign and speculated on just what Daley would now do. When the *Chicago Tribune* reported on December 19, for example, that "Daley is expected to resign tomorrow as Democratic county chairman to make the race for mayor," he did nothing to confirm or deny the story.

There was every advantage in saying nothing, because the impression given by the story—that he would surrender a measure of his political power—would disarm some of those who were accusing him of being an aspiring boss in the grand mold. But it also served Daley not to deny the report; no man could now afford to seem overanxious to succeed him. Ambiguity was an intuitive weapon that he used all through his career: His facial expression could mean *yes, no,* and *maybe* all at the same time.

A reporter from *Life* magazine asked him once about his reputation for never committing himself until he absolutely had to.

"That's a good way to be," Daley replied, chuckling, "don't you think? That's a good way to run any business."

Daley would rely on the regular Democratic organization to turn out the vote; keeping the machine disciplined and responsive was, in every one of his campaigns, far more important to him than discussing issues or engaging in debates that could only give publicity to his opponents. He loved Chicago and he intended to be its mayor. He also intended to keep absolute control of the Cook County Democratic organization and, let others speculate as they would about it, he understood at the guttiest level of his political insights that this was essential to the kind of powerful leadership he intended to provide. Indeed, until the day he died only Richard J. Daley could sign checks for the party organization; only he knew what the bank balances were and how the money was spent. Close associates,like Colonel Arvey, had previously advised Daley that becoming party chairman in 1953 would interfere with his plans to run for mayor later on; others, with the best intentions of political sagacity or friendship, told him the same thing. Still he said nothing, and his silence would be interpreted as the signal that he had taken their advice; there was never any harm in letting friends feel the warm superiority of giving him counsel, no harm, that is, as long as he did not really take them seriously. Daley knew what he wanted to accomplish, but he could reveal this—and then through actions rather than words—only after he was safely ensconced in the mayor's office on the fifth floor of City Hall.

Politics was a business and Daley always emphasized basics. That meant keeping the fifty ward leaders and their thousands of precinct captains active in canvassing the neighborhoods, which they provided with everyday services that bound their constituents' loyalty to the Democratic party on Election Day. The organization was strung out on the webbing of the patronage system, but its essential structure was the delivery of concern and favors at the neighborhood level. Daley firmly believed that voters were more concerned about street lights, street repair, and garbage collection than they were about politicians who discussed issues that were not of such immediate interest to them. He knew the electorate was made up of ordinary people trying to lead decent lives according to traditional values. Respond to them when they had problems—getting somebody into the hospital or somebody else out of a minor problem with the law, being with them when there was a birth or a death—and they would respond with votes. He looked on the precinct captain not only as the key to political control but also as an heroic, priestlike figure who knew what his people needed and ministered to them regularly. In later years, Daley kept in his office a framed copy of "Ode to a Precinct Captain," written by Edwin Lahey of the *Chicago Daily News.*

So, in the last week of 1954 Richard Daley was concentrating on the organization and on the first practical step that had to be taken in order to insure victory over Kennelly and Adamowski in the February 22 primary. Each candidate's petitions had to be delivered to the city clerk's office on December 29. Those with the earliest time of arrival stamped on them would earn their candidate the top position on the ballot. This was no small advantage, in the judgment of professional politicians; it could, all by itself, mean as much as five percent of the vote. Let Kennelly mount his knightly campaign; the prizes of the new year would belong to those with lesser objectives in the last days of the old.

Kennelly's manager, Assessor Frank Keenan, with the look of a pink-cheeked baby who had grown old and tough, also understood the facts of political life. He would sell Kennelly as the pure-hearted redeemer, but he would also get busy asking for contributions from the business interests whose properties were affected by his assessments, and he would not ignore the question of the petitions and the advantage of first place on the ballot. The primary would be close, especially with Adamowski draining votes away, and each little step was vital to final success.

Keenan saw to it that a group of men were at the city clerk's office even before it opened on December 29, to see the mailed petitions for Kennelly delivered and stamped with the earliest arrival time. They had counted on the U.S. mails, but they had not counted on Daley's capacity to anticipate events and to bend them to his advantage through plans that left nothing to chance. Kennelly's men smiled as they saw the petitions delivered; they did not know that their mail had been routed to the city collector's office first, a slight stratagem which gained the smallest and yet most telling of delays. When the petitions did arrive at the city clerk's office, Al Kahn, head clerk of the license division, brought them to a deputy, who stamped them 8:19 A.M. Kennelly's men did not know, however, that in another departure from routine in that most routine of offices, Daley's petitions had been delivered through a side door rather than through the main door of the office. An experienced mail clerk had also departed from his well-established routine. Instead of distributing the mail to various desks, he had taken the whole batch to the deputy who had immediately stamped Daley's petitions as having arrived at 8:12 A.M. A small incident, indeed, like a stray tea leaf in the bottom of the cup, a leaf that still carries a wrinkled prophecy about kingdoms and destinies, yes, a silhouette where one could make out the profile of Richard J. Daley himself.

"Television is our precinct captain," one of Kennelly's aides said, indicating the heavy reliance the incumbent would put on this just-maturing medium as his way of reaching the people.

"Can you ask your television set for a favor?" Daley asked.

Keenan, snarling at the contributions of some business interests and sending back for more, knew that he needed a great deal of money to turn out a large number of registered voters, especially from outlying parts of the city, in order to defeat Daley. He made direct appeals to Republicans to cross party lines in the primary and to vote for Kennelly; one newspaper advertisement invited the Republicans to "ask for a Democratic ballot."

Daley, with customary patience, waited for Kennelly to make a mistake. This was another maxim from powerful Richard's political almanac: Let your opponent talk until he has talked too much or made a serious error and then go after him. Kennelly, overreaching on the issue of the Chicago public school system, made just such a blunder in an address at the old Garrick Theater. He claimed that, if Daley was elected, the high schools would lose their accreditation from the North Central Association. There were indeed troubles in the Chicago school system, but this was not one of them. Earl Bush, who would be Daley's public relations director and press aide for the next twenty years, flew through a heavy snowstorm to the North Central headquarters in downstate Illinois the next day and returned with a statement from its head that refuted

Kennelly's claim. Now Daley would speak on the issue, and speak to the ordinary neighborhood people whom he knew so well. He could not imagine a candidate for public office who would upset the mothers of a city by making them think that their children would be kept out of college because of defective high school diplomas. It was the classic moment for Daley to strike: when his opponent had clearly made an error on a matter which affected the day-to-day lives of the people who cast the votes.

The pipes were skirling as Daley and his aides concentrated on the neighborhood ward organizations, fine-tuning them for the Washington's Birthday vote. "You never stop campaigning," Daley told a reporter, "if you're doin' it right." And doing it right meant the day-after-day organizational work; the future mayor was a realist about political life. He needed the neighborhoods and he needed the unions, whose leaders were among his closest supporters and advisers. Making the rounds with the working man was a staple of the Daley primary campaign. And as he did this, many businessmen hedged their bets by contributing to Daley's campaign as well as to Kennelly's.

Typical of Daley's activities was his attendance at a dinner given for him by the Plumbers Union, whose leader, Steve Bailey, had been a lifelong friend. Indeed, the Plumbers Union would remain as close to Daley as any labor organization throughout his years as mayor. These were, after all, people he understood, and people who understood and identified with him.

The plumbers, a thousand strong in their unadorned hall on the West Side of Chicago, had just finished a corned beef and cabbage dinner when Steve Bailey rose to speak. He presented Daley with an outsized stillson wrench, saying, "After you're mayor, if the City Council won't go along with you, you can shut the water off!"

This was a night for sentiment, thick and Irish as the embrace of warriors drunk with the sweetest thoughts of comradeship in battle. "I don't know a finer man," Bailey said. "I don't know a better-qualified man. What burns me up at times, Dick

Daley hasn't been presented right. He's outstanding in every respect. And no one can put a finger on him."

Bailey paused and referred to the campaign postcards with pictures of Daley and his family on them. "I've seen his cards, and the pictures of his children. Dickie Daley is square, honest, upright, and fair, and no one will ever take that away from me."

Now Bailey was plainly overcome, an old laird falling on the sword of his own emotion. ". . . and he's a father—" But he broke off as the applause erupted and the plumbers rose to their feet to hear Daley speak.

Daley was touched but not overcome by emotion. He remained enough in possession of himself to lay aside an Indian headdress before he could be photographed in it. "No one could be introduced by anyone like Stevie Bailey without being tremendously moved. We both came from the same neighborhood and we have seen men in all walks of life come out of our neighborhood and walk the ladder of success. Why?"

The candidate paused slightly before stating the refrain that he would repeat, with hardly a word out of place, through the generation of power that lay just before him: "Because basically we were taught some very sound fundamental principles and lessons at the feet and knees of our fine parents, the lessons learned from the good nuns and priests. They taught us the first thing—that you never walk through life alone, that you must, as you go through life, make friends—friends who help one another."

The plumbers did not need an interpreter to understand that this was Daley's way, without mentioning his name, of depicting Kennelly as an outsider, a man with no taste for such a clan and its gatherings. Daley built up to a final warm accolade for "my pal, Stevie," and, as the band struck the first notes of "Chicago, Chicago, that toddlin' town," Daley was on his way through the crowd to another meeting in another part of the city. The plumbers applauded him loud and long as, exchanging greetings all the way, Daley headed for the exit. The plumbers would do well under his administration; the plumbers, in dreams to dazzle the most ambitious among them, would prosper as a union, swelling their membership through enlisting anybody who had anything to do with water—what a long list when one considers the possibilities: dentists, nurses, and how many more?—and growing affluent on their dues and their own multiplied wages.

Daley had a touch with these crowds and really hit his stride in the campaign on February 14, when a large rally was staged at the hulking Civic Opera House, a huge pillared building hard by the Chicago River. The organization had turned out over four thousand cheering and singing party loyalists, who filled the seats and crowded the staircases and aisles for a Daley rally that would explode like a starburst shell above the last week of the campaign. The orchestra kept up a rhythmic beat of campaign songs, and the hall echoed with the hand-clapping of the party workers. At 8:20 P.M., Colonel Arvey stepped to the stage microphone to prepare for Daley's entrance, a rite that would be staged a thousand times with minor variations over the next twenty-one years. The house would be brought to the finest edge of excitement while Daley waited in the wings for the chairman, alone in the spotlight, to build up to the last introduction. Arvey declared, "I am a Democrat and proud of it!" And the Opera House exploded with cheers and whistles, with the homely roar of political professionals doing what they do best. And the band started to play, bringing the beat of ragtime and Dixieland together in "Happy Days Are Here Again."

At that moment, surrounded by aides and family members, Daley began moving, almost like a man leading a charge, down the center aisle. "Dick! Dick!" the crowds began to shout as Daley, waving and smiling, and the engine of his own phalanx, headed toward the stage. It was an entrance of entrances, simple and swift and filled with old melody and the promise of new power, the very set piece for the energetic man in the dark blue suit who now looked out with a broad smile at the men and women swaying and clapping and cheering to Roosevelt's old campaign song.

Daley's rhetoric was shaky at best, a long climb on a sheer facing of clichés, and yet, as always, he communicated his identification with the people and his love for their city. "My opponent says, 'I took politics out of the schools; I took politics out of this and I took politics out of that.' I say to you: There's nothin' wrong with politics. There's nothin' wrong with good politics. Good politics is good government. . . . Ladies and gentlemen of the Democratic party of the city of Chicago, let them be the State Street candidate. Let others be the LaSalle Street candidate. I'm proud and happy to be your candidate."

The excitement was an intoxicant to the Democratic workers as Daley concluded with a sentence that would set the crowd cheering wildly again and in a single moment would weld the identities of speaker and listeners together. Yes, something passed between the plain working-class crowd and the far from dashing but exciting figure of the solid man on the stage; he laid claim to the crown and the scepter, to the kingdom itself, as he said, "I'm a kid from the stockyards and I say to all of you, I'll stand with you!" A confirming shout came from the men and women who hailed the candidate as their leader, a shout that was as good as a coronation.

"Give 'em hell, Daley!"

And Daley, the king acknowledging and blessing his people Chicago-style, shot back, "Thanks very much, pal."

The campaign had a full head of steam and Daley, putting the pressure on in every ward meeting and precinct gathering, pulled the throttle full back on the machine.

Kennelly hammered at his favorite theme. "This election," he said, "is a question of the people against the bosses."

And so it was, as the bosses scurried at every level to get the votes out for Richard Daley, or at least to take votes away from Kennelly by diverting them to Adamowski on primary day. Everything, in Daley's judgment, depended on the performance of the organization, and on election evening he was proved correct. As Kennelly studied the returns and muttered, "They're unbeatable, just unbeatable, aren't they?" it was clear that Daley's margin of victory was due directly to the machine's strength. Of his winning edge of 100,064 votes, 99,000 came from eleven of the wards that were under the absolute control of the organization.

In Kennelly's headquarters Morris B. Sachs, a local clothing merchant who had run for city clerk with the silver-haired old mayor, leaned on Kennelly and wept like a man whose business has failed. He would brighten up and accept Daley's invitation to run with him for city treasurer a few weeks later, but now it was a time for mourning as the primary—and Kennelly's career—shuddered to a stop.

At the Morrison, well-wishers were gathering around the now official Democratic candidate for the office of mayor. It was a throng of fulfillment and prophecy, of old warriors like Congressman Dawson, who had raised the first battle cries against Kennelly; and of union leaders like plumber Stephen Bailey, steelworker Joseph Germano, William Lee, president of the Chicago Federation of Labor, and William McFetridge of the Flat Janitors Union, a gathering of chieftains who knew what they wanted and now almost surely had it. And there was Sargent Shriver and his wife, Eunice, of the Kennedy family, all their dreams and nightmares still before them. It was a night when things had come together in the Democratic camp; six weeks more and Daley would take Chicago as his bride.

But tonight he spoke softly and slowly, with a tone of humility that could not hide the bulge of his power. "I shall," he said, "conduct myself in the spirit of the prayer of St. Francis of Assisi. Lord, make me an instrument of your peace."

[10]

708,222

One has heard of elections in Chicago. They stretch back across political history like the coal-country slag piles that smolder and smell for years, eating their own insides and trailing smoke across the countryside.

In Chicago in 1955 many Democratic leaders, longing for the less restrained plundering of the administrations which preceded Martin Kennelly's, expected the election of Richard J. Daley to be the first step in a restoration of the freebooting days; they lusted like cartoon industrialists for the wealth that could be strip-mined out of the earth with little concern for social consequences. Richard J. Daley said nothing, of course, for the more he learned the less he said. Let others read what they might in his impassive responses; once he was mayor they would learn the truth. If he would never be averse to politicians making some money in the course of their work, he was sick of the pillage and rape of that great lady of a city he loved so deeply.

Yet this was precisely what his Republican opponent, the WASP prince Robert Merriam, said would happen if Daley became mayor. Chicago would collapse once more into a shameful orgiastic existence with Daley as its leader. One cannot imagine a campaign theme that could have offended or hurt Daley more. It also made headlines. The thirty-six-year-old Merriam, a Democrat turned Republican only the previous fall, became the delight of amateur politicians and self-styled reformers throughout the city. Robert Merriam, the war hero who had written a book about his experiences in the Battle of the Bulge, had a master's degree in public administration from the University of Chicago, where his father, who had run for mayor before him, was a professor. He was as culturally different from Daley as it was possible to be—the young idealist on the shifting edge of a campaign that could be the first, or the last, of his career.

Merriam wanted Chicagoans to recall the days when the city was filled with blood and money; when "Hot Stove" Jimmy Quinn earned his nickname by accusing the aldermen of being ready to steal everything they could get their hands on except a burning stove; when, during the election time in 1928, Senator George Norris asked President Coolidge to withdraw the Marines from Nicaragua and send them to Chicago. Chicagoans still shuddered at the memory of Al Capone, whose brother Frank was killed in an Election Day melee, or of Bathhouse John Coughlin, who, along with Hinky Dink Kenna, represented the First Ward, the juicy heart of the city. Bathhouse once explained the recruiting and sheltering of transients for multiple voting on Election Day as "Hobo, Floto, Voto." Coughlin, who wrote such songs as "Dear Midnight of Love" and "She Sleeps by the Drainage Canal," had said, "When I see a reformer I put a hand on my watch." It was the vision of a return to control by such men, of a Chicago, in the words of *The New York Times,* "disgraced but not ashamed," that Merriam presented to the voters.

Daley set up his political headquarters at the Democratic offices at the Morrison Hotel and opened a campaign office on Washington Street. It was a symbol of a distinction which he would maintain throughout his life; he would keep the jobs of party chairman and of mayor quite separate, although he was determined to hold on to both of them. It was, in fact, a daring strategy; not even Anton Cermak had attempted to maintain both positions. Daley's instinct for the acquisition of absolute power did not come from the study of political science; it was a prodigal gift in his genes, the sense he breathed in the most tender moments of his mother's care, it was the smell of survival in Bridgeport itself.

In his office on Washington Street, Daley maintained a small staff, headed by the indefatigable Earl Bush, who prepared statements on policy and wrote Daley's speeches; it included Seymour Fox, a Phi Beta Kappa television writer, James F. "Spike" Hennessey, ex-newsman and Democratic press agent, and Rita Fitzpatrick, who had been a star reporter on the *Chicago Tribune.* Present also was John McGuane, a political patriarch from Bridgeport, a witty man who had made a fortune in real estate, one of the few persons Daley ever seemed to trust almost totally. McGuane was a father figure and more; he was an example of the shrewd Bridgeporter, the politician who gave away money from his stuffed pockets at neighborhood picnics and offered as well the most restrained advice—fileted of the tiniest bones and trimmed of the thinnest sheen of fat—to the future mayor. He represented the values in which Daley believed; McGuane was a genie from the well-rubbed lamp of traditional home life, an elderly man still devoted to his mother, a man who would keep a framed pencil sketch of her in his office.

So Daley, who would never have anybody else who even seemed to resemble a campaign manager, had McGuane, who symbolized everything that was familiar, and Bush, who, in many ways, symbolized everything that was new. He trusted both of them as he dug in for the final weeks of speaking and visiting, of going to wakes and dropping in at ward organizations, of attending rallies and giving interviews, before the April 5 election. He was often accompanied by Matt Danaher, a neighbor from South Lowe Avenue, a young dark-haired Irishman in whose bright eyes one could not yet read the foreboding of the tragedy, of his graphlike rise and fall across the next generation. But in March of 1955 all that was distant from the man of twenty-seven who was caught up in the thrill of Daley's first hurrah.

Daley's style was a clear revelation of convictions which he reworked very little in the years that followed. He would not run his campaign for the media, and he would emphasize basic political organization and performance rather than public discussion and debate of what his opponents would describe as "issues."

On the other hand, Merriam, dark-haired and almost boyish looking, was the modern candidate, speaking of issues and using the media, especially television, to the fullest extent. He was the very opposite of the caricatured machine politician whom he cast in the villain's role in the campaign. On television, on the Sunday after the primary election, he vigorously attacked Dick Daley as "the machine candidate" and presented what he described as "evidence of the link between Chicago crime—Syndicate crime—and machine politics." He played a tape, made in the days of the Kefauver investigation, of a Chicago gambler's attempt to bribe a Southern sheriff. Merriam, righteousness signed on his full brow, claimed that the Chicago gangsters also operated in "narcotics, prostitution, the illegal sale of liquor to minors, 'B' girls, counterfeit cigarette stamps, tainted horsemeat." It was a list for a church door, a crusader's manifesto for a new era in Chicago.

Daley, his control sorely tested by such accusations, kept his own counsel. There was no point in refuting the opposition's charges; that was playing into their hands. Wait, yes, wait in the traditional strategy, wait as he had waited for Kennelly, and make the mildest of statements in the meanwhile. "The Republicans are trying to portray me," he said, "as a man who would unleash the forces of corruption on the city of Chicago. But my private and public life has been guided by my conscience and my God." That was enough to say, he decided, while he put his time in on making sure that the organization was operating properly.

Merriam, riding a tide of mass-produced campaign litera-
ture, attempted to capitalize on the slogan with which his television spots began, "It's time for Merriam." These words were
plastered on billboards throughout the city, and Merriam himself would set a wristwatch alarm to go off twenty minutes into
his public speeches. "Oops," he would say as it rang, "time for
Merriam!" He traveled around the city in a station wagon that
was equipped with loudspeakers, a telephone, a tape recorder,
and an electric razor.

Daley continued to work the ward gatherings where he
could meet individually as many of the precinct captains as
possible. He waited for the right moment to make his entrance
into these places too, even though they were often merely small
back rooms or clubhouses just a door from the neighborhood
tavern. The local alderman would have worked the crowd up
with a talk that emphasized the need for them to get to every
house in their neighborhoods, and suddenly Daley, smiling
broadly and greeting many of the workers by name, would
hurry into the smoky and noisy room.

Writer John Bartlow Martin recalls a story that Daley would
tell at these gatherings, a joke with the neighborly texture that
all his listeners could feel for themselves, the kind of story only
one of their own could tell. "There was a fellow who was hard
of hearin' and he had been doin' a good deal of drinkin', so he
went to see Doctor Hughes, over at Thirty-seventh and Wallace, and the doc told him, 'Pat, I'm tellin' you this: If you keep
up your drinkin', you'll lose your hearin'.' Well, the fella came
back in a month, and he says, 'Well, doc, I'll tell you, I been
enjoyin' what I been drinkin' so much more than what I been
hearin' that I thought I'd just keep on drinkin'.'"

After the explosion of laughter, Daley would speak a few direct sentences about the great tradition of the Democratic
party and his personal certainty that with the help of what he
always called the "presint captains," the election would turn
out favorably. Then, as quickly as he had arrived, he would be
gone into the fresh night air and on to a similar gathering
across the city.

Back in Bridgeport, Daley took delight in a campaign song that a neighborhood character and amateur entertainer, "Sambo" O'Connor, would sing for him.

> I'll talk to Gilhooley,
> He'll talk it over with Dooley.
> Dooley'll go around and see O'Shea.
> Then O'Shea will see O'Gara,
> He'll go to see O'Hara,
> Then he'll go to call on Pat O'Day.
> So O'Day will see O'Marra,
> He'll talk to McNamara
> For Mac is with the pols 'most ev'ry night.
> But you can't depend on Haley,
> So they'll have to see Dick Daley—
> Everything will be all right!

When "Sambo" died years later Daley attended his funeral, as did the entire Eleventh Ward organization, on orders.

Merriam, meanwhile, was attempting to dramatize that vote fraud had occurred within the machine during the primary campaign against Kennelly. He produced testimony and pictures from a Chicago character named Admiral Leroy, who had gone with a recorder and a camera to observe another celebrated Chicagoan, "Short Pencil" Sidney Lewis, as he erased votes that had been cast for Kennelly on February 22. In a turn of events that should have surprised no one, the Election Board, dominated by Democrats, investigated and censured Merriam and Admiral Leroy instead of the accused Short Pencil Sidney. Merriam came up with more evidence: He had mailed 31,986 letters to registered voters in sixty-five of the Democrats' strongest precincts. Of these, 2982 were returned with the stamping "Moved, left no address," or "Unclaimed." Merriam said that many addresses were nonexistent and that many addressees were dead, that a projection of these figures suggested that there were perhaps 100,000 "ghost voters" in the city. Daley replied to none of these charges.

Merriam had been influential, while serving on the City Council, in having a commission, the so-called Big Nine, appointed to investigate the relationship between crime and political activities in the city. It was a mill filled with grist, as he saw it, and he wanted to dump the contents on the campaign trail. The question of whether or not to keep the files of the "Big Nine" secret was to be taken up by the commission on March 4. A Democratic alderman flew back from Florida to tip the vote 5 to 4 against revealing the files.

Meanwhile, Richard Daley, still silent about such issues and accusations, was encouraging campaign workers with statements which bore the indelible mark of his having spoken them. "We will," he told one group, "continue to carry the message as the early Christians did—by word of mouth."

On March 8, Alderman Ben Becker, who was running with Daley for city clerk, had to resign under the pressure of investigation by the Chicago Bar Association. There was no evidence that he was guilty of fee-splitting, as charged, but, given the climate of accusation, Daley immediately let the trap door fall beneath Becker's feet. He closed it just as swiftly and, in a gesture that was as surprising as it was politically astute, he asked Morris B. Sachs to join his ticket, shifting John Marcin to the city clerk candidacy and asking Sachs to run for city treasurer. Sachs, who only a few weeks before had wept with Martin Kennelly in defeat, accepted with the nimble quality of an early-rising jogger. Morris B. Sachs, who never tired of telling of his immigrant background and his Horatio Algerılike life, Morris B. Sachs, who would claim that he sold Dick Daley his first pair of long pants, was well liked in Chicago and would, in fact, get 27,000 more votes than Daley on Election Day.

A few days before St. Patrick's Day, Merriam spoke publicly of "a group of dictators who may spend a million dollars—over two hundred dollars per precinct—to try to buy the votes they cannot honestly win." It was a melancholy accusation so close to the great Irish feast day but, as a matter of fact, St. Patrick's Day was not yet the great green celebration that it would become after Daley was elected. The parade, and a small one at

that, was held on Sunday, the thirteenth, and—onto what hard
times can a tradition fall?—it was led by a Frenchman, a barber
named Columbus deChatelets. Perhaps Daley mused on that
irony as he prepared for the dinner, to be held on the seventeenth itself at the Hilton, the dinner at which Mayor Ed Kelly
had once read a large section of his speech twice without anyone's noticing it. That day Daley had been asked about the
"Big Nine" files, which had been kept confidential through the
vote of Democratic aldermen. Daley said quietly that, yes, he
would favor open hearings on these files. "It would be a whole-
some thing," he said softly to a reporter.

The reporters were having a hard time believing that Daley
would not work more to win them over. He seemed, in fact, to
hold them in disdain, to feel, as he would even more strongly
in later years, that they exaggerated their own importance even
as they distorted reality in their reporting. He did not believe
that the press determined the outcome of elections and, raising
his spear, he attacked them in a variety of ways.

His office would not give out information about meetings;
Daley sometimes took delight in giving out false addresses for
supposedly significant gatherings so that the press would rush
to a vacant lot while he was at a meeting in another part of the
city. He laughed heartily at the dismay of the reporters; in his
perception, they were, and to a large extent would remain, the
enemy, and he would charge whenever he saw the sunlight
glint on their shields. Yet it was incomprehensible to the journalists that a candidate should regard them as the enemy; they
could not believe that a man running for office in a media-
conscious age would battle with them rather than woo them.
Some of them never understood that Daley genuinely mis-
trusted them and did not value them, in the final analysis of
what makes society run, nearly as much as they valued themselves. It may not have helped the chieftain's temper when on
St. Patrick's Day itself, the *Chicago Sun-Times* published the
first results of its straw poll: Merriam was in the lead with 50.9
percent of the vote.

On Tuesday, March 22, a state senate committee asked Downey Rice, investigator for the "Big Nine," to come to Springfield to testify. The Republicans, in a new strategy to make the files public, had introduced a number of bills to restore authority, lost in the twenties, to the Illinois attorney general to conduct criminal prosecutions independent of local state's attorneys. Back in Chicago, Merriam was getting headlines by denouncing Daley as "the front man for a pack of jackals who have been feeding off the city for the past twenty-four years." Adlai Stevenson, the elegant and heroic Democratic loser, the patron of the party's liberal spirit, was, in typical worrisome fashion, revising the talk he would give in Daley's behalf that evening at the Palmer House. He was genuinely disturbed at the tone of Merriam's accusations and, as the hour for the dinner of the Volunteers for Daley drew closer, he was still striking out phrases and paragraphs, attempting to make the speech a mannerly rebuttal of the charges against the man whose integrity and ability he recognized quite clearly. It was a vintage Stevenson who, smoothing a strand of hair, virtue and honor seeming to sparkle in his eyes, rose into the bright light of introduction that evening.

"This has," he intoned in his precise manner, "it seems to me, been a curious and very disturbing campaign, in which a contest has become an obsession, in which truth and falsehood have become sadly commingled; in which the real objective of right-wing Republican mastery of Illinois has been cynically masked by the heroic picture of gallant St. George spearing an evil Democratic dragon." He paused ever so slightly. "The fact that St. George was a Democrat until a few weeks ago makes little difference."

The night would be a graceful ride through his balanced sentences, a strange trip for many old-time campaign workers, who were ready to cheer on cue anyway, but it had just the right tone for many others, who thought that Merriam's campaign had become unbalanced in its efforts to blacken Daley's reputation. Few knew, for example, that Merriam had gone to see Daley personally just a few days before and had asked him not to reveal accusations about some embarrassing operations in a Republican ward, and that Daley had agreed. Merriam went right back on the attack the next day but Daley, to his aides' surprise, did not seem disturbed; he seemed rather to expect it and to feel that this was the way of it in professional politics, and that if Merriam continued hammering away in this fashion he would probably do more harm to himself than to his opponent. It was all part of the mystery of politics, already twice confounded in Chicago, and coming swiftly to a conclusion on this cold evening at the very beginning of spring.

Stevenson, meanwhile, was quoting Lewis Carroll and rolling out periodic sentences with the grace of a jeweler displaying a tray of fine diamonds. "That's why I say it is very disturbing. I don't believe the democratic process is served by intemperance, unreason, and deception." He paused again, in ambassadorial fashion. "I don't believe the way to lead is to mislead." It was a phrase for the papers, a quote for the independents, the right words from a highly respected source at a crucial stage of the campaign.

Daley himself continued on his round of wakes, small meetings, and rallies, punching out phrases which, according to his own style, were at least as memorable as those of the sophisticated Stevenson. On the twenty-fourth Daley declared with great feeling, "I will strive to be the mayor who would take Chicago on its journey of ascendancy to its great place in the world." He then went on, the strength of his purpose somehow splinting the broken thoughts into a whole sentence, to explain that Chicago was called the Windy City "because immigrants took off their coats and worked to build it."

It was the same tone of determination that came through in yet another tumultuous rally at the Civic Opera House on March 29. With eleven Democratic leaders on the stage and the house packed with a crowd caught up in the melodies of "Chicago" and "Hail, Hail, the Gang's All Here," Daley clipped off a few indignant sentences about his opponent.

Mark them well, for they would reappear, like good stories, in slightly altered form on many future occasions when Daley wished to rebuke his accusers. "He gave no evidence. He repeated charges against other groups and other people. He could not give a single instance . . ."

Daley would take exactly the same tone in a statement prepared for him by Earl Bush that was to appear in the *Chicago Sun-Times* on March 31. "Although he must know better, the Republican candidate has painted an ugly and distorted picture of the city you and I love. . . . This has been his campaign—to picture Chicago as evil and ugly and to portray me as a tool of vicious and corrupt men. . . . I spoke recently on the same platform [before the Church Federation of Chicago]. And I quoted to him one of the Ten Commandments, 'Thou shalt not bear false witness against thy neighbor.' . . . He did not give one single instance. . . . He gave no evidence. . . . He repeated . . ."

On March 30, the Wednesday before the election, the Republican majority in Springfield were satisfied with the way their plans were working out. They had summoned "Big Nine" counsel Irwin N. Cohen to testify, and he was to bring the suppressed files with him. The Republicans' questioning, in behalf of the four bills they were supporting, would force the contents of the files into the open, with plenty of time for the newspapers to spread their contents throughout the weekend editions. State Senator William Lynch, Daley's old friend from Bridgeport, along with Senator Donald O'Brien (the survivor of the Wagner automobile crash), was leading the opposition to the bills which the Republicans had sponsored as a device for getting the files into the open.

If Daley was worried about developments in Springfield, he did not show it that evening at the rally held for him at the Chicago stockyards. This was neighborhood stuff, the kind of evening to generate a sense of triumphant sentiment in the candidate, who was greeted by his first boss, the now graying Patrick Dolan, the commission merchant for whom Daley had worked so long ago. There was a broad smile on Daley's face as he passed, with the torchlit and singing crowd, through the old stone gate and up to the Exchange Building. Perhaps the twinkle in his eye as he began to speak was the smallest hint that he had been mightily pleased at the news of Senator Lynch's strategy that afternoon in regard to the "Big Nine" revelations.

The Republican majority leader, Richard Lewis, had smiled confidently as "Big Nine" counsel Cohen arrived, briefcase in hand, for the scene that would, according to Republican plans, turn into the brightest revelation of scandals in the Chicago Democratic organization. Cohen would have to reveal the contents of the files in connection with the Republican arguments for their bills to restore the state attorney general's powers of investigation. But Lynch, the in-fighter who gave no quarter, was on his feet before the proceedings could get under way. He demanded that the committee vote immediately on the bills, which, until that moment, he had been denouncing vigorously.

The Republicans were stunned and sensed that the trap was closing fast. The only reason they wanted to question Cohen was to support their bills, the very ones which Lynch wanted them to vote on without further debate; they would either have to forgo questioning Cohen—and abandon hope of getting at the "Big Nine" files—or be in the position of voting against their own bills if they voted against Lynch's motion. There was a rumble of consternation, and Senator Marvin F. Burt, a Republican from Freeport, tried to offer a substitute motion. Adding insult to what was already grave injury, Lynch roared, "Are you trying to play politics with these bills?"

A violent debate broke out as the Republicans fought to preserve their golden opportunity to subpoena the secret files. Republican Senator T. Mac Downing of McComb was fingering the subpoena nervously as his colleague Robert McClory, who would attain a measure of national attention many years later on the House of Representatives' Impeachment Committee, charged that Lynch's motion was "a subterfuge to end the hearings." Democratic Senator Roland Libonati, from the old First Ward, the onetime domain of Bathhouse and Hinky Dink, replied sarcastically, "I've been here twenty years and I never heard a man talk like him."

McClory responded coolly, "Is this a motion to close the book on the crime files? Then it ought to be defeated."

"You were no good in the House," Libonati shouted back at him, "and you're no good in here!"

Lynch and O'Brien then decided to throw yet another haunch into the ring of confused and snarling lions by demanding that there be "full disclosure" of the "Big Nine" files, which still remained in Cohen's closed briefcase. It was too late for the Republicans; they were forced to accept Lynch's motion in favor of voting immediately on their own bills. Cohen stood up, bade the senators adieu, and, with his still unopened briefcase, left the hearing room and returned to Chicago. Senator Downing put the subpoena back in his pocket, saying, "I was all ready to issue it. But it happened too quick."

So concluded a Democratic maneuver worthy of every Irish ghost in Bridgeport, a maneuver with enough roguish tilt to unsettle the most self-satisfied of the Republican WASPs. It was the sweetest kind of political revenge, and it was on a professional level. Alderman Thomas Keane, political dynast from the Thirty-first Ward, with narrowed eyes like those of an accountant who notices the slightest chit or notation in your records, Keane, who anticipated great favors from Daley after the election—the chairmanship of the Finance Committee would be a good start—appeared on local television and, in an obvious bid for the Catholic vote, spoke of Merriam's divorce and the fact that two of the Republican candidate's children were from his wife's first marriage. He added sardonically, "Daley has seven children and they are all his own." Such tactics, including inflammatory mailings from nonexistent groups, were common in the last days of the campaign.

The sense that the election would somehow begin a new era

for Chicago was heightened on April 1, when Colonel Robert McCormick, the conservative old publisher of the *Chicago Tribune*, died. He had been as Republican as they come, and yet he was a man who had admired and worked with Ed Kelly when Kelly was mayor of the city. It was a small augury of change, a sign that the men who had dominated the first half of the century would yield their places to others in the second half.

Daley, who had the support of only one of the four local papers, the *Chicago American*, was in the homestretch of his campaign. The *Chicago Daily News* began printing some leaked material from the "Big Nine" files on Saturday, April 2, as did the *Tribune* the next day. Merriam, brandishing a pointer, appeared on television, stating, "They've asked for evidence. Here it is." And yet, just as the old colonel had faded away, so the "Big Nine" evidence, like Merriam's last anticlimactic rally at the Chicago Stadium, was far less persuasive than had been promised. The new candidate was presenting old stuff; the fresh reformer was wearing down and looking tired as Election Day itself loomed.

Daley himself was in high gear, pushing the organization to turn out the vote on Tuesday, and in an occasion as sentimental and symbolic as any the chieftain would ever enjoy, he went on Saturday night, April 2, to the AFL Sheet Metal Workers hall on West Jackson for a meeting of Local 73, the union organization of his broad-shouldered uncles and of his father, Mike, a fifty-year member, who had once been blackballed for his organizing activities. He rose to speak in behalf of his son's candidacy. "Do a job for Dick on April fifth," the wiry old man urged the crowd. "Give him your vote, men, and do a job for Local Seventy-three and all organized labor."

Daley's Uncle Al, trustee of the union's welfare fund, led the applause as the candidate stood up amid the daguerreotype gathering on the stage and, in a choked voice, said, "No man is as proud as I am for having such a great dad as Mike Daley."

The night was not yet spent of symbols. If Colonel McCormick was gone and some of his power over the city with him, Chicago had still to witness the full ascendancy of the labor unions in its affairs. Was there the slightest flex of muscle in William Lee, one of Daley's chief backers, as he said to the partisan crowd, "For anybody who might have the mistaken idea that he's running as a labor candidate, let me set the record straight. . . . He's not committed. . . . We're not looking for a single favor or office from him."

Tuesday, April 5, turned out to be a fine day, and Daley and his wife, Eleanor, walked a half block up from their home on South Lowe to the small, old-fashioned fire station to cast their ballots. Merriam rose at 5:30 A.M. and spent the day inspecting polling places in what he thought were the "worst" of the Democratic stronghold wards. But he found no vote fraud and, at 6:30 P.M., returned to his headquarters to watch the returns come in. He looked at a blackboard where the story was already being told. With the polls closed for only an hour, Daley had a 60,000-vote lead. "It doesn't look good," Merriam said, "but you never can tell." The signs of death were already present, however, in the silences, and in the movements of disappointed workers and backers as they quietly left. The crusade was all but over; Merriam's political career was over, too.

At the Morrison, however, the bands were playing and the crowds were drinking and singing. Daley himself stayed far from the crowd, watching the returns with a small group of party leaders and family members in a hotel room. He talked to the various committeemen and workers who reported on how they had turned out the vote for him that day. It would become an Election Day ritual over the years, this procession of the captains bringing their treasure and spoils to the leader, who was now only minutes away from the absolute power that he had wanted so badly. At 8:58 P.M. Merriam conceded and everything that had been seeded into the soul of Daley's ambition so long ago, everything that was worth singing about in any Gaelic song of war, was his. He had received 708,222 votes to Merriam's 581,555.

There are those who say that as Daley claimed his prize, he stiff-armed his former associates Colonel Arvey, Joseph Gill, and Albert Horan out of the way so they would not appear in the pictures and seem to have any share of his power. But those who say this do not understand what Daley was like at this moment of victory, for he understood as well as anyone in the room that he had no peers in Chicago Democratic politics any more. He had the whole carcass, head and trunk, chairmanship of the party and mayoralty of the city, control that was deep and strong and that could not be challenged. Nor was he discourteous or interested in hurting anyone's feelings. He knew the size of his victory and he did not need small gestures to assert or prove anything about himself any more. He spoke softly into the glare of the lights and the flashing bulbs. "I promise no miracles—no bargains—but with unity, cooperation, and teamwork we will continue to build a better city for ourselves and our children. . . . As mayor of Chicago, I shall embrace charity, love mercy, and walk humbly with my God."

The bosses had thought that their hour of deliverance had come and that a restoration of the rights of plunder was at hand; this solidly built man, speaking so softly and solemnly about mercy and justice, surely, he would understand the way things might be again in bawdy old Chicago. But Daley had achieved his dream and he held all the keys. Alderman Paddy Bauler would spray the foam off his stein of beer that night with the declaration "Chicago ain't ready for reform." But he croaked something wiser and more vulgar later on: "Keane and them fellas—Jack Arvey, Joe Gill—they think they are gonna run things. . . . They're gonna run nothin'. They ain't found it out yet, but Daley's the dog with the big nuts, now that we got him elected. You wait and see; that's how it is going to be."

[11]

Marching Orders

Power is dangerous unless you have
humility.

—Richard J. Daley

Nearly three thousand people, a great smiling mix of officials,
friends, party workers, and family members, crowded into the
old City Council chambers on the evening of April 20, 1955, to
witness Richard J. Daley's inauguration as mayor of Chicago.
It was a night for sentiment as heavy as the smell of the spring
flowers on the evening air, a time when the chieftain gathered
together his father and an uncle, his wife and children, in-laws
and cousins, who radiated out like the diagrams of semifinal
athletic contests, some of them firemen and some of them policemen, others with their eyes already shining brightly in anticipation of municipal appointments; and all of them with the
unmistakable looks of the Irish whose clans had never admitted outsiders, with the well-satisfied expressions of victors who
knew that some part of the kingdom must surely be theirs now
that the whole of it belonged to Richard J. Daley.

It was the moment for which Daley had prepared so
thoroughly. The whole ceremony would last barely an hour,
but that was long enough to make quite clear that from then on
his, and his alone, were the kingdom and the power and the
glory. There had been politicians who had expected Daley to
make the city wide open once more, to return it to the days before Kennelly, when the "handbooks" could be found on

practically every corner, when smoke and sour odors seemed to rise above a city that lay sprawled like an old courtesan who was once a great lady, half inviting and half repugnant, filled with sweet promises and dark memories. The aldermen who had dreamed of ravishing Chicago once more learned, on this very night, that Daley had no intention of allowing them to return to their freewheeling ways. If his love for his city was part of his motivation, so too was his determination that he would control Chicago absolutely and unambiguously.

After his old friend from Springfield days, Abraham Lincoln Marovitz, now a Superior Court judge, had administered the oath of office and a sad-faced Martin Kennelly had handed him the gavel, Daley, mayor at last, opened his speech and began to read it as carefully and clearly as he could. He was, in this one moment, the Irish warrior hanging the enemy heads on the gate and the good boy placing a bunch of flowers at the feet of the Virgin. He was what he had always wanted to be and he had what he had always wanted; now his listeners would learn just how he intended to use his power. "I have lived all my life in a neighborhood of Chicago—all that I am I owe to the influence of my family, our neighborhood and our city. . . . Chicago is a city of neighborhoods and I resolve to be the mayor of all the neighborhoods—of all people of Chicago."

This was not just sentiment but the deepest of his beliefs, words like those he would still be speaking on the day he died, the very key to his passion for the city that he must have thought of as a woman. But one could be tender only if one was strong, and Daley wasted hardly a paragraph before turning to the City Council. "I have no intention of interfering in any way with the proper function of the City Council. But, as mayor of Chicago, it is my duty to provide leadership for those measures which are essential to the interests of all the people— and, if necessary, to exercise the power of veto against any measures that would be harmful to the people." This was to speak of things that could never be, for, in the new order of things, it was impossible for the council members to imagine, much less enact, any regulation, however small, which Daley had not approved in advance. The sentences were symbolic of the fact that, although technically Chicago was a city in which the City Council was supposed to be stronger than the mayor, it would not, in practice, be that way in the future.

Daley was not just proposing a program; he was giving marching orders. He took the power of preparing the budget into his own hands, and he pushed the council to implement the recommendations of the Home Rule Commission that had been set up during Kennelly's term. Daley was, in every sentence, redefining the aldermen's tasks as almost exclusively legislative; he was taking charge, planting his spear in the turf, and with the ease of a politician quite sure of how much power he has—in this case, since he was party chairman, all of it—announcing what he intended to do. He presented his program in this brief inaugural address; he would, over the next four years, carry out much of it.

But his main statement concerned the exercise of political authority and influence in the city. It would not be the good old days revisited; the council members would have to surrender the crowns of their independence and pledge allegiance to the new king with the uncompromised fervor of condemned prisoners begging for clemency. He would redeem his lady Chicago and keep her safe from those who were ready for rape and pillage. The new mayor, in phrases crafted by Earl Bush so that they matched his bludgeoning speaking style, concluded with what amounted to a litany, a chant and a hymn to the city that so many people misunderstood. "I mean the Chicago that is the great economic and financial giant of the Midwest. I mean the Chicago made up of contributions from people of every race, religion, and nationality. I mean the Chicago made up of fine neighborhoods. I mean the Chicago made up of splendid churches and temples of every faith. I mean Chicago—the medical center of the world—with the finest hospitals in the nation. I mean Chicago with its great universities. . . . I mean Chicago, with an unlimited potential, to be the magnificent city of the future. I mean the Chicago of 'I WILL.' That is the real Chicago." And, in a few moments he was finished, the benediction was given, and the smiling Daley moved with his family through the applauding crowd.

Daley moved into City Hall for good the next morning. He was no longer the candidate hesitant about revealing his intentions and his plans, and, in the next several months, his style of wielding absolute power began to define itself. It was not that he had studied the works of political scientists or essayists; he seemed rather to have an intuitive sense about both people and the way to exercise his power. "The first thing you have to understand about a politician from Bridgeport," an old associate of Daley's said later on, "is that he doesn't even trust his mother. Love her? yes; trust her? no. In fact, he distrusts her."

Let this be the inscription on the arch under which we are about to pass. Of all men, aspiring politicians may be the least secure, the most subject to sudden shifts in the fortunes of their patrons, professionals who must learn to scramble for cover— or at least for some connections—should the visitations of death, indictments, or indifferent voters threaten their power base. Politicians, plumping away for what must be done at the moment, are pragmatic survivors who live by something like the ancient rules of the sea, stepping lightly from sinking ships onto newly captured prizes with an ingrained understanding and acceptance of the principles that govern the division of spoils.

Nobody understood these rules, or the men who lived by them, better than the new Mayor Daley. His grasp of the political realities had gotten him to City Hall, and a glint of his hard-bought insights can be caught in his continuing to function as party chairman out of the Democratic headquarters at the Morrison Hotel. In his first news conference he would say something about resigning this post; indeed, a compact mythology has built up about his supposed soul-searching on the issue, but none of it is true. He would be mayor and he would

be chairman, for holding both offices was essential to his main-
tenance of absolute power. If he was going to dominate the
City Council, he had to be able to command its members politically. Control—that was essential to his view of the universe.
Control may have been the essence of his soul and personality,
for he had survived through dominating and modulating his
own impulses, through keeping his own judgments a secret behind his unmoving face; he would relate to the City Council
and to the Democratic committeemen in the way he related to
himself—with clear, absolute, and unquestioned control.

Taking the budget-making power away from the City
Council was the first indication of Daley's sure sense of how to
effect control. Power lay in budget making, in understanding
where every penny was spent, what jobs were represented by
what entries, and whose interests were intertwined with what
headings. Daley had learned a great deal about city budgets
while he served in the controller's office; he had found out even
more as Illinois state revenue director in the cabinet of Governor Adlai Stevenson. Reading a balance sheet was power in the
purest form and, unlike his predecessor, Kennelly, Daley could
always answer the most detailed question about a city budget
with full knowledge about how the numbers got there and
what they signified.

Having stripped the members of the City Council of their influence over the preparation of the budget, Daley moved
swiftly to bring their political activities under his control as
well. Politics is built on doing favors for people; many aldermen and committeemen, as well as some other city officials,
had been doing favors directly for those who approached them
on matters such as zoning regulations, driveway permits, or
parking areas near their businesses. Daley quickly let it be
known that such independent operations had to cease and that
he alone would exercise power in regard to whatever favors
were to be done at any level. If a Democratic committeeman
was approached by a businessman for a zoning variance, it
would henceforth be suicide to grant the favor without refer-

ence to Daley. The new mode of operation demanded that the committeeman—or the alderman, if that was the case—must bring the request first to Daley himself. If this was humbling for the officials, Daley's unfailing reply was devastating. After hearing them out without giving any sign of his reaction, Daley would say simply, "Tell him to see me." Thus the aldermen and the committeemen were totally under the chieftain's domination; as party chairman and mayor he could turn them into lepers before their former backslapping colleagues.

Long-time Fire Commissioner Tony Mullaney, a hulking man with white hair as majestic as the crest on a noble bird, had been doing political favors for years. The Fire Department was politically powerful, because it was responsible for such a variety of building inspections throughout the city. Merchants could not afford to have their places of business closed down for minor code violations and were quite willing to make donations to the department's favorite causes, some of which were, of course, influential firemen. Mullaney, sure of his power, did not respond to the instructions Daley had sent out and continued to make deals in his own red-trimmed empire.

"Write a resignation letter for Mullaney," Daley ordered Earl Bush one morning, and that was the end of the fire commissioner. Mullaney would make a public protest, charging that he had never even seen his own letter of resignation, but he was on the way out and an old friend of Daley's from Bridgeport, Robert Quinn, was ready to move in. The significance of such clear moves was not lost on other members of the city government.

There was a briskness about everything in the early days of the new administration which matched Daley's own swift stride. He was having the time of his life, always hurrying, always looking around to see what could or should be done next. Having remained somewhat aloof from the distrusted news media during the campaign, Daley now began, under Bush's urgings, to make the news every day, to take advantage of the newspapers and television stations for his own purposes. Press conferences were held every morning and releases spilled out of the mimeograph machines on every move and plan the new mayor had to improve Chicago. Daley was actually taking the first steps in a public relations plan that would give him a much sharper personal identification with the public at large; the possibilities of a profound reciprocal identification between the mayor and the people were understood, at least in outline form, and the constant publicity given to Daley was meant to capitalize on it. All of this, of course, also reinforced his power; it would, in time, make him a political figure stronger than the Democratic party itself. If he wanted, he could have won without it, but the party could never have won without him.

Gradually, he began to pull other loose ends back into his own hands. He had the chairman of the City Council Finance Committee, "Parky" Cullerton, a member of one of Chicago's oldest political families, introduce an ordinance to put an end to any investigative bodies like the "Big Nine." Cullerton's ordinance transferred all responsibility for investigating municipal wrongdoing to the mayor himself. There was a $200,000 appropriation to start things off, and the mayor was also empowered to hire his own investigators, who would report only to him. As a finishing touch, further action on any findings was left to Daley's judgment alone. It was the complete piece of legislation, and the thoroughness of it, awesome as the work of an avenging spirit on a sinful town, shaved away the last stalk of doubt about who was running Chicago. A similar gesture occurred when Daley disbanded the "Scotland Yard" unit of the Police Department; members of this group had been discovered tapping his Morrison Hotel offices during the primary campaign. There was a brawling definitiveness to such moves; they were worthy of the Celtic leader who, when he was asked why he had burned the cathedral in a certain town, answered that he had thought the archbishop was in it.

While Daley tidied up party discipline, he also set himself to the task of developing his programs for the city. He wanted, he said, to "convert programs into action . . . to do whatever has to be done as quickly as possible." He gave high priority to better municipal services. His political sense and his affection for the city convinced him that what the average person wanted was attention close to home: garbage collection, street cleaning, better lighting, and more visible police protection.

It has been observed that it is always better to come into office after a poor administrator, because then there is a great deal that one can do to impress the voter. Daley followed a weak administrator and his direct moves in the area of public services attracted immediate attention. He was cleaning Chicago up, and the people loved it; he was increasing the number of firemen and policemen, and the voters were grateful. It seemed a homely beginning and yet it is a perfect illustration of the two-pronged approach which Daley employed throughout his years in office. He appealed to self-interest with projects that were in themselves valuable; he did this with the neighborhoods, and he began quickly to do it with varied groups: the bankers, the builders, the merchants, and the union men—he had something for them all in his plans, projects that would make them prosper as they made the city grow. He accomplished his ends by consistently applying yet another characteristic strategy: divide and conquer.

It took enormous vigilance on his part, of course, but he was obsessed with the fascinating game of politics, and to his last day, when he sat between political rivals at the gymnasium dedication, he played it with a steady hand. It was simple and clean, like the stroke of an ax. He never appointed anyone to a committee or a commission without, at the same time, appointing a person of just the opposite political viewpoint or allegiance. If he placed a member of the Cullerton faction on an important board, he placed a member of the Keane family along with him; if he needed a chairman for a group, as he did early in his first term for the Chicago Dwelling Association, he chose someone—in this case realtor Jim Downs—who was actually opposed to the program. The effect of all these maneuvers was to keep most competing groups battling with each other so that ultimately they had to come to Daley to settle the issue. He kept the power of decision by pairing opposites; "Put Pat with Mike," an aide noted, "and, by God, sooner or later, they have to come back to Dick." Daley may have been like General Patton, with a high tolerance—if not an outright affection—for battles going on around him all the time. He was the only person who could settle any of them, as he well knew, so that every one of his appointments ultimately strengthened his own hand.

There were appointments that were rewards for old supporters. Who would do better, for example, as chairman of the Civil Service Commission than his friend Bill Lee, head of the Bakery Drivers Union and the AFL in Chicago? And who could object to AFL Vice-President Bill McFetridge's being made head of the Park District? As a matter of fact, it was very difficult for anyone to object to his appointments, for he almost always selected qualified persons; even those involved could not complain when they were paired with a rival, and even they did not quite grasp why everything ended up back in Daley's hands anyway.

He did not replace the department heads, except for Mullaney, in a hurry. He preferred to let attrition work its way and then to place a trusted successor in office. Here again, Daley showed his skill at maintaining control while supplying the city with able administrators. For the office of controller, for example, he reached out to Carl Chatters, president of the National Municipal Officers Finance Association, an appointment that was well received.

Daley soon earned a reputation as a recruiter of young talent as he invited a group of men in their thirties to head various offices in the city. They became known as the "Whiz Kids" and, if Daley beamed, it was not only because of the applause he received for quality appointments, but because all of them fit into his political plans too. These men were not the protégés of any other political leader, they were not members of one or the other political dynasty in Chicago; they were apolitical and thus totally dependent on Daley for their position and advancement. Their chief characteristic was their controllability; they reported to Daley and they did exactly—and only—what he ordered. It was small wonder that Daley approached each day with such zest; things were going well, they were going his way.

[12]

The Man Who Could Work Miracles

The toastmaster, Pat Hoy, had just introduced him and Mayor Daley, the slightest smile breaking above his black tie, hurried behind the dais, the spotlight moving unsteadily to keep up with him, toward the speaker's rostrum. As the swell of the ovation, as sweet to a politician as the sound of the sea, trailed away, Daley looked out at a classic scene: the ballroom of the Conrad Hilton Hotel filled with Irish politicians, lawyers, and other professional and business men. "There certainly is an elegant group here tonight," he began, his choppy phrasing slightly softened, "the finest, the most prosperous Irish in Chicago. I can't help but think of your mothers and fathers and grandparents, who would never have been allowed in this hotel." The crowd erupted in laughter and as it quieted, Daley, solemn as when pronouncing judgment, added, "I want to offer a prayer for those departed souls who could never get into the Conrad Hilton."

The acquisition of political power by the Irish had been rooted in the remembrance of deprivation and prejudice, of penal laws drafted by the "bloody English" and signs in hiring places, in the bluntest WASP script, that read "No Irish need apply." Daley had the power now, but he remembered the

thick catalogue of Gaelic hurts, and the emotion that sluiced
through his soul was a blend of tenderness and a lust for revenge that would soon have expression far beyond this ballroom and beyond Chicago itself.

This long day had begun early, because Daley so enjoyed his
job that he could barely wait for dawn. These first months in
office had been filled with excitement. The new mayor rose between 5:30 and 6:00; he would work for a while at his desk in
the remodeled basement of the home on South Lowe, sometimes making telephone calls, sometimes reviewing reports that
he had tucked into his briefcase as he was leaving City Hall the
day before. He would join his wife, Eleanor, known as "Sis" in
public but referred to by him as "Ma" in private, and their
growing children for breakfast.

One daughter had entered the convent shortly before
Daley's first election as mayor; hers was the sacrifice to the service of the Church that was as common as it was expected in
Catholic neighborhoods in the fifties. It was the virginal offering, the blessing of a vocation on the family, the pride of the
parents who had practiced their faith with devotion. She would
finally take the name Sister Richardelle and later, in a scene repeated in many Catholic families over the next generation,
would withdraw from the convent and eventually come back to
live in a white clapboard house next to her parents. She would
weep the most at her father's funeral; yes, she would feel the
loss intensely, but now, in her crisp habit, she was the loss, the
pure offering made to the Church without question by a good
Catholic family.

Daley's official limousine would ease into the reserved parking place in front of the house at about 8:00 A.M., and the members of the bodyguard detail—a long-established security procedure for the city's mayors—would step out to greet the mayor
and hold the door for him. In the early years, Daley often instructed his policeman-driver to vary the route that would take
them toward City Hall. He liked to look over the neighborhoods of the city to check on potholes, streetlights, or traffic

jams that needed attention; he made brief notations about these and any other problems that his practiced eye noticed, and he would promptly contact the responsible department heads and instruct them to do something about these situations.

As the black Cadillac entered the Loop area of the city, Daley would tell the driver which Catholic Church he wished to visit. It was frequently St. Peter's, run by the Franciscan Fathers, and the mayor, again accompanied by the bodyguards, whose fixed expressions mirrored his own, would hurry into a pew to attend mass and to receive the Sacrament of the Eucharist. "Do you pray for guidance for the day's activities?" a friend once asked him. "No," Daley replied, "I've done my homework the night before." He would then walk briskly to City Hall through the crowds of early morning commuters. Sometimes he would ask to be dropped off at another location so that he could approach the Hall, which had been sandblasted of half a century of grime early in his term, from another direction. It was all quick movement, the bodyguards moving in doubletime, until, after a flurry of greetings—"Hello. How are ya?"—Daley would enter the elevator that took him to his fifth-floor office at exactly 9:00 A.M.

Every morning Daley was briefed by Earl Bush on all the important topics of the day before he met in his regular press conference with members of the media. Daley was fully prepared for these questioning sessions and, although he claimed not to read the newspapers, he had gone over them very thoroughly.

The mayor worked hard and long hours, saving his business as chairman of the Democratic party for his luncheon trip to the nearby Morrison Hotel. In the early years it was a constant push toward getting things done, toward implementing his programs for a clean city, for more playgrounds and better lighting, for more policemen and firemen, and for construction—highways, apartment and office buildings almost beyond numbering, and a new international airport—and toward pro-

viding all the fine shadings of response that were demanded of
a mayor whose passion for work, part love and part obsessive
need, intimidated his aides. For if he worked, they worked,
often late into the night and on Saturdays and Sundays too.
Daley disliked the classic bureaucrat who, after all, attained
distinction not by agreeing with you but by saying *no* to you,
and he often complained, "There are too many people who are
telling me what I can't do. I want some men who can tell me
what I can do!" So his admiration, if not always his affection,
went to men who threw themselves heedlessly into the sus-
tained charge of each day's activities.

But let us pause here, freezing the frame of Daley, who looks
like a banker as much as a boss, in his glasses and never-doffed
jacket, as he sits almost at attention at the desk he likes to keep
as clear as a coffin lid. For this is the chieftain who, near the
hour of five, will hand a stuffed briefcase to a bodyguard and
head back home for dinner with his family, before leaving
again in the early evening for a quick visit to a wake or two and
then on to a dinner, often at the Hilton. Look closely at the absorbed face, at the geography of its crags and arches, as mysterious and filled with secrets as that of the moon. We must listen
carefully, straining for the slightest of sounds or signals, because Daley the person is better suited to the sensitive powers
of radar than to those of a portrait painter. One must feel one's
way, grasping a handhold as carefully as a man climbing a
glacier in the dark; one is aware of forces, some as surging as
the high-tide sea and others as resistant and enveloping as the
darkest quicksand. A journey along the ice facing and finally
into the caverns of Daley's soul is filled with both Irish music
and menace.

Creative people, according to researchers, live in a turmoil
of contrariety all the time, drawing on opposite feelings to
achieve the unique synthesis of their vision; but the often dis-
ordered public life of the artist reveals the tension within. With
Daley, the achievement of control in the unmoving face and
the life of traditional virtue and habits belied the wrestling po-

larities inside him. And yet the emanations that rise from his personality, like the wavy distortions of perception on a summer day, are those of ambivalence.

In Daley, one can feel the clash between the man of ideals for the city and for the nature of family and personal life and the man of the finest instincts for compromising with the human condition, for building his strength on a capacity to read accurately the weaknesses of others, for settling things as pragmatically as an executioner who looks aside as the blade falls and goes home to a good dinner. Before us sits a man who could feel tenderly for people, who would, on a trip to a far city, want to stop his car and give money to a wandering old man with white hair, but who could also turn away from the most tearful pleas if giving in to them might sap away a drop of his power. Here is the leader with genuine concern for the welfare of the people of Chicago, with a feeling for the way they live, who, in the last light of battle, is ruthless and uncompromising about anything that might adversely affect him or his family. Yes, the warrior chief can seal a politician's fate and sleep well the same night, just as he can be the most simple of men, cleaning up the bottles and glasses after a party or helping aides to lick stamps. At other moments, he can strike back coldly at anyone who failed, even in some small way, to show him due respect. Here we have the man locked in battle with his own intelligence and curiosity, the practical administrator with no taste for experts or professors or political analysts, the anti-intellectual who would fight for colleges for the young people of Chicago, who would, in fact, find it impossible to resist the lure of knowledge promised through any shortcut and who constantly bought books on how to learn languages in thirty days, who even purchased *The Syntopicon*, philosopher Mortimer Adler's ordered amalgam of human wisdom.

If Daley appears tightly controlled on the outside it is not for lack of a never-ending battle in his many-sided soul. That is why Daley the man of power who wants to give service to others also wants all the credit for it, why Daley, no stranger to inner ambivalence, indulges no such public feelings in those around him. It is in his exercise of power that we see the claw-toothed edges of the leadership he forges anew every day of his life.

Politicians are not great planners; they rather resemble tough boxing champions who have fought their way up through engagements in a hundred smoky clubs and who no longer ponder the ethics of gouged eyes and blows below the belt. To the champion, winning is the only goal and every move and strategy is committed to the service of raw and trembling reflex. So with Daley the responses were not so much planned as they were matched to the advantage of the moment; they were the boxer's reflexes for any developing situation, the undifferentiated use of force in the service of power, primal political violence as terrifying as the whistle of the chieftain's sword in a battle in which death is the prize of the hesitant.

Daley's vigilance was nourished by a complex information system through which he quickly learned of everything that was going on in all the municipal departments. He effected this by placing loyal Eleventh Warders in every office connected with personnel. These old neighbors, dependent on the mayor for their jobs, reported directly to him about what was taking place in their departments. So Daley already knew almost all of the things which other officials might later think they were telling him for the first time; still, he would listen, giving no sign of whether he was hearing it for the first or the fiftieth time—and pull the strands of his own executive power a little tighter in the process. Such knowledge was power, and each worker who delivered information gave himself over just a little more to Daley's control with each message.

Daley's watchfulness was as awesome as his capacity to seem inattentive to the money that was being made through deals and arrangements that were taken as a birthright by swaggering Chicago politicos. It is clear that nothing could take place—no promise could be made nor contract let—that did not have the explicit approval and full knowledge of Richard J. Daley. If this constituted a tax on his ability to balance his inner feelings about such matters, there was no surface evidence that he was perturbed; he would say his prayers and keep his unyielding control on the city and on everything that had to be arranged to make it function well. Daley, the chief, stood at the center of the encampment and could count the silver in every sack; he knew every animal—where it had been found and how it had been caught—that turned over every fire.

Those who worked for him were caught up in the mixture of what was so utterly attractive and warm in his Irish manner while they were totally dominated by the force of his power. The seeds of the ambivalence that would ride in their hearts for years were sown by Daley himself. Aides who gave their best energies to his demands, even when these demands were close to impossible, found themselves in chronic conflict. They liked Daley; they identified with his strength and they felt secure with his decisions and plans. They were dependent on him for their livelihoods, but they had been shorn of something—they were not sure what—in the process. They could give no name to the problem, to this root of ambiguity, to this combination of admiration and frustration that lay at the heart of the unquestioning loyalty Daley demanded. A few of the more sensitive tried to sort it out in psychotherapy; most of them, caught up in crushing economic, religious, and political forces, hunched down to their jobs, denying their doubts in favor of security, eagerly accepting the profound validation of their lives and hopes which Daley offered them.

The unusual qualities of Daley as a person cannot be minimized or lost under the shorthand designation of "boss" or "chief," for he can be understood only if one realizes the roiling complexity, the mixed heritage of antagonistic forces under a control that could generate a mood of tension as palpable as an electric field around him. It was this special presence, this concatenation of forces as heavy and brooding as a thunderhead, that men around him could feel; yes, it was something

Left: Daley's birthday, May 15, was celebrated annually in his City Hall office. Here, in 1961, he is surrounded by various department heads and some youthful members of the Shannon Rovers Pipe Band. The mayor's laugh was infectious. (*Chicago Sun-Times*/Kotalik)

Below: Daley, in his best sphinx pose, which gave nothing of his thoughts or feelings away, waits to begin a meeting with Chicago religious leaders during the racially troubled year 1966. In the foreground is Chicago's Catholic Archbishop, John Cody; and in the center of the picture sits the Reverend Martin Luther King, Jr., who was uneasy at the way the mayor was dealing with him, avoiding any face-to-face meetings while publicly supporting King's aims. (*Chicago Sun-Times*/Kotalik)

Above: Thomas Keane, chairman of the Finance Committee of the City Council, locks his diamond-hard eyes on the even harder eyes of Mayor Daley during a conference in the Council chambers. Keane was an expert on city finance and government and worked well with the mayor in a relationship that succeeded partly because neither fully trusted the other. (*Chicago Daily News/* Reporto)

Left: Daley glares at a questioner at the 1968 Democratic Convention, on the night that would explode in violence outside the Conrad Hilton Hotel while the world watched on television. It had been a year of horror, with the assassinations of Martin Luther King, Jr. and Robert F. Kennedy, as well as the burning of Chicago's West Side and Daley's famous "shoot to kill" order. Daley was infuriated by Senator Abraham Ribicoff's remarks about Gestapo tactics on the streets of Chicago. (*Chicago Daily News/*Farrell)

An uneasy handshake between Mayor Daley and Vice-President-elect Hubert
H. Humphrey in 1964. Humphrey emerged from the shambles of the 1968 convention with the Presidential nomination. Although Daley delivered the votes
for Humphrey on Election Day, he did not feel that he had been a good candidate. (Murphy Photography, Inc.)

Above: The typical flurry of excitement that marked a Daley exit from his campaign headquarters after a successful Election Night. Preceded by bodyguards, Chicago policeman, and a platoon of political associates and hangers-on, Daley enters his limousine as his son Michael looks toward him. Daley's car always bore the license number 708-222, the number of votes he received in his first election as mayor in 1955. (Murphy Photography, Inc.)

Left: Daley leads the applause as Senator Edward M. Kennedy is introduced at a 1972 Democratic fund-raiser. Daley never thought of him as a Presidential candidate after Chappaquiddick but still admired him and his family. (UPI)

Bottom left: Daley greets Democratic Party Chairman Lawrence O'Brien at a gathering of mayors in New Orleans in 1972. O'Brien made the rulings that led to Daley's exclusion from the Miami Beach convention later that summer. (UPI) like elemental power that made them step back when he passed.

And in the first term, this reservoir of energy was being poured into making the city a great metropolis. Bankers and newspaper editors were beginning to appreciate the drive of the stocky man from Bridgeport who seemed to know how to get things done. If his friends prospered, it was not so hard to understand; after all, this was standard political procedure. Nobody was surprised when Billy Lynch, his boyhood friend from Bridgeport and his old law partner, suddenly became the counsel for the Chicago Transit Authority, and then for a succession of other businesses which had a stake in the success of the city. Who could find anything illegal in Lynch's taking large fees from organizations like Murphy Associates, which would be involved in building so much of Chicago's new skyline over the next two decades? Was it odd for Lynch to become the lawyer for Washington Park Racetrack? Nobody breathed a dissatisfied word in front of the mayor, who was merely doing what seemed natural to him, giving a good deal to an old friend. Wasn't that the way it worked in the reality of political life?

"Would General Motors give a contract to Chrysler?" That was Daley's reply when an associate asked about all the city contracts that were going to his old friends. A man would be crazy, Daley insisted, not to take care of his friends and family; that was fundamental, an instinct that was deep in his nervous system. If Daley never made money from his job as mayor, it was clear that his friends would. These were to be great days for contractors, union men of all kinds, and do not forget bankers and architects, insurance men and the mixers of concrete; they would all receive of Daley's largess in the booming years ahead.

"What the hell do you want that much for?" Daley was heard to yell at some contractor friends who were making a proposal to the city. "No, that's too much," he went on. "You've got to cut it down."

And so another side of Daley and his contradictory nature was made manifest. His friends were welcome to the business of the city; that was one thing, but he bristled and made them back off if he thought that they were taking advantage of the taxpayer. The bids might be won by friends, but they had to be close to the competitive range or Daley would cancel the contract on his own; he did not keep power by failing to exercise it, even against those who were his allies and supporters.

A favorite device of Chicago contractors remained the so-called change order, a simple but effective procedure which guaranteed profits to them. A certain firm might win as low bidder on a city contract and, having begun construction, would request a "change order," citing unanticipated difficulties with the weather or other acts of God which necessitated a recalculation of their costs. Once the order was granted they were able to recast their estimates and practically fill their hods and wheelbarrows with the cash that became available. A healthy percentage of their profits could then be reinvested in Democratic party campaigns.

In his first term as mayor, Daley faced the city contractors head-on, old and favored friends among them, by advertising nationwide for bids for one of the largest sewage-system construction projects ever planned by the city. The local builders were enraged at this sudden shift in the accepted way of doing things, and a group of them filed suit when the contract was given to a California firm, alleging that it was incapable of carrying out the job. Daley made the new arrangement stick, however, not only as a better business deal for Chicago but because it re-established perspective on who held the power to anoint and dispense in all matters. It was a classic confrontation with the toughest of men and the highest of stakes; Daley emerged more clearly in control than ever.

Daley was particularly careful about campaign contributions. While he expected money from the businessmen who dealt so profitably with the city, he would accept no donations from tainted sources. Back in 1946 he promptly returned an envelope that had been dropped on his desk by a syndicate representative, and he remained on guard against any such contributions to the Democratic treasury, warning his aides constantly not to take money from questionable sources. It was not only principle that inspired this wariness but a well-educated sense of caution about the things that brought ruin to political organizations. Wariness and willpower combined to keep the financial records of the Cook County Democrats as clean as possible.

The mayor remained, nonetheless, the champion fundraiser, knowing exactly whom to approach and how to encourage donations to the Democratic party. Shortly before each Election Day he would call the committeemen together and distribute various sums of money which they were to use for "expenses"—a broadly defined term—in the last days before the votes were cast. It was always understood that whatever was left over could be kept by the committeemen themselves. Daley was as generous as he was prompt in paying the bills incurred in his own campaigns. He was, therefore, something of a rarity among politicians, who were noted for letting bills for various services pile up long after the election returns came in. If they won, they didn't need help any more and, if they lost, they generally did not have the cash to settle their debts anyway. "Get the money up front," became a slogan among those who, like printers, did business with political candidates. Daley always maintained the reputation of a prompt payer of these debts.

And the power, like Skeffington's in *The Last Hurrah,* could be felt in ways that had a humorous or ironic edge. Thus, when Daley wanted to preserve O'Hare Field (which he invariably referred to as "O'Hara") as part of the city even though it was several miles northwest of the Loop, he proposed to annex the land over which an expressway would link the terminal with downtown. When the townships which would have to yield property for such an endeavor balked, Daley simply advised them that they would have to police and maintain whatever length of the expressway ran through their village limits. The land was quickly ceded to the city. If, on other occasions, news

came to Daley that Fire Commissioner Quinn had closed a
theater when a show of questionable taste was about to open
in town, the mayor would be amused by his fellow Bridgeporter's activities and would later reverse Quinn's efforts to
enforce his own morality on the city.

Daley listened in his characteristically noncommittal way
one afternoon as a neighbor from Bridgeport—who worked at
City Hall—told him of the plight of a large family in which
the husband, an out-of-control drinker, had just died, leaving
his wife and children in desperate circumstances. There were
no indoor toilets; the house, which had a dirt-floor cellar, was
falling into splinters, and the numerous children were badly
in need of food and clothing. Daley reacted as both mayor
and neighbor. He called "Ma," who quickly began to orga-
nize friends to bring food and clothing and to arrange a
fund-raising dinner at a local restaurant. Meanwhile, Daley
was on the phone to a number of department heads organizing the material and manpower necessary to repair and refur-
bish the widow's house. His orders were simple and direct.
Some lumber could be found here and some shingles there;
surely electrical wiring and plumbing fixtures could be
rounded up from other sources and, yes, there were some city
workers who could lend a hand. It was all done swiftly, and
within a few days, the collapsing shack was being practically
rebuilt for the troubled family. Mayor and Mrs. Daley appeared at the fund-raiser and several thousand dollars were
donated to the widow and her children.

"People always help other people in our neighborhood,"
Daley said simply, warming to the vision of simple goodness
that he held, against all social upheaval and criticism, against
time itself, as the modest and decent ideal of the good life.

"People always wonder whether Daley ever stole anything
from the city," observed the Bridgeport city employee who
ended up coordinating the rebuilding of the widow's house.
"Sure, he stole things, like Robin Hood did, in order to give
them to the poor. He was Saint Crook."

On other occasions, Daley, his face still betraying no emotion, was less direct in his advice about taking things. A relative had approached him about an old friend who wanted to get a job with the Chicago Park District. "The trouble is," the intercessor explained to Daley, "she can't pass the test for it. There are some chemistry questions on it, and she's never had any so she always fails. Is there anything that can be done?"

Daley looked straight ahead as he said softly, "Well, tell her the next time she takes the test—to take the test."

And that, of course, was what the lady did; she took the test home, found the right answers, and got her job with the Park District. Daley smiled only slightly when he later learned that she had lied about her age and would have to work until she was seventy-one to get her pension.

But if there were stars of merriment bursting around the rising arc of Daley's success, other forces were already beginning to gather to challenge him in unexpected ways. He had mastered power in his own city. There seemed to be no problem that he did not know how to control. That was his business, his profession, his sense of calling, his whole life. But, pleased and comfortable within the limits of old-fashioned Bridgeport life and thinking, he could not readily conceptualize social problems of a different source and shape; he could not control history or the storms which, like hurricanes, were forming in remote and unfamiliar places.

In the fifties, the racial problems of America were a low on the weather map in places like Little Rock; they were not yet the raging fury that would blow across all the big cities just a few years later. There had been racial troubles in Chicago, but they had seemed controllable through ordinary political means, through the influence of men like Congressman Dawson. Daley, Bridgeporter to the core, could not yet read the signs of the problems that would explode in his city ten years later. In his first term, he was riding high and enjoying himself thoroughly.

[13]

The Time of His Life

The conversation was brief. Joseph P. Kennedy and Richard J. Daley never had to say much in order to get their meanings across to each other; they responded at a more basic level, on a plane of tribal awareness, as though they had lived before as brothers and warriors dreamed by the same savage king; and they shared the same deep acquisitive lust for land and family and power. It was good, some observers felt, that they were not rivals in the same business, for what united them as mystical allies would surely have pitted them against each other as mortal enemies.

Back in 1954, County Clerk Daley was in Kennedy's Merchandise Mart office asking him if he thought he should run for mayor of Chicago. They had already known each other for several years and had regular contacts when Kennedy was in the city. The financier asked a few direct questions about the likely opposition and what monetary backing Daley had and said simply, "I don't think there is any question. You should run."

Daley concluded the conversation quickly and hurried out the door and down the corridor; Sargent Shriver, who was present, can still recall the sound of Daley's rapid footsteps as he headed for the elevator.

Daley was already determined to run for the office, of

course, but he understood the need to discuss it with this influential man who had been such a success as a businessman, as an adviser to the classic Democratic hero, Franklin D. Roosevelt, and as Ambassador to the Court of St. James's. Kennedy had financial resources whose importance Daley clearly recognized; he was, through his ownership of the Merchandise Mart, an important man in Chicago, just as he was, for similar reasons, in big and small cities all across the country. They were alike in many ways, perhaps most profoundly in their understanding of power and its exercise in and through people. Neither Kennedy nor Daley was a theoretician; they had achieved success not because they had mastered scholarly analyses of business or politics but because, as chieftains out of another age, they reined their horses tightly as they gazed steadily into the eyes of other riders to take their measure. They could appraise other men and know, in a way they could never explain even to themselves, whether they were soft or hard, dependable or risky, controllable or not; they felt rather than thought out the judgments which told them both how far and to what destinations they might move with others. Both Daley and Kennedy built their empires on reading other people correctly.

These two men had long memories of the injustices that had been perpetrated against the Irish both by the English across the seas and by the WASP inheritors of the American establishment. If they could not complain publicly about the stories of discrimination they had both heard as boys, they could share the same sweet secret resolve, a pulsing determination to wreak revenge on the oppressors; it was like an oath they had sealed with their blood in a previous life to show the stuffy WASP leaders of American society that Catholics, especially Irish Catholics, were just as good as anybody else. This was their sacred unspoken pledge as they surveyed the Protestant Kingdom of America: They would ride together and take the White House for the Irish Catholics.

But such an aim required virtues which both Daley and

Kennedy understood: restraint and a willingness to wait for the right moment to strike. The year 1956 provided Daley with his first opportunity to place an Irish Catholic on the list of future contenders for the Presidency. The Democratic Convention would be held in Chicago that summer and Daley, mayor for just over a year, was delighted to welcome it. As the local Democratic chairman he experienced intense pride as he watched the delegates file into the International Amphitheater next to the stockyards of his youth and within walking distance of his home on South Lowe Avenue. Daley was committed in advance to the Presidential nomination of Adlai Stevenson; it was, in fact, the only time he ever let his preference be known before a convention, and this only because Stevenson was a native son of Illinois.

It was during the early days of the convention, however, that Daley sensed a good possibility of nominating Joseph P. Kennedy's son Massachusetts Senator John Fitzgerald Kennedy for the Vice-Presidential candidacy. The elder Kennedy, vacationing on the Riviera, had opposed the idea, fearing not so much that his son would be part of a losing ticket, as that the attempt would not be carried out well at the convention and that the result of a faltering move would do more harm than good. Daley, however, was convinced that Kennedy needed favorable national exposure if there was ever to be an opportunity to run him for the Presidency itself.

Richard J. Daley had other things to think about as he contemplated the possibilities of John F. Kennedy's Vice-Presidential candidacy. Only the previous month, Republican State Auditor Orville Hodge had been exposed as a thief of public moneys, largely through the efforts of Michael Howlett, a rising young Democrat with the body of a football player and the face of an Irish altar boy. The *Chicago Daily News* had broken the story and this had touched off a search through the activities of other governmental officials, a development Daley disliked as, indeed, he always pulled back from excessive probing into the personal or professional lives of fellow politicians. A move against any politician, the ancient Bridgeport logic said, was a move against all politicians, and so the discoverers of shady deals here or there could never expect a hero's welcome from the mayor.

But the enthusiastic investigators had turned up something which, if not so great in itself, contained the seeds of more trouble than Daley needed in this election year. Daley's candidate for governor, County Treasurer Herbert C. Paschen, had a "flower fund" in his office, from which he had borrowed several thousand dollars for a European trip, leaving an I.O.U. in the files. It may have been the leaving of a trail rather than the borrowing of the money that irritated Daley, but he was not long in reviewing the evidence, passing judgment, and carrying out a summary execution on the very floor of the convention.

Daley let the word out that Paschen was to be removed from the ticket, but Paschen, who was seated only a few chairs away from Daley in the Illinois delegation, knew nothing about it. When the reporters came to ask the mayor if the story was true, Daley confirmed it in his own monosyllabic way. His inner rage and turmoil were suppressed with the awesome power of his self-control as the reporters turned to Paschen and asked him about it. Bewildered, Paschen came to Daley, who, his arms folded across his chest and his eyes staring stock straight ahead, replied simply, "What did you expect?"

He had severed a head so neatly that it did not topple immediately from the victim's body; it had been a public execution, and if the swordsman had deemed it necessary, he also experienced his own concealed anguish at having to strike at another politician. (Daley would later appoint Paschen a judge, the kind of gesture of public re-establishment which he often made for candidates he had to remove.) It was, for observers, a flashing moment of revelation about the chieftain's style and temper.

For the last three days of the convention, Daley worked tirelessly behind the scenes in order to line up votes for Kennedy; this became a stronger possibility since Stevenson, eschewing political tradition, refused to name his choice and said he wanted the delegates to pick his running mate. The result of Daley's efforts was that Kennedy came within nine votes of the nomination and, after his support began to drain away, gave a gracious and good-humored speech in which, before a national television audience, he asked the delegates to make the selection of Senator Estes Kefauver unanimous.

It was the country's first look at the handsome and youthful senator and the zestful spirit which he embodied as a promise for the future. Daley said publicly, "The contest for Vice-President shows the vigor and vitality of the Democratic party." Privately he said, "If Sam Rayburn had recognized the right people, Jack Kennedy would have made it."

Although Kennedy was finally glad that he did not suffer the potentially fatal political experience of running on a losing ticket, he had been edged into the limelight of countrywide attention for the first time. The elder Kennedy had been alarmed, but he also understood that what Daley had accomplished had not been inept but had, in fact, nourished their mutual dream substantially.

In the years ahead, Daley was to supply basic political know-how while Joseph P. Kennedy supplied the organization and the technology for the run for the nomination in 1960. Daley was a master of precinct politics, and his subtle understanding of neighborhoods and blocks became the basis for the extraordinary computerized breakdown which the Kennedy organization would make of every precinct in the country. This strategic analysis was the fusion of experienced political insight with the electronic capability of the age. Daley did not trust the technical approach to winning an election, but he understood how precinct politics worked and his appreciation of old-fashioned vote-gathering was fed into the circuitry of the Kennedy campaign strategy.

But while this dream of kings waited, Daley was busy both as political leader of Cook County and as mayor of the city. Old faces began to reappear; in April of 1956 Frank Keenan,

an archenemy of Daley's when he served as campaign manager
for Martin Kennelly, was making a comeback. If the behead-
ing of Herbert Paschen was a combination of pragmatism and
impulse, the Keenan episode is, from start to finish, instructive
about the manner in which Daley preferred to operate with
party dissidents. Following Daley's 1955 election, Keenan had
been disciplined by the Cook County Central Committee. He
was replaced as committeeman from the Forty-ninth Ward
and his patronage powers were transferred to his successor, a
party regular named George La..e. But Keenan was tough and
unrepentant, and a year later he ran successfully against Lane
for his old office; an enemy had slipped back under the tent.
Daley's instinct—and a practical political move—was to welcome Keenan back into the fold. "The people have spoken,"
Daley commented to the newspapers. "The door is open."

It must also be noted that Daley was inclined to co-opt old
enemies rather than to run them off completely; he would
rather get them back in the ranks and under his power than
have mavericks running loose. At the same meeting with
newsmen, Daley was asked if he would accept the Democratic
chairmanship if it were offered again. Daley still observed the
pieties; he still kept his cards—in this case all of them aces—
close to his chest.

"I don't know," he answered, challenging thunderbolts from
on high. "I'm still thinking about it. I won't decide until
Monday."

Assessor Keenan, back in command in the Forty-ninth
Ward, now struck again on his own. He decided to take a stand
against the Democratic organization's slated candidate for
state's attorney, John Gutknecht, in favor of another former
friend of Daley's and now a Republican rival, Benjamin Adamowski. In a letter to Daley, Keenan wrote that "this was the
only honorable course to pursue."

Was the mayor surprised? "I am not," he said through
clenched teeth to reporters.

Did this kill chances of reconciliation? the journalists wished to know. "Keenan is the one to answer that question," said Daley as he turned away.

By now it was clear that Keenan was not going to be brought back into line very easily. But, as Daley habitually felt, there was no need to respond immediately. There was every advantage in waiting; anything could happen before the November elections.

What did happen was that Adamowski, aided by Eisenhower's landslide second victory over Stevenson, was elected to the office of state's attorney, a position Daley hated to lose because the man who filled it could make investigative mischief for many local Democrats. But the story is not yet fully told, no, not at all, for a few weeks after the election, the outgoing state's attorney, Gutknecht, indicted the intransigent Keenan on charges that finally led to a federal trial for income tax irregularities and a subsequent prison term. Daley would never initiate such an action, although he might not try to stop it either. He believed that an unwritten political code existed, one precept of which forbade turning in any politician for censure or indictment. That was one reason he never fully accepted Michael Howlett, who had exposed the illegal activities of state auditor general Orville Hodge. Such efforts, like those of reformers and do-gooders, might open closets from which any number of other skeletons might clatter out onto the floor.

Keenan's political career was at an end; he took to painting and selling pictures from his prison cell. Back in Chicago, however, he was an object lesson, like a wrongdoer swinging at the gates of the city, where Daley began immediately to make plans to unseat Adamowski in the 1960 election; that, in the judgment of some observers, became almost as important an objective to the mayor as the election of John F. Kennedy in the same year.

The Republican party in Chicago was in a state of near-collapse. There were only a few Republicans in the City Council, and with Daley presiding and Thomas Keane, recently anointed as chairman of the finance committee and floor leader, standing by, crusading Republicans were often made to jump through parliamentary hoops like circus animals. City Council meetings were held, after all, to ratify the business that Daley had already approved in advance. Still, these meetings were something to see as Daley made his usual fast-paced entrance through a cordon of bodyguards and stood with eyes lowered as an invited clergyman gave an invocation. Daley almost always made a point of thanking the clergyman, whoever he was, and at whatever occasion he was present. One of his favorite phrases was "Could you send me a copy of that, please?" There was little chance that the mayor would look at it again, but there were advantages in flattering members of the cloth.

Daley would then make a few opening remarks, often welcoming the schoolchildren who filled the galleries, brought by their teachers in order to observe their municipal government in action. It was always a pleasure, Daley would say, "to see these fine youngsters" with their interest in the democratic process. He would then lead a round of applause for them. He was not averse to their presence for another reason; they were part of what came to be called a "ruly crowd," a nonhostile group whose members would obey the rules and not begin any unfriendly handclapping or hooting.

When the City Council chambers were remodeled, Daley's place was equipped with a device through which he could signal the controlroom to shut off an opponent's microphone if he seemed to be talking too long. Daley had already been dubbed "Hizzoner" by the newspapers, although they were still hesitant to print his sometimes tortured sentences exactly as he uttered them. Years later, they would get them down clearly, as, for example, when he said to an objecting minority alderman, "The point of order is not well taken."

Let us observe a typical scene of Republican desperation in a session early in Daley's mayoralty when Republican Alderman John J. Hoellen, who would run against Daley for mayor in 1975, attempted to revive a resolution, which the four minority council members had previously proposed, to investigate the activities of the City Traffic Court. Hoellen, a man given to chronic exasperation, attempted for two and one-half hours to get a motion before the council, one Democratic alderman after another rising to interrupt him with a point of order. Several times as Hoellen attempted to speak, Daley, his eyes twinkling, said, like a patient father to a child, "Not now, John." Finally, near the meeting's end, Daley laughed as he introduced Hoellen: "Is everybody ready? Gentlemen of the council, here's John."

Hoellen promptly entered into an argument with floor leader Thomas Keane, who countered with the charge that Hoellen had failed to attend his committee meeting on the previous Monday. Hoellen then accused Keane, a past master of just such actions, of running through the agenda in five minutes and ending the meeting before he could get there. Keane, his face reddening with anger, shouted back, "That's a deliberate lie." Daley, smiling sweetly, intervened to close the discussion with a soft-spoken reminder that the aldermen must act like gentlemen at all times.

Things went just that smoothly for Daley throughout his first term, and by the time he was to face re-election in 1959, the Republicans were hard pressed to find anybody who was willing to run against him. Finally, a Republican leader, Timothy Sheehan, agreed to make the race although the outcome was never in doubt. The usual contributors to the Republican party were funneling their donations into Daley's treasury. Perhaps the clearest symbol of Daley's domination of city politics was found in his invitation to speak during the campaign before the highly conservative—and solidly Republican— Union League Club. Political writer John Dreiske began to speculate in his *Chicago Sun-Times* column about whether or not the two-party system had any future in Chicago.

Daley continued to campaign vigorously, leaving little to chance, and hugely enjoying the torchlight parade which, despite the spitting snow and rain, provided a resounding climax to his run for a second term. Daley marched along with the bands, the drum-and-bugle corps, the delegations of veterans and boy scouts, and even a contingent of shivering Little Leaguers, along with thousands more who carried sputtering red rail fuses to the Lithuanian Auditorium in the heart of Bridgeport.

A few days later, the mayor, under a full head of steam, spoke of the season of greatness that was almost upon the city of his lasting passion. "The events that will take place this summer—the opening of the St. Lawrence Seaway, the Pan-American Games, the International Trade Fair, the visit of Queen Elizabeth—will focus the eyes of the world on the people of Chicago." He was the proud knight now, lighting a sea of candles for his Lady of the Lake. "We stand on the threshold of a great future, of tremendous expansion, for our destiny"—and now he spoke his pure vision with a full heart—"our destiny is to be one of the great cities of the world."

It was all over early on Election Night. At Republican headquarters, the gloomy silence was broken by a man who began to sing "When Irish Eyes Are Smiling." Someone from across the room yelled "Shut up!" and the gloom patched itself together again.

"They tell me it's no contest," Sheehan said to a group of reporters. The Republicans shook their heads.

Chairman F. X. Connell said grimly, "We get seventy-nine votes a precinct and they've now gone from two hundred three to two hundred fifteen a precinct." They had been hit broadside by the organization, and Daley took all but one of the fifty wards as well as 71.36 percent of the total vote. It was a victory crushing enough to please any leader, large enough to permit Daley his usual soft-spoken humility as he stood with his family members at the Morrison Hotel. One could hardly hear his voice at such moments; it was as though the novice was making his first profession all over again and only hushed phrases would befit the almost sacramental profundity of the moment. The words, it must be admitted, did have a familiar ring. "I thank the people of Chicago. With the unity, cooperation, and teamwork of all the people of this city, we will continue to build a better city for your children and mine." Then the slightest of pauses. "As mayor of Chicago, I shall embrace charity, love mercy, and walk humbly with my God."

Nineteen fifty-nine was a fair year, indeed, and except for the death of his father, an event that shook Daley greatly, he enjoyed it all. The spectacles of the summer all came to pass. Great boats from around the world were anchored off the lakefront, the games went off on schedule, and Daley beamed through it all. The high point came on July 6 when Queen Elizabeth and Prince Philip arrived in the Royal Barge at Congress Street on the lake's edge. There were parades and dinners, and the newspapers and the television screens were filled with images of the mayor greeting the royal couple. The Irish boy from Bridgeport, who explained to his anti-British friends that Chicago was honoring a head of state rather than the throne of England, carried off the day with a blend of grace and pride. He had, after all, brought a Queen to his great city and there were rave reviews about Chicago in the London papers. The old image of a gangster-ridden city was being altered at last.

Bridgeport broke through as Daley bade the Queen farewell at the final dinner, saying, as though he were speaking to a relative who visits too infrequently, "Come back and see us again and bring your kids with you." It was, in fact, the way he spoke to any royalty who came to visit Chicago regularly over the years; Daley became a quasi head of state himself, so nobody minded when, in the last year of his life, he spoke to Princess Beatrix of the Netherlands in the same fashion. It was his way, the only way he could speak what he felt. "We remember when your mom and dad visited us," he said as though talking across a fence in his neighborhood. Perhaps Daley was as comfortable with royalty as any American leader could be; was not his ruler's soul brimming with dreams of crowns and scepters, of conquerors' rights and portions?

The year 1959 was the time of his life for Richard J. Daley, and his re-election and the almost constant public summer tableaux—event crowding upon event—were crowned perfectly when the Chicago White Sox brought the World Series to his own neighborhood in October. Life could not have been sweeter than in the long warm autumn of that last innocent year.

Now Daley was anxiously anticipating the election campaign of 1960. He did not know that all during that championship season a young burglar named Richard Morrison was preparing a major crisis for Daley in the new year. Morrison was no ordinary burglar, you see, because he was working with the cooperation of a group of policemen from the Summerdale district of Chicago.

[14]

The Green Necktie

Richard J. Daley was not surprised, but he was shocked by the news that a half-dozen policemen had been working in league with the common thief Richard Morrison. It was not just that his old foe State's Attorney Benjamin Adamowski would use the case as though he were a Polish guerrilla who had just found the plans of his opponent's fort; no, it was more than that. The mayor wanted no scandal, not now of all times, when things had been going so well and he stood, armor in place, ready to help lead a holy war for the White House. There was more, however, much more to trouble his soul, for he was closely identified with the Police Department and its members, whom he unfailingly described as "good family men."

Indeed, the Police Department in very real ways was his family; the number of policemen related directly to him or his wife was not easy to calculate. The Chicago Police Department was an extended family for the mayor and this only made his instinctive admiration for its members more intense and more compromising. For how could he move against the police without feeling that he was, most unforgivable of sins, moving against his very own? There were stories about how many commanders, captains, and patrolmen of various grades would tumble to the ground if one shook the Daley family tree. As a close associate would recall, "You'd hear about some cop who was in trouble and then you wouldn't hear any more about it. When you asked, somebody would say, 'Oh, he was Daley's third cousin,' or 'He was related to his uncle on his wife's side,' or something like that."

Beyond blood relationship were the ties, firm as a sailor's knot, established by the large proportion of policemen who were Irish and the high percentage of Bridgeport neighbors who were policemen. Thus, if Daley felt betrayed by a handful of policemen from the Summerdale district, he was doubly uncomfortable at the prospect of turning an investigator's eye toward the blue ranks with whom he was involved on so many profound levels.

Daley was related to the police by blood and guts, by a finely tuned inner affinity with them and their lives. Was his mind, one must wonder, in its deepest loops and coils, in its vigilance and commitment to a rigorous morality, was it, in its most ancient seeds of instinct, that of a policeman? Did the order he would give so many years later, "Shoot to kill," spring from the pure root of the policeman personality? There is no doubt that the kinship was deep, because the "pleece," as Daley called them, were the men he trusted; their floral piece stood alone in the church at his wake and he was borne to his grave on the shoulders of men almost all of whom had been policemen and bodyguards.

Daley made a distinction between honest and dishonest graft which can be illustrated in his attitude toward the cop on the beat. If, for example, a storeowner said to a policeman, "Would you mind checking the door on my place every night as you go by?" and then gave him a ten-dollar gift on a regular basis, Daley would voice no objection. That, he felt, was the way the world worked and no great harm was done. On the other hand, if a policeman approached storeowners to shake them down for extra protection money, Daley would be outraged, feeling that this active seeking of graft was an intolerable violation of the policeman's code. The mayor applied this distinction to municipal workers and officeholders at every level.

But there was something worse than a police scandal here, and it is small wonder that Daley was visibly upset and that he seemed to react more strongly than the occasion demanded. His inner moorings had been strained by the scandal; he became tense with reporters, holding brief, stand-up conferences with them; nor was it out of character that he was visibly irritated by a *Life* magazine article which described him as the last boss and told the whole country of some of his malapropisms, of how he had referred to a "tantrum" bicycle, "Alcoholics Unanimous," and "walking pedestrians."

It didn't take him long, however, to turn the situation to his advantage. He commissioned trusted aide Earl Bush and Fred Hoehler, superintendent of the Chicago House of Correction, to find the best police chief in the country to succeed Timothy O'Connor, who was being dropped as a result of the scandal. Bush and Hoehler approached O. W. Wilson of the Criminology Department of the University of California at Berkeley, who, after some persuasion, agreed to head the search committee. This committee finally recommended that Wilson take the job himself and, with a promise of *carte blanche,* the highly respected Wilson accepted. Daley beamed as the story even made the front page of *The New York Times.* He had actually emerged from the problem looking better; he promised even more equipment and training to the police force to which he was related in so many ways; and, having cast his chieftain's glance into the eyes of the dour-looking Wilson, Daley was convinced that he had a reasonable man here, a man with whom he could deal after all.

Daley, of course, ran the Police Department during most of his years in office. While Orlando Wilson had some independence, he still understood the mayor's expectations, and Daley was able to do business with him without undue discomfort. The mayor's face never changed, however, at news conferences when, in response to questions about a police matter, he would say solemnly, "That is entirely in the hands of the superintendent of police." He never added out loud, "After I've told him what to do."

Daley had other concerns; the Democratic primaries were about to begin and all his powers of concentration would be needed if he was to help John F. Kennedy get to the Presidency.

The previous fall, Daley had been asked by Mayor Robert Wagner of New York to give a talk at the state Democratic Convention at Troy. Daley was astounded to find the tables below the dais filled with Democrats far gone in drink, a scene that was totally unimaginable back in Chicago, where the mayor tolerated no such lapses in public discipline. Daley would say later to Wagner, "Why don't you take charge here?" but, at the moment, he studied the noisy and distracted audience and decided to put aside his speech, which had been prepared so carefully back in Chicago. He spoke extemporaneously, criticizing the Eisenhower administration to the crowd whose behavior so surprised and upset him.

He was again speaking off the cuff when, on his return to Chicago, a group of reporters asked him which candidate he would support in 1960. He was solemnly vague, mentioning, as much for his own amusement as for the information of the reporters, the possibility of Adlai Stevenson or perhaps even someone from outside the field of politics altogether.

Would he be making any more speeches outside Illinois?

"No," said Daley, "I'm going to stay here and watch home plate—I mean home base." His face brightened into a smile. "I guess my mind is on the White Sox."

His mind, of course, was very much on the upcoming election campaign. He had his eye on Kennedy, but many other Democratic leaders—men like David Lawrence and William Green of Pennsylvania, both as Irish and as Catholic as Daley—were nervous because they still felt that a Catholic on the national ticket might harm the chances of their local candidates. They were not yet committed to a Kennedy candidacy, and Daley, also aware of the local situation, was unsure of Adlai Stevenson's intentions about a third try for the Presidency. Daley understood that he had to clear up Stevenson's plans, that he had to get a decision out of the former governor whose anguish in self-examination was as well known as his sardonic wit. This season, Daley had to know his plans early; the mayor was ready to support the native son of Illinois if he chose to go to the post, but he had to have a definite commitment from him since he had alternate plans which would demand all his attention if Stevenson's answer was no.

Colonel Jack Arvey and Daley traveled to Stevenson's farm in Libertyville, thirty miles north of Chicago. "Adlai," Daley said, "we have to know your plans. Are you going to run for the nomination for the Presidency?"

Stevenson had made up his mind. "No," he said, "I am not."

"We have to make sure," Daley responded, "because we will give you our support if you make the race."

"No," Stevenson said again.

"Okay," Daley replied, "that's it. We are free to make other commitments."

Stevenson agreed, giving what, despite his romantic cast of mind, he recognized as more than a casual pledge; one did not make casual pledges to men like Daley and Arvey, old professionals who had little taste for the densely qualified reasoning that characterized the former governor's approach to things. If he always strained and shifted to choose exactly the right thing to do, Daley and Arvey settled every day for what they had to do to keep a political organization running. With Stevenson nothing was ever settled to his complete liking; that was one of the reasons that rank and file politicians—the men who would be delegates from Illinois at the 1960 Democratic Convention in Los Angeles—were uncomfortable with him. Stevenson was not an ordinary politician; it had always been a problem to get him even to shake hands with Democratic leaders, to get him to play the game as it had to be played if it was ever to be won.

As Daley and Arvey drove back to Chicago, they felt that they had been released by Stevenson; he had, with what fine balancing of his inner scales of thought they cared not, withdrawn from active contention. Daley would return to City Hall and await the visits of all the other hopeful candidates while he quietly thought about the best strategies for nominating and electing John F. Kennedy. If Stevenson had just let his glorious dream die at his own hands, Daley was fashioning a vision of a shamrocked White House, a heady dream of revenge and triumph. He would remain noncommittal as everyone from Lyndon Johnson to Stuart Symington made trips to Chicago to seek the support of the man they all recognized as a potential kingmaker at the July convention. Daley, of course, understood that it was easy to smile, shake hands, and remain silent.

Meanwhile, John F. Kennedy and his campaign directors had decided to run in selected primaries throughout the country in order to demonstrate his strong grass-roots appeal and to build up enough delegate strength to make it virtually impossible for the July convention to deny him the nomination.

"You concentrate on Presidential issues," his father told him. "Say what you think is the right thing and I will speak with the leaders about the political implications."

Joseph P. Kennedy had been given the role of dealing with the political chiefs; with Charles Buckley of New York, as well as with Green and Lawrence and, of course, Richard J. Daley. There was a drumbeat of excitement to the Kennedy campaign and Daley, in low profile and in the subtlest communication with Joseph P. Kennedy, was enjoying it all. He kept his uncommitted stance in public; what, after all, had he ever had to gain by revealing his plans prematurely?

Years later, Lawrence O'Brien, Kennedy's campaign manager, would recall that he was not at all sure of Daley's support even when the convention opened in the Sports Arena in Los Angeles. O'Brien and Robert Kennedy did, however, learn a lesson in political protocol during the campaign when they came to Chicago to hold a regional meeting without clearing it first with the mayor. Such presumption on Richard Daley's good will or good humor was naive. No matter where his Irish heart was, Daley had no good humor or good will for anybody who failed to acknowledge his sovereignty on his own home ground.

The reasons were cold and simple, as impersonal and unyielding as a bank vault. First of all, Daley was chairman of the party and attention had to be paid so that no observer would ever think that anyone, even a Presidential campaign manager, could bypass him. Secondly, the 1960 election could not be won without Illinois, and Daley knew that Illinois could not be won without Chicago. Last, and perhaps most important, if anything was to be done in Chicago, Daley reserved the right to do it in and through himself. Were any obligations to be incurred in the arena of Chicago politics, they would be incurred to Daley and to nobody else. So the mayor, for O'Brien and Kennedy, became suddenly silent and inaccessible, a strategy in which he enfolded himself as a guru wraps himself in the insulation of his meditation. One might pull and tug only to feel that there was a shadowed and immovable mass beyond the door or at the other end of the phone; it was an attitude he maintained until O'Brien, sensing his error, finally made what Daley considered the proper approach to him; he asked the mayor's permission to hold the meeting in his city. The incident was a lesson and a symbol of Daley's most basic feeling for power: It had to be his in an absolute and uncompromised way in his own territory—that is what made it his own territory.

In 1960, Daley was deeply invested in the candidacy of John F. Kennedy, but not to the extent that he would allow Kennedy's campaign organizers to commit political blunders in his own backyard. Beyond his yearning to place an Irish Catholic in the Presidency, Daley recognized Kennedy's attractive qualities; he was just the kind of candidate at the top of the ticket who would, in the long run, do most for the local candidates. And here, of course, Daley was intent, as an animal is for the kill, to remove the troublesome Benjamin Adamowski from the office of state's attorney.

A major decision in the Kennedy campaign was to run in the West Virginia primary. It would test the Catholic issue and would provide an opportunity to knock Hubert Humphrey out of the race. The media dramatized the religious issue and, when Kennedy, after intense campaigning, won the primary, much was made of the triumph as proof that the demon of religious prejudice in American politics had been exorcised for good. Democrats breathed more easily everywhere. Back in Chicago, Daley chortled over the results. He had been for Kennedy's running in West Virginia, but he had never worried about the outcome. He laughed in the manner of a man who has known a good secret for a long time, a secret so sweet that he had longed to set his own self-control aside and tell it to somebody. Now, with the votes in, he could reveal the source of his certainty that John F. Kennedy, despite the interpretations of the media, would win in West Virginia. "I knew all along," he told Earl Bush, "that Kennedy would have no trouble, because Al Smith won the primary there in 1928."

In June of 1960 America was reeling under the impact of international events. The U-2 incident had occurred and President Eisenhower, the father figure now in his seventieth year, was surveying the wreckage of the Paris summit conference. A decade past midcentury the country was filled with a yearning for something fresh, for a new start. The promise of this was found in the primary campaigns and in the emerging figure of John F. Kennedy, for he seemed to represent something different, the ascendancy of a younger generation, the arrival of a fresh spirit. And yet, not all Democrats looked upon him as the man to lead the party in the Presidential campaign. Eleanor Roosevelt spoke out for Adlai Stevenson, saying that the collapse of the summit meeting showed the country's need for the "wisdom, maturity, and experience" of the man who had been defeated twice by Eisenhower.

On that same day, Mayor Daley's office announced that he would be meeting with Pennsylvania Governor David Lawrence when the latter was in town to talk to the Loyal Order of Moose. Lawrence was still unsure about Kennedy despite the massive write-in vote he had received in the Pennsylvania primary; Daley, who knew that Kennedy had over 600 delegate votes already, wanted to deliver Pennsylvania and Illinois with their combined total of 150 votes to the Kennedy camp and so place him, at the start of balloting, within close reach of the 761 needed to secure the nomination.

Up in Libertyville, Stevenson was receiving calls from groups who wanted him, even at the eleventh hour, to make a fight for the nomination. They would be ready to put great pressure on the convention if Stevenson would declare himself openly. But Stevenson, the idealist whose heart had been twice broken, the hesitant visionary who disdained the rough and tumble of organization politics, would not lead a move in his own behalf; no, in the fever of his ambivalence he would accept the convention's call, but he would not seek it actively.

"Mr. Mayor," a reporter asked Daley just a few days before he was to leave for Los Angeles and the convention, "is it true that you are going to support Senator John F. Kennedy for the nomination for the Presidency?"

Daley replied softly that he would make his choice known at the caucus of the Illinois delegation on July 10. He pursed his lips, for the more he wanted to keep a secret the more he would drape it with the ribbons of sacred rights and piety. "The right to come out for someone is a very personal and individual one. In fairness to other delegates, I feel I should wait and listen to everyone in the delegation."

In fact, he had resolved to turn the winch on the delegates in order to unite them, from upstate and down, behind John Kennedy. He wanted it unanimous, if that was at all possible, in order to have maximum effect on the convention.

The Stevenson issue arose early in the convention at Los Angeles, where his supporters had organized large demonstrations outside and inside the hall. Daley would soon be deluged by telegrams from Illinois that would urge him to switch to Stevenson; these wires were part of a well-orchestrated effort to take the convention by a mixture of storm and popular acclaim for Stevenson. Daley was to feel the pressure intensely, even after the Sunday caucus of the Illinois delegation, the results of which he announced as fifty-nine and a half for Kennedy, two for Stevenson, one uncommitted, and the rest for Missouri Senator Stuart Symington. The Sports Arena itself was ringed by chanting Stevenson demonstrators as the delegates filed into the recently built hall. "We want Stevenson!" echoed in their ears as they made their way to their places. Stevenson himself was now installed at the Sheraton West, where he had received many callers urging him to run; he had consented to speak to the Minnesota delegation in their caucus, but he would not take up the standard. The split in the California delegation gave his backers renewed hope that they could cluster around the thirty-one delegates who had announced for Stevenson and stop Kennedy and take the nomination in the excitement and noise, in the emotional swell they might just be able to build up—if only Stevenson would act decisively.

The phone in the Illinois delegation rang. It was a call for Daley from Eleanor Roosevelt. Could she come to see him?

"No, no," he said, his great feeling for her late husband flooding into his voice, "the day will never come when you will have to come and see me. I'll go and meet you."

It was his old-fashioned gallantry that moved him, even though his instincts, fine as those of a sea bird tracking a school of fish, told him exactly what she wanted. Accompanied by one aide, he traveled to her hotel and went to her suite.

Drawing upon all the sentiment and power at her command, Mrs. Roosevelt, in her voice that rose and fell liquidly, in words that were shaded by the slightest lisp, implored Daley to turn away from Kennedy and to give his support to Stevenson. Daley, doubly pressed by such pleading from a woman for whom he had so much respect, spoke in his own distinctive tones, softened now with a tenderness and concern for her feelings. "I can't change now. I asked Adlai whether he would run. He gave us his answer a long time ago."

She appealed to his every Democratic memory and instinct,

battering at Daley's self-control, hoping that emotion would wash away his resistance. He was as close to dismay as he ever got.

"I can't change my commitment now," he repeated, holding off her entreaties, despite the turmoil which her request had caused for him. Daley's word had been pledged and, despite his uneasiness, he held his position.

He seemed shaken as he made his way down the hotel corridor after the meeting ended. He would have to face harsh criticism from many liberal Democrats who would feel that he could have done more for Stevenson at the convention. In Daley's view it was Stevenson, feeling now this way and now that, who had, from the heart of his noblest view of politics, caused this emotional tangle.

On Tuesday the Stevenson supporters, who had obtained a large number of passes and filled the galleries with chanting followers, did everything they could to create the impression of a stampede for the former candidate. Stevenson had begun to call Daley; there was, after all, adrenaline bubbling once more in his bloodstream, and he wanted to express his new interest to his old friend. But Daley, his instincts fluttering like the pennants of a storm warning, would not accept the calls; this convention had to be run professionally, with the kind of control and discipline which were the fiber and bone of his own political organization. No, now was not the time for Stevenson to declare his interest.

But Stevenson, perhaps with the faint hope of a man who would finally yield only if the party swept away all his doubts and disclaimers, longing for unqualified affirmation in the face of his own reluctance to accept the tainted rewards of compromise, made his way, against all tradition, to the arena on Monday afternoon in order to claim his seat in the Illinois delegation. The crowd, already well infiltrated by his own enthusiasts, greeted him tumultuously as he made his entrance.

The members of the Illinois delegation had always found Stevenson a puzzle; they might admire him, but they did not like him, for he was not the kind of politician with whom they could do business, not the party regular who could be clapped on the back, not the kind of man who could be touched or even nudged good-naturedly in the ribs, not a man for the familiar quarters of masculine intimacy. The Illinois delegates, aware of the implications of Stevenson's arrival out of due time, sensing this as another effort to pressure them into supporting him, sat on their hands.

Daley looked around at the rows of his fellow delegates and then rose swiftly and grabbed the Illinois standard. He might have his differences with Stevenson, he might, in fact, be dead against this effort to upset the balance of the convention, but he would not have a son of Illinois, a distinguished Democrat and former national candidate, humiliated before the convention and a national television audience. Daley led the cheers for Stevenson himself and, without looking back, he knew that every delegate was following him, joining in the noisy frenzy, the counterpoint of the band pounding through the din as Stevenson was borne to the rostrum. It was a moment of intense emotion, to be matched only by the demonstration on the next night after his name was officially placed in nomination by Senator Eugene McCarthy.

Now Stevenson looked into the charged distances of the arena and with a blade of cleverness slashed the swelling balloon of his followers' enthusiasm. He would not be easily courted by their cheers and pledges. He placed the knife against the fine edge of their hopes. "I am grateful," he said in his quicksilver voice, "for this tumultuous and moving welcome. After getting in and out of the Biltmore Hotel and this hall, I have decided I know whom you are going to nominate. It will be the last survivor."

The vessel of his supporters' expectations, which had been bobbing against the ceiling like a new balloonlike invention at an old-fashioned fair, sagged and crumpled down over the crowd. The high moment—the instant during which he might have declared himself—flicked by, and the destiny of the convention passed once more into the hands of the party leaders.

Stevenson would take his delegate's seat directly behind

Daley and, as the television cameras witnessed, the former governor, his face animated despite the stress of the experience, asked the mayor, the canopies and drawbridges of whose face were drawn tight, if he had personal support among the delegates from Illinois.

"No," Daley said tersely, feeling a curse from the camera's eye, "no, you have no personal support here. You said you weren't going to run."

It was a difficult moment and Daley would bear the brunt of public responsibility for a fate that Stevenson so painfully and publicly had chosen for himself.

The next night they nominated John Fitzgerald Kennedy to run for President of the United States. This was more than a political victory for Daley and the other Kennedy supporters. The banner had been run up for an Irish crusade, and Daley, the lilt of "Happy Days Are Here Again" filling the arena, smiled broadly as he checked his voting card. He had predicted the exact delegate count for Kennedy on the first ballot.

Sargent Shriver was named the head of the Kennedy campaign in Illinois but he recalls that, although he was quite active, the real coordinator of the campaign was "Richard J. Daley. Period."

Kennedy was at home with Chicago Democrats, who responded with the full energy of their ancient party loyalties. Smiling broadly, he mixed easily with these men, who had never before been at ease with a Harvard graduate. Daley exulted in the younger man's success; watching them, one saw two Irishmen in a golden season of politics.

When Kennedy concluded his first televised debate with Nixon in Chicago, Daley, certain that the vigorous and witty appearance of Kennedy had won the contest, stood waiting with a question: "Would you be willin' to go out to the northern suburbs to meet a couple of thousand Democrats? I've got them waiting for an answer on an open phone now."

Kennedy agreed immediately. "I can debate that SOB Nixon anytime, but I can't meet Chicago Democrats all the time. Let's go." So, aides trailing in their wake, the two smiling men headed into the night, the older chief and the young prince caught up in the fun and challenge of the campaign.

Daley knew that the race would be a close one, and that just as Illinois was crucial to victory, so too was it symbolic of one of the major problems facing John F. Kennedy. Two cultures eddied into each other in the flat black farmland of Illinois: one, of the big city, smoking, noisy, crowded with immigrants and their offspring, of strangers with foreign ways caught up in the hustling nightmare of technology and ambition that all but obscured their goodness; the other, that of rural America, where the simplicities seemed to abide in the spired small towns and where traditional virtue in clean overalls and starched Sunday clothes overwhelmed whatever perverse infections and lonely madnesses were hidden within the tree-shaded farm houses. Two ways of life stared suspiciously at each other across the borders of Cook County, strangers to each other's religion as well as politics. Downstate Illinois was strongly Republican and uneasy with the idea of a Catholic's taking over the White House. On Reformation Sunday in that long warm fall of campaigning, Protestant churchgoers would be asked to stand up and be counted among those who did not want to let the Presidency, which seemed to be theirs by right, slip into the hands of a Roman Catholic. The downstaters were committed to their own ideals, they were, in fact, pious, and they knew as well as Daley that they were engaged in a holy war. The religious issue, the contrast between big cities and spacious farmlands, the challenging future against a highly prized past: These were the Illinois issues that John Kennedy had to face and overcome everywhere.

The downstate Republicans wore a mantle of righteousness, but as professional politicians they were hardly different from their Democratic counterparts in Chicago. They may have been more stuffy in their self-presentation but gouts of rogu-

many of those who worked close to him. He wanted something that was almost impossible to provide, and on short notice at that. Most of his aides, caught up in the spell of his personality, tried to do what he wanted even when it seemed impossible. Bush found out the cost for the air-time Daley wanted and reported back to the mayor.

"Go over to Mr. Kennedy at the Merchandise Mart, and he'll give you a check," Daley said, as he passed on to other matters.

When Bush arrived at the offices of the patriarch of the Kennedys, the older man took out his pen and wrote him a check for $125,000, just as simply and purposefully as Daley had requested it. As a result, Kennedy's speech at Chicago Stadium was seen nationwide.

Kennedy underestimated the planned exuberance of the Chicago Democrats, who made so much noise that he could barely complete his prepared speech because of the constant interruptions for applause and cheers. In the control booth, the sound engineer said, "You Democrats are so loud you'll bust the goddamn machine."

Daley needed the elder Kennedy's financial help again for a program he hoped to activate on Election Day itself. Fearful that the downstate counties might illegally deprive Kennedy of votes, he planned to station poll-watchers in every precinct in the state. It was a huge undertaking, but he was out of patience with what he considered the hypocritical practices of the Republicans. He might have the reputation for juggling elections himself, but they had the long-practiced skills for it. In the last week of October Daley had lost his temper at a gathering of the Joint Civic Committee on Elections, a group of do-gooders, in his judgment, who presented what Daley considered unjust accusations about the rolls of Democratic voters.

"A lot of things are being said here," the mayor declared in exasperated tones, "that are not true."

He turned to a representative of the committee who had been alleging Democratic wrongdoing, and, referring to him only by his last name, Daley said acidly, "Let's not kid ourselves, Brill, a lot of this is being done for partisan purposes."

He was like a great beast closing in on a prey that had been paralyzed by fear; it was the time-tested strategy for handling accusations, because it put the accuser in the defendant's box.

Daley continued, "Everybody knows you're a Republican. Why don't you admit it?"

Brill answered, "I do admit it."

The mayor was not interested in anything as simple or limited as a factual answer; he pressed ahead with the full force of his personality. "Don't try to kid me that you're not a Republican."

Brill countered by saying, "We want party challengers—Democrats and Republicans—to put into the precincts on Election Day. We do have Democrats in our organization."

Ah, just the opening the old warrior needed. "Who are they?" Daley demanded. Brill said he would get a list, but Daley moved in on this delay. "If you had an impartial committee, you'd have the names. There aren't any Democrats on it. You're not kidding me."

Brill then asked Daley for Democratic credentials.

"Let's keep the record straight. Connell [the Republican chairman] already gave you credentials."

Brill was clearly on the defensive now. "Mr. Mayor, you're trying to make us partisan."

Daley snorted. "Once you take the credentials of either party, you're partisan. You're in there to stop people from voting Democratic. You're not on the square."

It was a classic encounter for the old campaigner, and it ended abruptly when an aide reminded him that he had to attend a funeral. It had not been bad work, however: He had put the do-gooders on the defensive, disrupted the meeting, and, like an Irish chief not satisfied with his victory, he had turned the place into a shambles before making a quick departure.

The last band had played, and a hoarse and weary Richard

Nixon had spent the final campaign afternoon on a national telethon while, in the evening, John F. Kennedy gave one last speech from Faneuil Hall in Boston.

A great quiet descended on the country as the polls opened the next morning; within a dozen hours the nation would begin to hear the first results of the Presidential election. Daley and his wife walked the half-block to the small fire-house on the corner to cast their votes and, after a visit to the Bridgeport Democratic club, Daley went to his office at City Hall. At about 2:00 P.M. Sargent Shriver, who was to fly to Hyannis Port to be with the Kennedy clan for Election Night, stopped to see the mayor.

"How does it look?" he asked.

"It is going to be very close," Daley replied, "but we do have our poll-watchers downstate. That's the thing we have to worry about. They will certainly try to take the election, but we're ready for them."

Daley was more than ready for them, as his precinct captains and other workers turned out practically everybody who could pull a lever or mark a ballot. Chicago was also crowded with poll-watchers from both sides; Republicans and Democrats exchanged no presumptions of good will about voting. The hush of the afternoon ended as the evening television coverage began to deliver the first results and to offer projections about the final outcome of the election. "It looks like we have a cliff-hanger," newsman Chet Huntley was saying on NBC.

Daley, in the Morrison Hotel party headquarters, knew that he was right. A long night lay before the country and, while Kennedy's electoral vote total hovered just below the number needed for victory, Daley was busy on the phones getting reports from all the precincts in the city, as well as news from downstate. The city had gone massively for Kennedy, and for hours Illinois remained in the Democratic column.

Daley, however, began to make some calculations which were just as fine as any he ever did for a municipal budget.

The mayor understood that the Republican intelligence was almost as good as his, and that their strategists would be watching every development in order to estimate as closely as possible the number of votes they would need to be victorious in Illinois. Late in the afternoon Daley had been informed that in a scattered number of downstate precincts the workers had stopped counting the ballots and had taken them home. There would be a delay in their reporting of their vote totals; the vote tallies might not come in until after midnight. The Republicans would have time to make an estimate of the margin of votes they would need to take the state and could supply them in these delayed returns. They could top the final Cook County vote by taking advantage of this time lag.

"It's hard to milk the cow for eight or ten thousand votes at that time of night," Daley remarked later. What could he do in this last, perilous game, in this last contest in this most cherished crusade? He would hold back some votes, almost twice as many as the Republicans were likely to report on the basis of the projected Cook County total and the time delay in which they could find the ballots they needed. Daley had seen this strategy used before, most recently four years before when, at a late hour and finally with more votes than they had registered Republicans, Will and DuPage counties had supplied a thin margin of votes to defeat the Democratic candidate for governor, Richard Austin.

This was a tense game, however, a gamble for a man who was not impulsive, but who was willing to roll the dice on the message delivered to him by his deepest Irish instincts; victory would be more enjoyable if he beat the dry and self-righteous downstaters at their favorite game.

Back in Hyannis Port, Sargent Shriver blinked back tears as he heard the television report that Illinois had slipped into the Republican column at about 4:00 A.M. He felt that with the loss of Illinois the whole contest was lost, and he glumly headed for bed.

In Chicago, however, Daley was not even sleepy; he was

waiting—how accomplished he had become at it!—and he still had some high cards that he wanted to play. It was all going just as his instincts had told him; Will and DuPage had submitted their tallies and they had been stamped final. This was the moment for which his chief's intuitions had shaped him. He reported the withheld votes because now it was too late for additional returns to come in from downstate. He had outwaited them. Illinois slipped back into the Democratic column for good. The Republicans spluttered in astonishment and rage, but John F. Kennedy was President-elect of the United States.

There would be charges of vote fraud, yes, and predictions that Illinois would end up in the Republican column when the electoral votes were cast in December. By the twenty-first of November, the recount had actually increased Kennedy's lead slightly and Daley was on the attack again.

"This proves definitely that the Republican party and its candidates are bad losers. If they are talking about a recount, the proper thing to do is to recount the entire state. If they recount the state or any part of it, Kennedy will still carry it and the Democratic candidates will still win."

The week before, Daley had offered to put up a million dollars for a recount if the Republicans would do the same. "It is noteworthy that their leader, Mr. Nixon, is standing by the will of the people," he added.

Daley would be the subject of a thousand anecdotes and humorous stories about multiplied vote counts; the legend that emerged would make him the plunderer of innocent and virtuous Republicans, and Nixon would even take to saying that he could have upset the election in Illinois, but that he had not wanted to precipitate a constitutional crisis; no, he would save that for later. But none of this meant as much to Daley as the knowledge that he had been such an important part of John F. Kennedy's winning campaign. He would, in the months ahead, seek much for Chicago but ask for only one thing personally. It was a very Irish request: He wanted to be photographed with his family and the President in the Oval Office.

There were great and tragic days ahead for both Kennedy and Daley but now, in the last gold of autumn, Daley was celebrating with a tribal ritual. He came to the City Council meeting two days after the general election wearing a bright green necktie. When the reporters asked him about it, he grinned and said, in a statement that came closer than anything else he ever said in public to describing his pride in seeing an Irish Catholic in the Presidency, "It's an old family tradition. My mother always told me whenever anything important happened, to wear a bright green tie."

Then he paused and the torches of the last parade seemed to flicker in his eyes as he said, "Wasn't it a great victory?"

[15]

The Man Who Could Not Work Miracles

Chicago was working, there was no doubt of that, and Richard Daley had gained a national reputation for understanding modern urban life by the time he ran for mayor a third time in April 1963. It would be a fight to the death with Benjamin Adamowski, who had been defeated for state's attorney in the 1960 election. Like two scarred warriors, shifting their furs to wield their axes better, they moved toward each other across the late winter like enemies on a drifting ice floe. Daley would win by the smallest of his victory margins because so much of the Polish vote went to his opponent, and Adamowski would surrender his dreams of elective office for good, but it was a wrenching campaign and a wearing one, the first sign, perhaps, that the stars were moving into a configuration of tragedy, that there was a hook and a curse in greatness and fame, and that blood was on the rising moon.

Daley wept uncontrollably at the news of the death of John F. Kennedy, and the country itself, its young leader slain, shuddered and erupted like a volcano that would spew fire and ashes across the decade ahead. Some balance had been shattered and Daley, the man who knew how to use power so well, was soon to face a vision of dread in which he could no longer control men and events as he once had; he was to enter into a world which he could not fully comprehend. It was not of his making, nor could its groans be translated into the basic language which he spoke along with so many millions of Americans; it was no longer a world of dependable verities, for fate was howling in the galaxies and bringing home the stinking plague of all the racial injustice and wrongdoing of the centuries, spilling it across the land and setting its great cities afire.

There were still good days ahead, long stretches in which Daley would become more personally popular in Chicago than ever before, but things would never be the same. It was, in fact, Daley's skill in exercising power that would plunge him into the heart of the racial drama of the sixties; it was his power that would lead civil rights activists to believe that he could make integration—as he had so much else—work in his city; it was his power that drew the scorn of the liberal journalists because they judged it always to be evil in motive and outcome; it was his power, that burnished and singing sword, that would inflict a wound on himself and his beloved city.

That power was undiminished, however, as he welcomed the members of the Metropolitan Housing and Planning Council into his fifth-floor City Hall office. He was self-contained as he nodded across his absolutely clear desk as its members filed into the room, which, except for the flags and the pictures of his family, was unadorned. He was silently counting the votes in this group of mortgage bankers, real estate men, college professors, and clergymen, who had come to give him their advice about the housing problems in the city. His eyes did not flicker as he appraised them and judged them to be a collection of do-gooders. He looked around and, one by one, began to ask his visitors where they lived.

"Glencoe," said one to the unsmiling mayor.

"Winnetka," said another.

"River Forest," added a third, as Daley gazed steadily at the group.

The list of suburban addresses, of comfortable places beyond the city limits, finally came to an end. Out-of-towners, all of them. Daley paused as the last member finished and then, in soft but mocking tones, he asked, "By what right do you come down here, when none of you live in the city, and try to tell us how to run it? You don't vote here. You don't pay taxes here. I don't think you should be telling people how to live in the city when you don't live there yourself."

"It's the principle involved," offered one of the visitors, but Daley cut him off before he could go further.

"The principle? What principle could you mean when you don't have any right to be here at all? Do you want the city people telling you how to live?"

Chagrin hung like tear gas in the air as, without even letting them take a seat, Daley dismissed them from his office with a curt "Good morning."

He had learned how to handle groups like this long ago; they had no power, in his judgment, and they didn't know what they were talking about. He acted differently just a week later when he was visited by another group, The Woodlawn Organization, an activist community group that had been organized by Saul Alinsky and Monsignor John Egan of the archdiocese of Chicago, and which included numerous clergymen, with the Reverend Arthur Brazier as their leader. These people lived in the city and they represented votes; they had, in other words, learned to speak a language Daley understood very well, that of ballots. The Woodlawn Organization's members had, a few years before, sent thirty-two buses of elderly blacks for their first voter registration to City Hall itself. The Chicago Transit Authority had mysteriously canceled their bus contract just the day before they were to go, but they rounded up school buses and vans and got there anyway. Daley respected that idiom of power and so he made time for this group. He even summoned various aides from the building and planning departments; he was as gracious as an old family doctor as, through his barely parted lips, he inquired about their needs and explained the city's plans. Not much more came of the second meeting than of the first, of course. But such was Daley's political art that he judged that he did not need the first group at all but needed the good will of the second. Click, flash, all over in an instant.

There was more here than even the members of The Woodlawn Organization understood. Alinsky had gained his initial reputation through organizing the stockyard workers. Daley had then been a state senator and they had got to know each other well. That relationship survived and, even during the years in which he was training community organizers such as the Woodlawn group, Alinsky met secretly with Daley once or twice a month. Although Alinsky gave the impression of being publicly opposed to the mayor of Chicago, he had reached a practical accommodation with him and would not utter a word of personal criticism until several years later.

Perhaps this skill, this way of managing and deflecting people, this controlled manner of pitting competing forces against each other, this mastery, after so many years, of letting the bloodthirsty animals of commerce and real estate and labor, yes, and even the syndicate too, glut themselves in order to make them produce the buildings and the jobs that kept residents in the city and maintained its tax base, perhaps, as one thinks about it, this ability to control powerful groups through prodding and indulgence, this chieftain's genius for looking closely one moment and looking away the next, perhaps this was filled with virus, a penalty like that in the blood of royalty, that finally exacted its own enormous price of misunderstanding and shame for Daley. For there were finally problems too big for the mayor whom the black leaders called "The Man"; there were forces that not even Richard J. Daley's skills could pound into a weapon for his own use.

Daley was perceived as the most powerful mayor in the country; he had, by the mid-sixties, become a national figure who would accept a series of invitations to law school forums, including one at Harvard during which he blew his critics out of the water and stunned the audience into silence with the power if not the grace of his webbed phrasing.

As he was being introduced several students in the audience began to hiss. Daley stared into the heart of the audience, the slightest smile on his lips.

"Hiss," he said. "My mother always used to tell me that was the sound of truth when it hit the furnaces of hell."

The audience quieted down as Daley moved in on them.

"Here you are at one of our greatest universities. You are from good backgrounds. You are talented. You have everything. There is just one thing missing." Daley waited a moment. "You haven't done anything. You haven't used your ability or your advantages. You haven't done a thing with your lives yet."

The students, as well as scholars like John Kenneth Galbraith, who was in attendance, were under his spell as he pushed forward in his own way with a masterful analysis of urban problems. The applause was long and loud and Daley, enjoying the taste of Puritan blood, went back with a group of students to a dormitory lounge for further informal discussions. What his hosts did not realize was that Daley was far from intimidated in a Harvard setting; he didn't think most of the professors there knew anything about city government anyway.

He delivered Cook County with another staggering plurality for Lyndon Johnson in the general election of 1964 but, like that President, he stood on the very edge of problems whose roots could barely be counted, much less chopped off cleanly. The winter of 1965 washed into a spring flood of civil rights marches and, after Selma and the march to Montgomery, Martin Luther King, Jr., bolstered by President Johnson's efforts in behalf of the voting rights bill, turned his gaze northward, to the big cities that were to be his next targets.

Chicago was the scene of massive black discontent with Benjamin Willis, the gray, self-satisfied, and very well-paid superintendent of the Chicago public schools. Problems with the schools were hardly novel in Chicago, and Daley had long ago developed strategies to handle them, largely through the appointments he made to the school board itself. Frank Whiston, a local real estate entrepreneur, was its president and Thomas J. Murray, president of the local Electrical Workers Union, was vice-president. The latter, in a manifestation of the power, cold and fearful as a star, that would be found if the city were sliced open, threatened the very school board of which he was a member by saying, when the introduction of blacks into the Washburne Trade School was proposed, "If the Board of Education interferes in union membership practices, the trade unions will pull out of Washburne and start their own school."

The board had, however, after much pressure from blacks angry over the crowded conditions of their schools and portable classrooms (nicknamed "Willis Wagons"), agreed by a seven-to-four vote in May 1965 not to extend Willis's contract beyond August 31 of that year. Ten days later, however, when the board met for its official vote on the matter, three members, including Mrs. W. Lydon Wild, a close friend of the Daley family, switched their votes, after Willis promised to retire on his sixty-fifth birthday at the end of 1966. That was the way things were handled in this city, which, with its expanded parks and beaches, with its new buildings and plazas, seemed to grow more beautiful externally, even as the inner forces of its component parts, like the furies of the sea, pressed and thrashed more intensely against each other.

And Dr. King could be handled as well; that was the political judgment at City Hall when news came of his plans to spend three days in Chicago in July. It was vintage Daley, right down to the fact that he was not in the city but at a conference of mayors in Detroit on the day Martin Luther King, Jr., led his first march to City Hall. He would not have a confrontation with King in any way; nor, in the statement he issued, would he mention Benjamin Willis, the awful bone in King's throat. Rather he would say of King, "The presentation of his position against poverty and discrimination, for which he was deservedly awarded the Nobel Prize, is a position that all right-thinking Americans should support."

It was difficult for Dr. King to feel that he had met an opponent in that message, which, like a torero's cape, hung on the air with nothing behind it.

King himself was not in complete control of the plans of the Southern Christian Leadership Conference. Decisions in Chicago were being made by the charismatic Jim Bevel and by Andrew Young, who controlled the finances of the movement. Dr. King, flying in and out, went along with their strategies; he was not clear on what he could accomplish in Chicago, and divisions within the movement about whether to confront or avoid Mayor Daley also weakened his position.

Daley was, it must be admitted, in a difficult position, because he felt, with the kind of sincerity that might fill his eyes with the purest tears, that he had worked tirelessly to improve Chicago, and had endorsed programs as good as or better than any others in the country to alleviate the problems of the black people. With some measure of justification, he could ask whether any other mayor or city had a record of achievement and purpose, even in the area of civil rights, to equal his and Chicago's. No matter what he did—as, for example, when he worked to increase the number of minority doctors on the staffs of Chicago's hospitals—he received criticism. He could never do enough to appease those critics who found in him the Erich von Stroheim of big city bosses, the bulldog of a man they loved to hate and sneer at. His personality, at once awesome and intriguing, had made him a powerful and appealing enemy to many journalists. His undiluted hatred for the media was nourished by the steady diet of criticism he received: He was never a "new leader" but always an "old boss"; the party was never an effective "political organization," but always a grinding and grasping "machine." Daley must have felt that the devil dwelt in newspapers and television, that evil bubbled in the maw of their constant activity. Outriders with cameras and microphones and trailing cables seemed constantly to be closing in on either side of him to catch the slightest grimace or mispronounced word; these circling hordes seemed to be enemies with no sense of fair play as they hacked away even at the paneled walls of his private life; they were everywhere in wait for him. They became, along with his bodyguards, part of his everyday existence, and he would come to terms with them—the snarling and defiant terms of a chieftain who has decided to challenge rather than to placate his enemies.

Before Dr. King arrived in Chicago in July 1965, Daley had proclaimed in a news conference, "There will always be law and order in Chicago as long as Daley is the mayor." It was to be a month and a summer of omens for the sixty-three-year-old Daley, who looked for political solutions, the only remedies possible in the short run, as he saw it, the efforts to let men talk out problems against a background of reality, with a sharp sense of the way things were as well as with hopes for the way they might be. Daley could not change the balance he had effected between merchants and labor leaders, between builders and haulers, and between all the other grappling factions of Chicago life whose cooperation was vital to the city's deliverance from strikes and stoppages; he had to keep every whirling, self-interested group in the air at the same time, for only then would the city prosper and find its destiny. It was strenuous work that required every bit of his obsessive commitment to the city, and it demanded political insights and action; he could not have a reformer like Dr. King, no matter what his zeal, visit his beloved city, disrupt it, and then move on. Besides, Daley had received disconcerting reports about Dr. King's private life and language; these were not messages that would win the affection of a staunch old moralist.

Still, things were changing. Adlai Stevenson fell dead on a London street that July while American astronauts circled the earth in further explorations that would lead the country to the moon. There was something in the very air of this summer that was unsettling and, beyond that, something surreal as well when sixty-five demonstrators, led by comedian and civil rights activist Dick Gregory, marched past the police and fire stations at the corner of 35th Street and South Lowe Avenue toward the Daley house itself. The marchers were in the heart of Bridgeport; many of them teenagers who had been moving every day from Buckingham Fountain near the lakefront to City Hall to protest against Superintendent Willis, but now they were walking into a hard white residential area, floating like a dream on the edge of nightmare past the small and simple homes of Daley's own neighborhood. A large crowd of local people gathered around the marchers, and as the jeering and tomato-throwing began, Captain Howard Pierson, commander of the local Deering police district, began arresting the demonstrators on the grounds that they might start a riot.

The next day, at a news conference, Daley denounced the marchers; he was under control, spreading his phrases out as carefully as a mason does his mortar, every inch the respectable citizen who was more amazed than outraged by the turn things had taken.

"People in their homes have a right to privacy. Surely the family of a man in public office shouldn't be subjected to this kind of action. There is no reason for this kind of marches late at night or early in the morning. I don't think it helps their cause to be marching in residential areas. I think they are surely trying to create tension." Then Daley urged his neighbors to be calm. "Our neighbors are fine people, middle-income working people." He looked around and added, "And they have no feelings one way or another about all this."

Daley was, in fact, echoing the convictions of the vast bulk of city dwellers; the view from Bridgeport was exactly what he saw himself. The downtown marches in the heat had been pounded into the senses of these people through all the communications media; in the tension they drew closer together, drawing on the beliefs and values which they had accepted and by which they had tried to live. They had been taught to work hard as well as to accept the inevitable unfairness and tragedy of existence; nobody, as they saw it, had given them, in their struggles as immigrant groups, a free ride or an easy hand up out of their simple and often quite poor lives; they had come to value property as a sign of their achievement and their individual identity, so they cringed when any group, no matter how genuine its grievances or how deep its pain, seemed to challenge any of this.

And the linchpin of all this, as the meteor shower of August began, was Richard Daley, man of the past, conservator king of the neighborhood he would not change—and yet man of the future as well, riding the edge of his city's transforming progress that would make it the most changed of cities in America, the all-seeing man with the blind side, the man who wanted to stop time and conquer it as well. Two opposing forces inside him were caught up in this first siege of night marchers, in this troubled scene below the streetlights he had made shine more brightly. He had a right to look puzzled as two arcs of history converged in his own personality and his own neighborhood.

Yet another change occurred that August when Archbishop John Patrick Cody stepped off the Panama Limited from New Orleans to take over in the city as the successor to Albert Cardinal Meyer, who had died in April. Cody, a heavyset and obsessive worker, became Archbishop and later Cardinal of Chicago at exactly the wrong time in history. He was an old-fashioned prelate who had teethed on a ring of ambition, and who had climbed to the top of the largest Catholic diocese in the country just as its foundations began to swell and crack from the pressures of change. Daley had learned how to deal with Catholic prelates across the years, but he had not been terribly pleased in the previous year when the first changes in the Latin Mass of his boyhood had taken place; he liked clergymen in their place and he paid them great honor and every courtesy, from his tipped hat to his weekly contributions. He could not know that Cody, as hungry as Daley for power, would involve himself in the civil rights issue in a way that would exert great pressure on the mayor. Daley could not understand the new, socially conscious Catholic priests—so different from their obedient and docile elders—who, along with the clergy of other faiths, applied community-organizing techniques on a wide scale in the parishes—which were co-extensive with the neighborhoods—of Chicago.

Nor could Daley have predicted what would happen on Thursday evening, August 12, when the Perseid shooting stars were at their height. An alarm bell rang in the fire station at 4000 West Wilcox and, as the firemen scrambled aboard and the hook-and-ladder truck pulled out onto the street, nobody noticed that the tillerman was missing. The huge truck fishtailed and slammed into and uprooted a traffic sign pole, which struck and killed a twenty-three-year-old black girl, Dessie Mae Williams of 4047 West Jackson, who had been waiting for a bus. It was spark enough for the explosive atmosphere of the Lawndale area of the city, and disorders began that night. The Los Angeles suburb of Watts was already burning in a five-day siege that would take thirty-one lives and cause $200 million in damage. Daley wanted nothing like that in his city, and he immediately moved in to take personal charge of the efforts to contain what might easily burst into a major riot. Things were not helped at all when somebody started distributing leaflets on the West Side with the inscription "Allegedly Drunken White Fireman Kills Black Woman."

On Friday, after he had studied reports about the seven persons who had been injured the night before, Daley gave an order to move an all-black unit of firemen into the station under a white commander. The mayor, grim-faced but determined to preserve order at all costs, shuttled between his office, in which he held meetings with his aides throughout the weekend, and his home, where he had set up an informal command post. He called Governor Otto Kerner and Police Superintendent O. W. Wilson and suggested that National Guard units should be brought into the city to stand by in local armories in case they were needed. Daley even ordered that the riot areas be swept clean of broken bottles to maintain local traffic and to remove potential ammunition for rioters. The mayor also called upon religious and community leaders to cooperate in maintaining order, after seventy persons were injured on Friday night. On Saturday teams of priests and ministers worked the streets, along with civil rights leaders, at two-hour intervals to maintain calm. The area's taverns were closed and five hundred policemen were brought in, along with ninety-five black detectives, many of them in plain clothes, to stand guard and mingle with the residents on Saturday night. The long, tense weekend came to a close and Daley congratulated all the men and agencies who had worked to keep the neighborhoods calm. Daley, with a combination of restraint and action, had saved his city. It was the last time it would be spared so easily.

If the threat of racial problems was not enough, the year ended with a hint of still other difficulties that would fall like shadows across Daley's years in office. Justice Department officials named two Chicago Democratic leaders as possible future targets of the methods they had used on Momo Salvatore Giancana the previous spring. He had been sent to jail for refusing to testify before a grant jury which had granted him immunity from prosecution; the same pressures were scheduled to be put on John D'Arco, Democratic committeeman from the First Ward, and Pat Marcy, secretary of that Democratic organization. Would it help the party, the reporters asked Daley a week before Christmas, if these two men resigned their posts? Daley gave a characteristic answer.

"We said that this is a matter for the people in their respective areas. They select their leadership. And as long as I'm chairman of our party, I feel that the people in their respective areas have a right to select the men and women they want to represent them."

He had switched, like an agile surfer, and ridden a different wave in to the shore.

But, the dogged questioners continued, would this embarrass the Democratic party if they appeared in crime investigations?

But Daley was halfway up the beach and on the way to lunch already. "Well, I'll face that situation when it arises."

In January, Dr. King announced that he would be returning to Chicago in order to work out of a slum apartment; he also hinted that he might move the headquarters of his Southern Christian Leadership Conference from Atlanta to Chicago. Well, Daley would "welcome" him again, employing the same strategy that had proved so successful in defusing King's visit the summer before; hadn't even the *Christian Century* observed that Chicago, "including its nearly one million Negroes, smothered King with apathy"?

In the meantime, Daley would celebrate as his old friend and former law partner, William Lynch, was named a federal judge for the Northern District of Illinois. Yes, Lynch was a friend to give comfort and good counsel, a friend who had prospered on the business Daley had directed his way after he became mayor, a rare kind of friend who might just respond generously to all the favors the mayor had done for him. Lynch had indeed prospered, and yet he seemed to resent his bene- factor, even though he was bound to him and the Daley clan very tightly. There may be no resentment greater than that ex- perienced by the one who profits from a friend who, like Daley in relationship to Lynch, has been more successful. Lynch was tied to Daley in a hundred ways and yet was never his equal; he would bristle, to the grave and perhaps beyond, in his in- debtedness to the mayor.

Daley made a statement of welcome to Dr. King, noting that all city departments would be ready to extend help to him after his arrival. Daley then referred to King's recent visit with Po- lice Superintendent Wilson.

"I believe," he said with the look of an altar boy, "this is the first police department in the country that he has met with."

What about King's statements that he would "break any law" for the cause of civil rights?

"I am hopeful and confident," Daley answered in his softest and most controlled voice, "there will not be any reason for breaking law. All of us are for the elimination of slums. This is the number-one program of the present administration and has been for the ten years we have been here."

He paused again, a touch almost of innocence gilding his proud tones. "We are not perfect but we feel we have done more than any other metropolitan city in the country."

It was also in January that the new archbishop, in one of his first changes, removed the activist priest Monsignor John Egan, from his directorship of the Office of Urban Affairs and made him pastor of Presentation, a black parish on the city's West Side.

King took over a dilapidated six-apartment building in the Lawndale section of the city during February. This was to be a dramatic demonstration of his program to end slums. He asked that the tenants pay their rent to his organization; the funds would be used to renovate the building. Dr. King described his move as "supralegal trusteeship." Judge James Parsons, the first black on the federal bench within the continental states, termed it "theft," while the mayor explained that the original landlord had been charged with violations of the building code. Daley added that there "are legal and illegal ways" to battle slum conditions. King's efforts with the building were a conspicuous failure; no rents were ever paid to the Southern Christian Leadership Conference and, although King spent about $1000 on the property, its condition seemed to deteriorate rather than improve. Finally, an injunction was issued which prohibited members of his organization from entering the apartments at all.

King was charging hard because his presence in Chicago was important to his national work, which included fund-raising from certain liberal sources who delighted in picturing Daley, the ogre of their pale imaginations, as an adversary not much different from a brutish Southern sheriff. But King was stumbling through the cape that Daley worked so masterfully.

"Your goals are our goals," Daley would declare as he anticipated most of King's demands.

This was Daley's regular strategy, part of his locking eyes with the press over crossed swords: Try to keep unfavorable stories from ever occurring.

To this end, the Building Department was correcting code violations while the Legal Department was drawing up papers against slumlords, and the Sanitation Department was checking on problems with garbage collection. During March, Daley held two conferences of local religious leaders in order, he said, to improve communication on the pressing issues of slums and poverty. After the second gathering, King declared that he was "happy" about some parts of the meeting but warned that "this does not in any way negate the fact that Chicago has a long way to go."

Daley was meanwhile absolving Chicagoans of the "collective guilt" King mentioned during the meeting. "These problems," he said, "were created thousands of miles away from here, in Georgia, Mississippi, and Alabama. This deprivation of education can't be laid to the people of Chicago. They had nothing to do with it."

King had indeed been contained, although Daley's political approach did not get at the basic problems in the city. These were, of course, problems so impacted that no mayor, not even the resourceful and energetic Daley, could have diagnosed or treated them in a short time. He felt that maintaining peace in Chicago was a service to all its citizens, black and white alike, and that preventing disruption, while planning programs, was a more than adequate response. The pressure on the city slackened as Daley's responses frustrated King's efforts to make Chicago a demonstration site.

Attention was drawn further away in June when James Meredith was shot while on a civil rights march in Mississippi; shot with him was a young Chicago priest, Father Richard Morrisroe, one of the scores of clergymen who had aligned themselves with the purposes of Dr. King's movement.

Everywhere he looked, Daley found the priests and the nuns, who had represented discipline all his life, marching and demonstrating for the civil rights movement. One of the clearest statements of his own Bridgeport view of things was uttered to a young nun who was marching for open housing. "Look, Sister," Daley said, "you and I come from the same background. We know how tough it was. But we picked ourselves up by our bootstraps."

While King was moving back and forth from the South, Daley was questioned again about the First Ward Democrats who were in the headlines once more. Justice Department officials claimed that United States Attorney Edward Hanrahan, a recent Democratic appointee, had failed to seek immunity for these men in order to question them about government charges that they had made large payoffs the previous year. At a press conference, the mayor was asked whether he was proud of the kind of leadership that the Democratic party had in the First Ward.

"I am proud," Daley answered, poised to catch another wave again, "of the leadership I have exerted in this entire community."

Well, the reporters wanted to know, trying to hold on to him, what about the leadership in the First Ward?

"The leadership in the First Ward is selected by the people of the ward."

"But the Justice Department has said that—"

Daley broke in quickly. "The leadership of the First Ward is selected by the people."

"But," another questioner asked, "do you have an opinion on whether that leadership is good?"

"Opinion on what?" Daley retorted. "I know nothing about the facts."

And so the questioning went, with Daley giving his practiced answers about the good record of the party and the democracy of its selection process. It was only when the questioning turned directly to the First Ward committeeman that he demonstrated the agility and one-two punching capability of a no-holds-barred brawler.

"Are you satisfied with D'Arco's record in the First Ward?" a reporter asked.

"What is his record?" Daley responded quickly, moving onto the offense, like a fighter picking up a bar stool. "Have you documented it? What's he guilty of?"

"He is accused," the reporter responded, "of having refused to testify before a federal grand jury."

"Do you know that of your own knowledge?" Daley shot back.

"Through newspaper accounts," the reporter answered, a little lamely.

This, of course, was just the kind of answer the reluctant mayor needed. "Let's get on the record here," he said. "Let's get talking common sense. Let's get talking the kind of conversation you would want talked about you."

He was warming to his subject now, a tone of righteousness in his voice as he took the press head-on again. "Let's have some evidence on these charges here, and I'll answer if any of you have any evidence of what we're talking about."

It was a classic rout, a prototype of the endless encounters between Daley and the media.

The summer, blown glowing red by the storms of the sixties, began with 100-degree temperatures that persisted into the first week of July. Dr. King was back, and he had announced plans for a rally at Soldier Field on Sunday, July 10. King had been complaining that "Mayor Daley has gone into partnership with me," and he wanted this gathering, in the huge, Coliseum-like stadium on the lakefront, to be the set piece for a series of marches for open housing in various white suburbs of the city.

The forty thousand who came on that blistering Sunday fell far short of filling the arena, but that lack was made up for by a strong message from Archbishop Cody, read by one of his auxiliary bishops, Aloysius Wycislo. Cody had been under intensifying pressure to offer support to King, but he had his own problems in the fact that over a thousand of his priests had been so dissatisfied with his imperial approach that they had organized an association of their own that very summer.

Cody had turned to the priest he had taken out of the Office of Urban Affairs, Monsignor John Egan, who, on Saturday afternoon, had gone to his office and typed a message that committed Cody strongly to King's efforts. He read it over, decided it needed no changes, and sent it to the archbishop. Daley was surprised and not pleased to hear the words that echoed and re-echoed in the half-filled stadium: "Your struggle and your sufferings will be mine until the last vestige of discrimination and injustice is blotted out here in Chicago and throughout America." Reform Rabbi Robert J. Marx was also present to support King, as was Dr. Edgar Chandler, the ex-director of the Church Federation of Chicago.

What none of the religious leaders understood as well as Daley was the simple fact that they were out in front of their people on this issue and that many of their communicants would simply not follow them or their activist priests and ministers as readily as they supposed. Still, it was an enormous boost for King, whom the mayor was to meet the very next day in his office. Before that appointment, Daley decided to make a few calls to other prominent Catholics in Chicago. The mayor let Archbishop Cody feel a little contrary pressure—nothing too obvious, of course, just influential men and established contributors who would tell the archbishop just how they felt on the complex racial problems that were besetting the city, and that too much archepiscopal support might damage the chances of the city's own constructive programs.

On Monday afternoon, with the temperature headed once more over the 100-degree mark, Daley looked remarkably cool in his dark business suit as he welcomed Dr. King into his office at City Hall. Daley had several department heads and aides present to supply information on current programs and, in a clear and controlled voice, in the manner of a man who felt very sure of himself, he began what would be a three-hour meeting.

Daley read from a forty-page memorandum, prepared by Earl Bush, which outlined the programs which the city had developed to deal with the problems of discrimination and blight. Dr. King sat uncomfortably with a group of his associates as the mayor read off the list of ordinances, plans, merit-review hiring policies, and other specifics, pausing regularly to raise his head and say, "We've got this. Now why don't you help us in it?"

It was difficult for Dr. King to respond, because Daley had put him at a distinct disadvantage: How could King complain when Daley was inviting him to support programs that were important; and where, in this massive presentation, could he find a handhold, a branch or a rock, which he could use to hoist himself above the frustration line?

King raised the issue of a civilian review board for the police but Daley, remembering the reassuring feel of his initial handshake with O. W. Wilson when he took him on as police superintendent, explained that he had to leave this to the police and that Wilson was opposed to it.

Then Wilson spoke his piece, just as Daley wanted, taking the fire that would otherwise have been directed toward the mayor. King would turn to an aide of Daley's at the conclusion of the meeting and say, "It isn't enough that he's doing these things. He's got to let us do them."

King had, in fact, already decided to go along with a campaign of direct action in the suburbs in favor of open housing; he had, as he also explained, to "have some victories with his nonviolent approach"; he had "to bring something back to show that progress was being made."

After the meeting ended, Dr. King faced the press and said, "We are not satisfied," adding that he felt that the mayor "doesn't understand the depths and dimensions of the problems we're dealing with in the city of Chicago." Daley had been "warm and sympathetic," King said, "but he made no specific commitments."

King was making the best he could of the bewildering encounter in which he had been badly outmaneuvered by the mayor, who had turned out to be far tougher and smarter than he had expected; King's own political interests had, in fact, been jeopardized by this sweet-sounding standoff. Just the day before, he had said that the black vote would elect the next mayor of the city; now the present and future mayor had lathered him and shaved him so closely that it was almost painful.

Daley faced the reporters after King and, although somewhat annoyed by King's presentation, he described, like an innocent man falsely accused, the work that the city was already doing. He was, in fact, speaking directly to the people of his city as well as to the country.

"We asked them, 'What would you do that we haven't done?' They had no answers. I asked for their help and suggestions, and they frankly said the answers were difficult. I asked them, 'Why can't we sit down and you tell us?' There wasn't any answer."

Daley was asked about King's pledge "to fill the jails if necessary" to call attention to rights demands.

"We asked," Daley said again, like a virtuous boy answering a teacher's question, " 'Why do you have to do these things?' and there wasn't any answer."

It was 100 again the next day when, in the Lawndale section of the city, firemen, concerned about water pressure, turned off the hydrants which the black children had been using to cool themselves off. Tempers flared and rioting quickly broke out; policemen coming to restore order were fired on, and Chicago's West Side was ablaze. Three days of looting and shooting followed, and on Thursday the National Guard was ordered out; Dr. King canceled a speech in Geneva, Switzerland, to return to the smoking city. Many ordinary people felt—how else, given the conditions, could they interpret it?— that this would never have occurred if King had stayed away from Chicago. On the other hand, the licking flames were searing proof, in this hottest of summers, that the underlying problems were too complex to be handled merely on a political level, that something far more than Daley could ever produce would be needed to remedy things.

So on Friday, King and Daley met again in an effort to ease the West Side tension, agreeing on the formation of a citizens' committee to make recommendations to improve relations between the police and members of the community, as well as on the installation of spray devices on the hydrants and a speedup, with additional federal funds, of swimming pool construction in the black areas. They had been critical of each other, these two men caught up in events with which they could only compromise but which they could never completely control, events which, for both King and Daley, were filled with the smoldering dread of the fire next time.

It was a summer in which the devil seemed to be everywhere, a long hot season during which Richard Speck butchered eight nurses and his tattoo, "Born to raise hell," summed up the times themselves.

In August, after months of preparation, Dr. King started a series of marches through selected areas of the city, all of them filled with middle-class, white, and largely Catholic homeowners. These were Gage Park and Marquette Park on the South Side and Cragin in the northwest section of the city. The nonviolent marches would be aimed at the real estate dealers in these neighborhoods, and they would be centered in the churches, whose cooperation King depended on very strongly. Had not Archbishop Cody pledged to stand behind him and were not several Catholic priests working closely with him in preparing and carrying out these marches? But neither King nor the other clergymen had counted on the resistance that they would find among these churchgoing people; they did not grasp the reluctance to change which these people felt, nor their potential for violence even when the marches were filled with singing nuns and priests.

The probe of nonviolence was inserted into these neighborhoods, but it was soon tangled in the deep and twisted roots and vines of an entrenched culture. The massive effort trig-

Daley puts his arm around his wife, Eleanor, known popularly as "Sis," a strong and able woman who was a perfect match for the mayor. Deeply religious and devoted to family life, Mrs. Daley provided not only emotional support but regular counsel to her husband. (*Chicago Daily News*/Riddle)

Daley, the exhorter, with every ridge and crag of his face quivering as he stitched his sentences together. Sometimes the syntax verged on the disastrous, but no one ever misunderstood his passion or his meaning. (Murphy Photography, Inc.)

Above: A 1970 photograph of the mayor and his four sons. Like an Irish king, Daley believed in the privilege of bloodlines, and helping his sons get ahead in life seemed natural and virtuous to him. From the left, they are Richard, John, William, and Michael. At the extreme right stands another Eleventh Warder, Michael Bilandic, who would succeed Daley as mayor. (Murphy Photography, Inc.)

Right: Two survivors exchange a few words at a 1972 Democratic dinner. P.J. "Parky" Cullerton, city assessor for many years and member of a powerful Chicago political family, keeps a thousand secrets beneath the crevasses and plating of his ancient face. (Murphy Photography, Inc.)

Daley performs a yearly ritual for the last time, greeting the 1976 St. Patrick's Day Queen, Cathy O'Connell, in his office. Around them stand members of the Shannon Rovers with their leader, Tommy Ryan, at the extreme left. On the night of his wake the full complement of the pipers would play Daley's favorite piece, the "Garry Owen," in the Nativity of Our Lord Church. (Brighton Krug)

A young girl, one of the hundred thousand mourners who passed through the church to pay their respects to the late mayor. She holds a memorial card of the occasion, on the reverse of which was printed the prayer of St. Francis "Lord, make me an instrument of your peace," a favorite of Daley's that he always carried in his wallet. (*Chicago Daily News*/Stein) gered violence; Dr. King was struck by a rock and several clergy were cursed and spat upon. At Marquette Park, where, in the mysterious way of such things, many groups, including contingents of the American Nazi party, appeared, it finally took 960 policemen to extricate 600 marchers from a threatening crowd of some 4000. At Gage Park 313 policemen were mustered to supervise the march while in Cragin the members of one Catholic congregation turned on their pastor at a meeting during which he was trying to prepare them for the meaning of the demonstrations. A few days later, he was called to the chancery office and criticized for his role in the march.

The support of the Catholic Church which had been offered so positively by Archbishop Cody only the month before, seemed, except for the dozens of individual priests involved in their own areas, to have been modified considerably. Archbishop Cody seemed farther behind Dr. King than the civil rights leader had expected. Even the priest who had replaced Monsignor John Egan in the Urban Affairs Office, the highly proper Father Edward Egan, seemed to serve as an informant to the archbishop about which priests and nuns participated in the marches, rather than as an intermediary or a supporter. Many would say that King's failure—for such it finally was—was connected, in great part, to his feeling that he had more in place with Cody than he actually had, and that the lack of follow-up support was fatal to his cause.

King, who after the Marquette Park march would say, "The people of Mississippi ought to come to Chicago to learn how to hate," left the city without the victory he wanted. The local SCLC leadership was anxious to move on.

He would return briefly before the elections, but his work had been successfully contained not only by the mayor but by the people themselves. What King failed to appreciate was the faithful way in which Daley mirrored the values and outlook of the neighborhoods, so much like his own, which stretched in every direction away from City Hall. King did not realize that

Daley spoke even for many black people who held similar views about dramatic change and who would continue to vote for him in succeeding elections. It was all far more complicated, this hard shell of power and energy that was Chicago, than King had anticipated.

And Richard Daley, late in August, would tell hate groups to stay away from Chicago. He had finally obtained an injunction to regulate open occupancy marches in the city, and he reported that his mail on this decision was overwhelmingly in his favor. And, as to the agitators, he said, "The Commies are in there. You've got the Nazis. You've got everyone else. You've got the haters. That is what they thrive on. They go from one part of the country to another but these are not the people of Chicago. Anyone who says that does not know the people of Chicago."

So the long hot summer came to a close and Daley had his victory, a triumph on Bridgeport terms, won in a tough fight in which he had taken on King and the liberal press and had spoken for his neighbors, who would now identify with and vote for him with deeper loyalty than ever. And yet the chieftain had somehow brought a strange curse on the things he prized most of all, his own name and his city. Martin Luther King, Jr., would return in the gutting fires that would follow his own assassination. And Richard Daley's tested techniques would not work so well in times which, despite his massive shoulder against the wheel of change, were being grotesquely transformed by forces that were beyond his political control. They would be a mystery and a puzzle, these events which he somehow could not control, and they would have their way with him yet. If he was the mayor chosen because he was thought to be the father figure who could save everybody, he would now suffer every denunciation, because neither he nor anyone else had that much power.

But at the end of that August in 1966, he felt that outsiders had violated the city that was his love. He told the press, "We could do well without them and we hope they go back to the place they came from in order that we may go ahead with our programs to make Chicago a better city."

Did he also mean certain civil rights leaders?

"You can answer that," he snapped.

Well, in addition to the Nazis and the Ku Klux Klan, did he also want Martin Luther King, Jr., to go back "where he came from"?

Daley was annoyed at the questioner. "You said that."

Still another reporter remarked that King was "an out-of-stater too."

But the chieftain turned away and asked, "Any other questions?"

[**16**]

1968

PENTHEUS: But *I* say: chain him. And I
am stronger here.
DIONYSUS: You do not know the limits
of your strength. You do not know what
you do.

—Euripides, *Bacchae*

Lyndon Johnson was in bed, the coverlet spread with reports,
but he was listening intently to Richard J. Daley, who had
been an overnight guest at the White House and who, his hair
slicked down and his dark business suit without a wrinkle, was
talking as earnestly as he ever did.

"I'm tellin' you, Mr. President, this is destroyin' the country," the mayor said in dry, flat tones. "You've got to get out of
Vietnam."

"I can't, Dick," Johnson replied. "We've got to see this
through."

An aide entered at that moment and the conversation broke
off, an exchange full of shadows and prophecy between two
bull elephants of power who were both being stalked by the
same hunter, who were both coming into watery focus in the
gunsight of history itself.

It did not seem so as the New Year of 1968 began. In an interview with the *Chicago Sun-Times*, Daley looked back on
1967 as a year to savor as one does a vintage wine. Not only
had Daley been re-elected by his greatest victory margin so far

over another sacrificial Republican victim, John Waner, but Chicago, the city of his heart, had witnessed none of the rioting and burning that had struck cities like Detroit, Cincinnati, Newark, and Atlanta.

"I think the way you avoid it is the way we tried to take care of the problem in 1967. We have positive, constructive programs, and you do not permit anyone to violate the law or take the law into his own hands."

He sounded confident because, after all, this strategy of absorbing the inconvenience of demonstrations had kept the city from burning down.

"You respect everyone's right under the First Amendment and permit everyone to petition and to demonstrate, but not take over the streets of Chicago."

Yes, and he would keep Chicago safe in 1968. He had not wanted the Democratic National Convention, but Lyndon Johnson had asked him to take it on and—loyal as he was, and confident as he was in his powers—he had accepted.

So Daley went on, "I said four years ago and I repeat it to you today: There will be law and order here. It will be with fairness and justice. But," and he spoke deliberately, in the tone of a man who does not make foolish wagers, "there will be no one coming in from outside this city to take over Chicago at convention time or at any other time."

The interview went on to other matters and, at its conclusion, the reporter, Frank Sullivan, who would later become Daley's press secretary, asked, "Mr. Mayor, many people wonder where you get the energy to do all the things you do. Can you explain?"

Daley's face broke into a wide smile as he answered, "I think it comes from my Gaelic ancestry."

So things had gone well despite the convulsive unrest about Vietnam which was highlighted by Minnesota Senator Eugene McCarthy's surprisingly good showing against President Johnson in the New Hampshire primary. Who could predict the crush of events that would come in March, in the month of the

St. Patrick's Day parade in which Daley would walk up State Street with the Lord Mayor of Galway and actor Pat O'Brien? Senator Robert F. Kennedy would announce for the Presidential nomination on the eve of that Irish feast and, ten days into spring, on the very last day of the month, Lyndon Johnson would declare that he would neither seek nor accept the Democratic nomination for re-election.

Anything could happen now and Daley, sensing that he would have a hand in Presidential destiny once more, turned the possibilities over in his mind the way a chieftain eyes a roast on the spit of his camp fire, impassive in his certainty that there will be plenty of food for everyone. Had not Robert Kennedy said, just a few days before Johnson withdrew, "Daley means the ball game"?

The mayor had enjoyed himself immensely when reporters had asked him about it at a news conference. "He means," Daley said with a smile, "I'm a great White Sox fan."

In the Catholic liturgical cycle, the season of the Passion of the Lord had begun; all the religious symbols were draped in purple as Daley went to mass during that first week of April. On Wednesday, the first prayer of the rite had been taken from the Psalms, "Lord, you rescue me from raging enemies, you lift me up above my attackers, you deliver me from violent men." The next evening, just as Daley sat down at a formal dinner at the Drake Hotel, the first news bulletin came that Dr. Martin Luther King, Jr., had been shot on his motel balcony in Memphis. The world seemed to shift under the mayor's feet, for who could tell what devils would come streaming out of the fury of this tragedy?

The next morning, a Friday and the thirteenth anniversary of his first election as mayor, Daley and the city were on alert; he ordered the flag to be flown at half-staff on all municipal buildings and arranged for a memorial service at the City Council meeting that day. He spoke of King's greatness and of the great sadness of the day; it was with deep feeling, with an Irishman's sense of darkness falling around an event, that he concluded, "All of us must soften the grief of Dr. King's family and associates by demonstrating that his life was not in vain."

The West Side, however, had already begun to crackle and smoke like an overloaded electrical line in the moment before it explodes. High school students and other young black people began to gather at Garfield Park, wave upon wave of them coalescing in their protesting truancy into an angry and swirling mob.

"Break out windows if you want to," one speaker told them, "but don't loot. Looting discredits the avenging of King's death."

But it was too late to temper the grieving beast as it clawed into Madison Street, smashing and looting all along the way, lusting finally for the limelike kiss of fire in the heart of the black community itself.

The first alarms started coming in at about 4:00 P.M. and soon half of Chicago's fire equipment and firemen were heading toward the now flaming West Side.

"You can't tell where the fires are," Chief Fire Alarm Operator David Sullivan told reporters. "They're walking west and burning as they go."

Sullivan would remain at his post for twenty-three hours, logging almost 600 fires but knowing that he and his assistants had missed dozens of others. If fire was a witch, chaos was her twin as columns of dark smoke rose above the river of flame that roared along the broad avenues on the western side of the city. Reports began coming in about similar problems in other cities, and about Chicago's firemen being pelted with rocks and bottles; and now a report that one had been shot in the leg, and that blacks had been shot too and some were dead, and the sun went down early in the smoke as the ashes of terror settled everywhere.

At three o'clock Daley had telephoned Governor Samuel Shapiro to ask that the National Guard be sent to the Lawndale area, and at 4:20 P.M. he went on radio and television to speak to the people of his city. He drew on his deepest reserves of self-control for this moment because that is what he wanted from the people.

"Stand up tonight," he said gravely, "and protect the city. I ask this very sincerely, very personally. Let's show the United States and the world what Chicago's citizens are made of."

Chicago was a ghostly and quiet city the next morning as Daley was driven to the West Side to inspect the smoking ruins. He stopped and talked to policemen and firemen and watched as workers from the Sanitation Department began to clean off some of the streets. Daley looked shocked and drawn, his usually pink complexion gone white, as his eyes, bloodshot and unbelieving, viewed the desolation.

"Why did they do this to me?" he is reported to have said.

Daley was not just a city official making an impersonal inspection; no, he was the next of kin, the spouse weeping at the rape of his bride. He was not just Churchill-like, standing in the rubble as the hardy figure of identity for millions of Chicago's citizens; he was the uncomprehending victim, seared in his soul by the fate that had overtaken his city, the suitor, ardent still, who had brought gifts and flowers, the best he could find, for the city he saw as sweet and virginal, for this great Lady of the Lake for whom his devotion had been pure and absolute. In his passion he had become the most vulnerable of lovers and the fire and the looting constituted infidelity, the breaching of every truest pledge; this wife he had loved as Yahweh loved Israel had been ravished by those he, the landowner and householder, felt he had helped most; how, indeed, could they have done this to him?

That afternoon Lieutenant General George R. Mather arrived at City Hall. He had just flown over the city in a helicopter and he asked to be connected with the White House switchboard in order to get President Johnson's official approval for bringing in troops from Fort Hood, Texas, and Fort Carson, Colorado, as well as for taking command of the now federalized National Guard troops. Shortly, army convoys would be rumbling through Chicago's streets, something that had never before happened in its history. Chicago, the city envied by municipal administrators all over the country, the city that was like a dream of goodness and orderliness to the mayor, was, in effect, under martial law.

Daley, studying reports of further killings, of Molotov cocktails being manufactured and thrown just a few miles from City Hall, felt consumed in a nightmare. But now he must work diligently to restore order and to prevent further violence. He ordered a curfew from 7:00 P.M. until 6:00 A.M. for everyone under twenty-one years of age. Was the mayor in favor of shooting looters, he was asked late that afternoon.

"Well," he answered slowly, "it's a pretty serious thing to be talking about shooting looters, but I am hopeful there will be sterner action taken by the military and the Police Department today and tonight."

But that night it grew quiet, silent as a city glutted on blood and plunder, as quiet as animals when they see the tents of the hunters, as silent as a house after the visit of death.

The next day was Palm Sunday and after attending mass, the mayor, along with Fire Commissioner Robert Quinn, boarded a helicopter for a forty-five-minute inspection of the ravaged city. Stepping out, grim-faced, Daley said, "It was a shocking and tragic picture of the city." There was the slightest of pauses as he found words for his sad wonder at it all. "I never believed that this would happen here. I hope it will not happen again."

It was Holy Week and he, along with his closest aides and the police and the army, would work long days in order to keep the city from reigniting. He got some breaks here because two black gangs, the Blackstone Rangers and the Englewood Disciples, had refrained from any rioting, and the black sections of the South Side had remained quiet as well.

It was a draining week. Daley had not only to attend to the still combustible situation, but he had also to come to some terms with his own massive grief at what had happened to his city; he was too busy for mourning and too preoccupied to express the anger that bubbled in the fouled juices of his betrayed heart. It was his trusted public relations man, Earl Bush, who would take the hostility that had been jammed in his veins and arteries for days.

Bush had been in Jamaica on vacation when the burning had begun; the sketchy reports he could get through sources there did not seem to demand that he cut his stay short. When he returned, on Easter Monday, he found Daley sitting in repressed rage at his desk. The mayor's lips were pursed, an unmistakable signal of an inner storm, of lightning flashing and wind howling in the caverns of his gut.

"Bush," the mayor said, just managing to maintain control, "where were you when I needed you most? You're fired."

Bush, who had worked with him since Daley was county clerk, began to explain, but Daley was having none of it. The matter was closed for the moment. He would hire Bush back a few days later but, by that time, the mayor would have managed his own public relations for that one fateful morning, one that he would never forget.

Just the Saturday before, Holy Saturday, things had seemed to be under control. Daley had dinner with General Mather, Superintendent James Conlisk of the Police Department, General Dunn of the Illinois National Guard, and a few others who had worked closely with him during this most difficult of weeks. Then the mayor left, without any aides, for a quiet Easter weekend at the estate which he had purchased a few years before in Grand Beach, Michigan, a ninety-minute drive to the other side of the great shimmering lake.

The mayor thought about the last few years as he tried to relax over the weekend, with grief and anger, and yes, personal hurt mingling in his Bridgeport soul. It was an interlude in a long struggle and he needed to find his center of gravity again. The chieftain brooded about the state of the city and the state of society; he thought about all that the city had done to avoid trouble over the last year. Daley had accepted the idea that it was better to let people act out their grievances in demonstrations than to find them blowing up the city; he had seen that, with patience and permissiveness—a word of almost scalding shame for an old South Sider—you could get through a great many difficult times. Suppose a group tied up State Street for a few hours; you could adjust to that and no one would be hurt, either. But what had all the city's tolerance delivered but nine dead, millions of dollars in property damage, and disgrace as obvious as mud on the flag? Daley looked back across the lake toward Chicago, where at sundown he could make out the silhouette of the still unfinished 100-floor John Hancock building. And the chieftain, like a man destined to do this from the moment of his birth, slipped back into his armor. He had made up his mind; he knew what he would do on Monday morning.

When the mayor arrived at City Hall the next day, he looked grave and determined. He had gone along with tolerating small infractions of the law in order to avoid larger and more destructive problems, but now he felt that this philosophy had slowly eaten away at the nature of both law and authority. The fires of Passion Week had proved that to him. After he had summarily dismissed Bush, he called in one of his closest associates, City Corporation Counsel Raymond Simon.

"Ray," the mayor said, "this has got to stop. This kind of thing that we've just been through will never happen again in Chicago. I don't care if I'm mayor for only seven more minutes. That doesn't matter." He paused slightly and plunged on. "The people must obey the law. Any progress that we're goin' to make must be within the law. We've let people think they can get away with anything and that if they're caught nothin' will happen to them." He was under a full head of steam now. "The pendulum has gone too far that way. What the hell, we've made more progress in race relations and civil rights than any other city in the country. Now I'm goin' out and make a statement about this and everybody is goin' to understand what we mean."

Without notes but with the deepest conviction that something had to be said to restore a sense of law and order to the city, the mayor hurried out to face the reporters who had gathered for a news conference. He was clearly upset, the chieftain with a gift for fighting but hardly any at all for subtle public statements; he had awakened under an angry star, and he would ride directly for it and plunge the lance of authority into the ground at the reporters' feet. He began by naming a nine-member committee to investigate all aspects of the rioting; then he criticized the police and the administration of the public schools for conditions which he said were "indescribable" on the day the riots began. But he was only warming to his task as he moved on to utter some of the most famous words of his career. If he meant them as a symbolic statement about the need for a hard stand by authority, they were heard and reported in quite another way.

"I have conferred with the superintendent of police this morning and I gave him the following instructions, which I thought were instructions on the night of the fifth that were not carried out." He took the plunge, swiftly and directly, onto the rocky bed of his own rhetoric. "I said to him very emphatically and very definitely that an order be issued by him immediately and under his signature to shoot to kill any arsonist or anyone with a Molotov cocktail in his hand in Chicago because they're potential murderers, and to issue a police order to shoot to maim or cripple anyone looting any stores in our city." He hardly paused between these phrases that had already stunned the reporters. "Above all, the crime of arson is to me the most hideous and worst crime and should be dealt with in this fashion." He went on to express his regret that policemen had some choice about using their weapons during the riots. "In my opinion, policemen should have had instructions to shoot arsonists and looters—arsonists to kill and looters to maim and detain." To a reporter's question about children, Daley answered, "You wouldn't want to shoot them, but with MACE you could detain youngsters." So it went and the journalists, uncertain that they had heard him correctly, would now spread his own words—"shoot to kill . . . maim"—across every newspaper and television screen in the country.

The words had escaped; they had a life of their own now. As for Daley, he left shortly afterward for a lunch with his old friend Judge William Lynch at the Tavern Club, high above Michigan Avenue. There, across the smooth linen and bright silver, he poured out his frustration to his fellow Bridgeporter. Across the dining room, Monsignor John Egan, pastor of the black Presentation parish, was lunching with Don McNeill, a Chicagoan who had become famous as the host of the "Breakfast Club" radio program. McNeill was arranging for a group of twenty black children from Egan's parish to spend part of the summer on his estate in Barrington, northeast of Chicago. Neither he nor Monsignor Egan had heard anything about Daley's news conference as yet. They were still discussing their plans when a waiter brought the message that the mayor would like to speak to Monsignor Egan. He walked to Daley's table but was barely able to greet him before the mayor, his face now livid, threw a question at him. "What are the churches comin' to when people representing the Church Federation of Chicago are not goin' to stand up and put an end to this shootin' and killin'?"

Monsignor Egan was stunned, and only when he saw the newspaper headlines as he was leaving did he understand what the question was all about.

Earl Bush was, of course, rehired almost immediately to deal with the massive reactions that had come from all over the country to Daley's "shoot to kill" statement. On Wednesday, after a day of claiming that he had been misunderstood, Daley read a statement—drafted by Bush and Simon—to the City Council to clarify his intentions. "It is the established policy of the Chicago Police Department," he said carefully, "—fully supported by the administration—that only minimum force necessary be used by policemen in carrying out their duties. But this established policy was never intended to support permissive violence, destruction, and a complete denial of that respect for law which is vital to our democratic way of life. . . . We cannot resign ourselves to the proposition that civil protest must lead to death and devastation—to the abandonment of the law that is fundamental for the preservation of the rights of all people and their freedom."

It was all clearer now but the first impulsive words on Monday—how high the price for the man who had prided himself on control—the words "shoot to kill" and "maim" would not be forgotten by his critics or his friends. He had spoken from his guts, from his warrior's stomach, and he had, in a powerful way, spoken directly to the churned-up feelings, to the heartburn and nausea of an America that was sick of rioting. He had uttered words that he may have been born to say to people who seemed to need to hear them. The press reaction ran heavily against him, but the mail was overwhelmingly in his favor. Perhaps he had found his star in this painful spring, perhaps he was moving closer to living out a contradictory myth of greatness.

"So my thanks to all of you," Robert F. Kennedy said to the cheering crowds in the ballroom of the Ambassador Hotel in Los Angeles. He had just won the primary contest on June 5. "And on to Chicago and let's win there!"

In a few moments more shots that would be heard around the world rang out, and Robert Kennedy lay mortally wounded on the floor of the hotel kitchen. America seemed a possessed country and the seeds of paranoia, plentiful as puffs of cottonwood in the spring, filled the air. The clamp on the national psyche had been tightened again; how much more violence and blood and terror could its people stand? It is among the cruelest of truths that Richard Daley, convinced in his heart that the war was wrong, had to live out the role of the party loyalist who supported it publicly, that the political leader who had built a career on his strong man's capacity for self-control was abandoning these deep instincts for reactions from a dream of half-remembered ancestral battles. It was the devil's own jest that Daley, who took his greatest pride in the good name of his family and his city, would find them both painfully compromised by summer's end; it was a season of destiny in which men, in a surreal landscape of violence and noise, took positions in a tragic myth that lay as brooding as a thunderhead across their converging paths.

Not that there had been a failure of prophecy or omen. On April 27, 6500 people had come to the Civic Center Plaza, where just the year before Daley had unveiled Picasso's famous steel artwork, in order to protest the Vietnam war. Police had finally broken up the gathering in a violent charge that was a ghostly rehearsal for the days of the Democratic Convention in August. Daley had just returned from a luncheon meeting at the White House with Lyndon Johnson when, on August 2, he was asked to comment on the newly released report of the commission that had examined the Civic Center disorders. This document stated: "Allowing public officials every benefit of the doubt, the commission concludes that they sought to destroy the march."

The mayor said simply, "Much of it is not true. I had a long conversation with Superintendent Conlisk and I know it isn't."

Well, then, what of the incident?

Daley, committed to law and order more deeply than ever, confessed that he was "sort of amazed" at the "constant effort of these people to confront the police."

By August, the mayor had many reports about the plans of the National Mobilization to End the War and other groups, including the Yippies, to come to Chicago to demonstrate against the war. Even as he criticized the report of the Civic Center episode, his representative, David Stahl, was meeting with Yippie leader Rennie Davis and others in the downtown Palmer House to negotiate permits from the city for the use of various parks and for parades during the week of the convention. But the air had been filled with terror and madness for months, and paranoia was in every city official's heart; the mood of paranoia was rising like mist and drawing rational men to abandon their ordinary reactions and to throw themselves into the chasms of irrationality.

Daley had heard all about the Yippies' plans for a "Festival of Life" to be held in Lincoln Park on the near North Side of the city. Rock bands would play as thousands of young people would arrive to live out the alternate life-style of the counter-culture while the Democrats held a "Convention of Death" on the South Side. The leaders of the various movement factions, often at odds with each other, represented the changes in atti-tude, values, and behavior that produced revulsion and out-rage in the blood of Mayor Daley. Had he not told a member of the City Council, during one of its meetings, that he needed a haircut? Had he not commissioned an assistant to take one of his own sons out for a closer barbering when the young man appeared at City Hall with hair a little longer than usual? Of such plain symbols, one made a simple and upright life. And the planners of the demonstrations had a profound sense of how to manipulate symbols in order to promote overreaction in the institutions of authority they wished to disrupt.

What could be worse than the language of their manifestos, the paragraphs packed with defiant obscenities? City officials were familiar, for example, with the statement that had ap-peared in the January issue of the *New York Free Press,* an un-derground newspaper: "We've got to get crazy. Craziest moth-erfuckers they ever seen in this country. Cause that's the only way we're gonna beat them. So fucking crazy they can't un-derstand it at ALL."

Promising great disruptive crowds—had they not marched successfully on the Pentagon just the previous October, making the troops and their bayonets look ridiculous as they defended the building against unarmed protestors?—these leaders knew exactly what they wanted: Through their "politics of ab-surdity," they would transform Chicago into a metaphor for their interpretation of America. They would celebrate a free culture—of blaring music, drugs, and lovemaking—in the Chi-cago parks while they forced the Democratic party to nominate a Presidential candidate under heavy guard in an old-fash-ioned arena next to the stockyards.

While Daley remained concerned about all of this and con-tinued active negotiations with Davis and others, he had other preoccupations. Not only had the International Brotherhood of Electrical Workers called a strike that affected telephone service in the city and threatened to prevent the installation of phones in the convention hall, but there was also the threat of a cab strike and a wildcat walkout of black bus-drivers on the very eve of the convention.

There was something more important than all this, however, and that concerned the selection of a Presidential candidate. With Robert Kennedy dead and Lyndon Johnson out of the race, the party was faced with Hubert Humphrey or Eugene McCarthy, neither of whom appealed to Daley as the kind of person the country needed at the moment. McCarthy, part poet and part monk, the antiwar leader of legions of college youths, seemed impossible, even though Daley was as much against Vietnam as was the senator from Minnesota. Humphrey, Vice-President to Johnson these past four years, was deeply involved in Vietnam, and it would be difficult for him to extricate himself from the issue successfully. Besides that, Humphrey was too garrulous for the close-mouthed Daley, and he represented a free-spending attitude, a left-of-center liberalism, of which Daley was automatically suspicious.

Then there was the bare possibility that Edward Kennedy, still in the deepest mourning for the death of his brother, might be persuaded that the moment for his entrance into Presidential history had arrived. This was the candidate who offered everything the Democrats needed to win, and, beyond that, a restoration of the Irish kingdom which Daley had helped to establish with John F. Kennedy eight years before.

On July 24 Daley talked to reporters about the possibility of Edward Kennedy's running on the national ticket and, yes, Daley would support him, if . . . It was a trial balloon meant to float eastward along with the calls Daley had already begun to make to other political leaders and to Kennedy himself. The senator was not ready to declare; he would have to think about it; he would not refuse it yet.

Back in Chicago, Daley was working on the unions to get

them to install telephones and Teletype machines in the amphitheater, and he was also supervising the erection of barricades around the convention arena, as well as the cleaning-up
of the streets and the boarding-up of empty lots on the route
that the chartered buses would take as they transported the
delegates from the downtown hotels to the amphitheater.
Everywhere signs would welcome the candidates to Chicago,
each sign with the legend "Richard J. Daley, Mayor"; there
would finally be tabs of welcome even on the telephones in the
hotels, posters and flyers and badges everywhere, all embossed
with the name of the mayor who was increasingly determined
that law and order should prevail in his city.

And yet the omens kept recurring. On August 5, as the Republicans gathered in Miami Beach for their convention, Rennie Davis and David Dellinger and other movement leaders in
Chicago were informed that the city parks would not be available to their followers for sleeping during convention week. On
the following Thursday, a Chicago street was renamed in
honor of Martin Luther King, Jr. That night, in Miami Beach,
the National Guard was called out because of disturbances
near the Republican Convention. There were reports of deaths
in connection with this action, reports which, along with the
other intelligence that was being supplied to Daley by various
government agencies, did little to reassure him about the possibility of avoiding violence in Chicago in the last week of the
month.

The Republicans nominated Richard M. Nixon and Spiro T.
Agnew, men who were also moving into their special parts in a
bizarre scenario of American history. They would run, appealing to the law-and-order wishes of the average American, the
very theme that Daley had been echoing, while the gods of
irony grinned across the skies.

On Saturday, while his assistant David Stahl met Davis and
his team in a coffeehouse in the Loop for further negotiations,
Daley headed for Springfield and the state fair. It was Governor's Day and the mayor, as close to consecrated to the

Democratic party as a man could get, chose to defend authority again in a nation in which it seemed to be disintegrating rapidly. He spoke up for Lyndon Johnson, saying in his almost breathless, run-on fashion, "Our Democrats are solidly behind Lyndon B. Johnson all the way. I know I am—one hundred percent. No man wants peace more than Lyndon B. Johnson. He has two sons-in-law over there." Then there was one last stab, an assault on these tribes of the counterculture, these straggling bands with whom he secretly shared a dislike for the war, but whose manners and style he could not abide. "I don't care," he said, "what the intellectuals or the university professors say."

Then he was done. The next day Senator George McGovern announced that he was stepping into the race for the Presidential nomination, that he would attempt to become the candidate of those who had supported Robert Kennedy.

During the next few days discussions continued with the leaders of the demonstration movements. On Tuesday, Davis and his colleagues met with members of the Chicago Park District and were told that their request for permits had been "taken under advisement." On Wednesday, Davis, who held a master's degree, and who had worked previously in Chicago in a community action project, "Jobs Or Income Now," among white Appalachian people in the Uptown section of the city, sent Mayor Daley a telegram, requesting a meeting.

Daley, of course, preferred to leave negotiations at a lower level, but Davis had begun to feel a need to meet Daley, this mysterious and powerful presence, face to face. The meeting never took place, but Davis felt that he understood the mayor and his police force; he had, in his earlier work in the city, experienced a running battle of mutual harassment with police at the Foster Street station. He had, a few years before, been involved in a march of three hundred people on that very police post. At close quarters, he began to realize that policemen, no matter how restrained or professional—were these not the qualities they had exhibited during the civil rights marches of

1966?—could be drawn across an invisible line into the territory of overreaction and shame. Davis was convinced that authority would back up on itself in Chicago, that the security would "become insecure," that, if the protestors played it right, the police, and Daley with them, could be drawn into perpetrating the very violence they were pledged to prevent. People were beginning to play their predetermined roles more actively; a mood of live melodrama began to pervade the city.

On Saturday, August 17, the Yippies began to move into Lincoln Park. On the next weekend, convention delegates would start to arrive. The clock was moving swiftly as the dissidents, using the park as a staging area, began to drill their followers in protest techniques, hold strategy meetings, and seek, in every way possible, publicity which, after all, was indispensable to their purposes. Meanwhile, Daley had succeeded in getting the union to allow its workers to install 3200 telephones and 200 Teletype machines in the amphitheater. On Sunday, the leaders of the National Mobilization met, and the next day they filed suit against the city for denying them the right to assemble and for denying them equal protection. The case was assigned to Federal Judge William Lynch, Daley's old friend. The demonstrators took some pleasure in this as well as in the sound of his name, which matched so well the theatrical events they were attempting to mount.

On Tuesday the *Chicago Tribune* broke the news of supposed assassination plots against a number of political leaders and municipal officials. Some of these stories had originated in the county jail; the very notion of assassination was, nevertheless, enough to raise the anxiety level of the city. On Wednesday the Russian government sent its troops into Czechoslovakia, and on Friday night's news Eric Sevareid would compare conditions in overrun Prague with those in Chicago. In the meantime, Rennie Davis rejected the offer of alternate parade routes that had been presented to him by Corporation Counsel Raymond Simon, although he accepted the permit to assemble in Grant Park on Wednesday afternoon, August 28. On Friday, Judge Lynch dismissed the suit against the city while a few blocks away, again in the Civic Center Plaza, the Yippies nominated a pig, Pigasus, for President. The Chicago police finally broke up the gathering, but not before the demonstrators had achieved a massive publicity coup with intimations of anarchy in every television image and newspaper photograph.

On Saturday morning the disputes with the television networks were settled in Daley's office. The television executives had not been happy to have to transport all their equipment from Miami Beach to Chicago. Upon their arrival they discovered the problems of the telephone strike and the restrictions imposed on them by the city for the sake of security. Now they were permitted to have whatever they wished as long as they did not interfere with police directives. They were still not pleased with the curtailment of their activities, but some of the tension seemed to have eased.

At the same time Daley had been trying to contact Senator Edward Kennedy, who was at Hyannis Port. He had talked to him on Friday, but the senator had not agreed to a candidacy. Daley could hardly believe it and wanted to know if Kennedy would come to Chicago. He called Kennedy again on Saturday, urging him to come and to signal his willingness to run, but the senator remained adamant. Daley was astonished but agreed with Kennedy's proposal that he send his brother-in-law Stephen Smith to Chicago to represent him. This had to be done very quietly, so reservations were made at the Standard Club, the pinnacle of Chicago's Jewish Establishment. Who would look for an Irish Catholic there? Daley would keep his delegation, which was due to caucus the next day, uncommitted.

The next day Smith and writer Peter Maas were met by Neil Hartigan, then an assistant to the mayor, a North Side protégé of Daley's who would later become lieutenant governor. He escorted them to the Standard Club and Smith called the mayor. Daley could not believe that the senator had not yet made up his mind. Smith, in a difficult spot, since he represented Kennedy but had no wish to offend Daley, explained that he felt that the senator was truly undecided and that he could only be persuaded by a genuine draft.

"But you have to raise your hand," Daley responded, "in order to get a draft goin'." The mayor talked again to Kennedy and then told Smith and Maas, "I'll hold the delegation another twenty-four hours."

Having heard the mayor's promise, author Maas was intrigued when, at a reception later in the day, he met Adlai Stevenson III, an Illinois delegate. Stevenson excused himself, saying that he had to attend the caucus. "Oh," Maas said, "who will it be?"

"We're going for Hubert," Stevenson replied, unaware of what would greet him at the hotel meeting room where the caucus was to be held.

If Stevenson was surprised at what developed, Humphrey, confidently expecting 118 delegate votes to be pledged to him that very day, was thunderstruck. The Vice-President appeared, along with the other candidates, to make his presentation but, as far as he knew, it had been settled a long time before. He had no knowledge of Daley's extensive dealings with Edward Kennedy. The caucus was coming to the moment of voting when Alderman Thomas Keane rose and moved that the meeting be adjourned. He said that, inasmuch as Chicago was the host city, backing a candidate so early "would impair Windy City hospitality." His motion was immediately seconded and passed. Daley had held the delegates without batting an eye; few orders had been carried out so quickly since "Let There Be Light."

Stevenson still looked surprised when he returned to the reception to report that a decision had been delayed. Humphrey was clearly upset, wondering if he was being crunched again by the Irish bosses just when he was so close to the prize he had always wanted. Daley seemed a child of innocence as he explained the action of the Illinois caucus: "Because of Illinois's friendliness and hospitality and because Governor Shapiro and I are going to give welcoming speeches . . . Monday night, we decided to greet delegates uncommitted and postponed action."

On Saturday night Lincoln Park had been swept clear of protestors in accord with the city ordinance that closed all parks at 11:00 P.M. Although some had suggested that the city officials just forget about the regulation during the week of the convention and allow the demonstrators to spend the nights outdoors and off the main streets, the final resolve had been to enforce all regulations, to make all visitors, newsmen included, obey the laws of Chicago. The marches on Sunday had gone almost good-naturedly, and no major incidents occurred as the delegates settled in for the work of the next several days. On Sunday evening, having controlled the Illinois delegates without any apparent effort, Richard J. Daley, standing beneath a huge portrait of himself, was host at a cocktail party. He was concerned about the city but he was even more absorbed, as he automatically shook hands, smiled, and said, "How are ya?" with Edward Kennedy's reluctance to accept his strong and repeated invitations to join the race for the nomination; it was a nagging problem because Daley was sure that he could deliver the nomination, and was just as positive that Kennedy could win the election if—if only he would raise a finger to invite the draft.

As darkness fell, it became much cooler along the lakefront; there was a distinct chill in Lincoln Park as the police, well trained for such maneuvers, prepared to close it down for the evening. They moved carefully, using loudspeakers to invite the demonstrators to leave. But misunderstanding was to be bred to miscalculation on both sides in that black, cool night; a police car unrelated to the sweep operation entered the park on a shortcut, only to come up against a line of protestors. The latter, sure that the car was riding point for a larger assault by the police, began to rock and stone it, shouting their slogans, half exulting in a crazed ballet of mass action at last.

When the police skirmish line finally began to move through

the park near midnight, a maddened dream of confrontation, cruelly inevitable, swept police and demonstrators up in a crashing jumble of fists and clubs, of curses and screams, with the salty taste of blood as its seasoning. The demonstrators, in a major tactical error by the police, were driven out of the park and into the neighboring streets; newsmen, there to report the action, were clubbed and beaten as the helmeted officers, wearied of double shifts, sick to death of foul names, rocks, and bottles, and drawn off professional balance by the outrageous presence of the demonstrators, pursued them through the streets west and south of the park. Rennie Davis, hearing of the violence, realized that their plans were working, that authority was betraying itself in the streets, that the Yippies and their followers had found their destiny, and that the next great setting would be outside the Hilton Hotel on Wednesday night. Had not Abbie Hoffman written in his calendar "Wednesday night—police riot"?

So Chicago, bracing itself for more danger than the protestors actually represented, was drawn, like a seasoned lineman who should know better, offside. There would be a continuing series of confrontations, all of them reported in great detail by the newsmen, who, having been bloodied themselves, began to identify with the oppressed. Daley, who had formerly said that the newspapers always distorted things, began to believe the headlines himself. The demonstrations, most of them small skirmishes in reality, were blown out of proportion by the overreported rhetoric and activities of the Yippies and the other protestors. A collage of violent images fed upon itself so that the presence of National Guard troops in battle dress, the jeeps armed in barbed wire, the arrival of Army troops in the bellies of the same kind of transport planes that were used in Vietnam—all of these merged in the public mind with a hundred images of Daley in every mood of toughness and displeasure, and of his blue-shirted police force, as grotesque and threatening in their riot gear as Martian visitors. Rennie Davis had been right: The bait of the demonstrators' insolence, of their Vietcong flags and their plastic bags of human excrement, of their shouts of "Fuck the pigs!" and their combination of innocence and psychopathy, this bait and its poisoned hook were swallowed by the authorities and the media, and by the final acceptance of all the participants of roles they would never have chosen for themselves.

Edward Kennedy had refused, again to Daley's astonishment, to do anything to encourage the convention to turn to him, while Daley, under pressure from all sides, kept trying to hold the convention together despite the ineptness of Representative Carl Albert, the uncertain permanent chairman. Daley had signaled him to close the proceedings on Monday night even before a chaplain, waiting just off the podium, could deliver a final prayer.

On Tuesday night Daley, providing the television directors with just the image for which they were searching, drew his hand across his neck to indicate that he wanted the session closed despite a spirited demonstration that was going on for the youthful black, Julian Bond of Georgia. Whatever he wanted to do to prevent further violence or injury, the mayor seemed to do it in a way that made him seem the successor of every red-necked Southern sheriff who ever set police dogs against children. Everything Daley believed in, everything he prized, was being soiled publicly at, of all things, a Democratic Convention in Chicago.

The final nineteen-minute confrontation, marked by an assault on the demonstrators at the corner of Balbo Street and Michigan Avenue in front of the Conrad Hilton Hotel, came just before 8:00 P.M. on Wednesday night. It would be styled, in a later report, a "police riot," a verdict that would make Daley wince and fume to the last of his days. He would always claim, and with much justification, that the events of convention week had been badly exaggerated by the news media, that, in fact, no shot was ever fired, that the convention itself was never disrupted, and that, unlike the Miami Beach convention of the Republicans, there were no deaths connected with it.

But on Wednesday as the networks started feeding tapes of the Balbo Street confrontation into their coverage of the convention proceedings, the country perceived everything in a different way. As the tapes were played and then replayed (with no indication that they were being rerun), Chicago seemed filled with oppressive violence. One television editor intercut scenes of the violence with live shots of Daley talking and laughing on the convention floor, leaving the impression that he was a dictator, someone like Hitler perhaps, doing his equivalent of the little jig the Nazi leader supposedly did at the fall of France.

It was a night not to be redeemed easily, for Daley fed the media even more destructive images when Senator Abraham Ribicoff of Connecticut, speaking for George McGovern, denounced "Gestapo" tactics in the streets of Chicago. Daley, whom Ribicoff had praised as the greatest mayor in America the day before, let go of the public control which he had maintained so steadily all his life. Flanked by other shouting members of the Illinois delegation, Daley, his face distorted like a patched and cracked canvas sail bellied out by the hot winds of indignation, yelled back at Ribicoff in the way a manager would berate the blindest of umpires. The reputation of Chicago, yes, and his own reputation for polish and wisdom and control, all of these were being destroyed in this tortured night of the long knives, in this Götterdämmerung of fury and misunderstanding, in the ballooned images that filled the television screens of the nation and the world.

If the media had taken some measure of revenge on this mayor whom they saw as a symbol of oppression, the people of Chicago, especially those from neighborhoods like Bridgeport, began to rally around the leader who had held his ground, as they saw it, in the face of long-haired and rebellious youth. "We Love Mayor Daley" signs (printed by his organization) began to appear throughout the city; they would even be unfurled at Notre Dame football games far into the fall.

On the night of the twenty-ninth, Daley's people saw to it that the amphitheater was packed with loyal followers, most of them carrying the signs pledging love to the mayor. The convention had been tormented by a thousand demons, but it would at least be free of them on this night of acceptance speeches and a touching memorial movie about Robert Kennedy. Daley was also on the attack; the media had, as he interpreted it, shown selective views of himself and of the police force. Now he would ask CBS for time to enter Walter Cronkite's booth and talk to the country about what had happened. The force of his righteous anger would be felt even as, in classic fashion, the passages between his thought processes and his larynx became clogged with some by-product of his anger, some chunky mass on which sentences broke apart and ideas were stripped of their coating of reason. America listened to Walter Cronkite; well, now they would listen to him.

Cronkite seemed strangely subdued, like a man who has awakened to find a bear inside his cabin. Daley wasted no time in describing the glories of the city and the problems of the Police Department. "We're fortunate in Chicago," Daley said. "Our kids get involved. They go to the aid of a girl that's attacked or something else. And I aid them and admire them for what they're doing." Did Cronkite know what the police had to go through? Well, it was extreme provocation. "And the language. You can't tell—you can't show it on this thing. The language that was used last night until four o'clock, you wouldn't repeat it. It think it's a disgrace in this day and age that people staying in the Conrad Hilton Hotel had to be subjected to this kind of, of propaganda all night, using the foulest of language that you wouldn't hear in a brothel hall. These poeple don't speak. These are terrorists that are intent on what they want to do, they're against the government, not all of them, but the majority, and the leaders—did you see some of them, what they have on their forehead?"

"No," Cronkite answered just before Daley charged again.

"Did you walk around? Well, you couldn't repeat what they have on their forehead, both young men and young women. This isn't our young America."

Cronkite had not been able to comment much, nor could he

begin to answer when Daley asked him directly, "How is it that you never show on television, Walter, the crowd marching down the street to confront the police? Would you like to be called a pig? Would you like to be called—with a four-letter word? Well, that's what happened."

Cronkite, speaking softly, finally broke in: "Now, here's a question I want to ask you. Who is 'they'? Your police—Frank Sullivan, who is in charge of public relations for the police—said today, 'Communists.' Now, is this—"

Daley, the old brawler, moved into the breach of the commentator's speculative pause. "There isn't any doubt about it. You know who they are."

"No," Cronkite countered, "I don't actually."

Daley pushed vigorously forward, "Well, you know Hayden? . . . the head of the Mobilization? Surely you know Dellinger, who went to Hanoi. Why isn't anything said about these people? They're the people who even now see their cues and pick them up in Grant Park. Rennie Davis. What's Rennie Davis?"

Cronkite, fighting to keep control of the interview, replied, "Well, I don't know that they're Communists."

And Daley, quicker than a conjuror, again like the man who wrecks the barroom and slips through the swinging doors, replied, with a touch of offended innocence, as though Cronkite had introduced the notion of Communism, "Well, certainly, neither do I."

But do not mistake the tangle of words, as worn and splintered as a pile of driftwood, as a failure in communication. Daley was talking again to the pained stomachs and aggrieved spleens of middle Americans, standing up for the values which they felt had been threatened by the demonstrators of convention week. Messages would start coming in from various professional organizations—from the American Psychological Association, for example—canceling their conventions in Chicago during the next year because of the disorders. Critical mail came from the professors and do-gooders who had vexed him all his life. But the great bulk of messages came from average Americans who were as sick of demonstrations as Daley was and who saw in him one of the staunchest defenders of everything in which they believed.

The convention would have its bitter aftermath, even though in November Daley would deliver Chicago to Humphrey by over 400,000 votes. But the two would never get along again, and they would blame each other for the loss of the Presidential election. Daley would remember his lengthy negotiations with Edward Kennedy and would say ruefully that the Democrats would have taken the White House if the candidate had borne the same name as a recent President. And, finally and even more disastrously, the Democrats would sponsor reforms to govern the convention of 1972, during which Daley would be denied a seat as a delegate, and from which would come a campaign monumental in its proportions of disaster. All that lay ahead. Now, Daley had to defend his city and his policemen, the "good family men" who had been so unjustly vilified during the last week of August.

He would meet with the reporters, as he had done almost every morning for all his years as mayor, outside his City Hall office. "On behalf of the city of Chicago and its people and the Chicago Police Department, I would like to issue a statement and I expect that in the sense of fair play it will be given the same kind of distribution of press, radio, and television as the mob of rioters was given yesterday." He glanced out into the bright lights and went on. "For weeks—months—the press, radio, and television across the nation have revealed the tactics and strategy that was to be carried on in Chicago during the convention week by groups of terrorists. In the heat of emotion and riot some policemen may have overreacted, but to judge the entire police force by the alleged action of a few would be just as unfair as to judge our entire younger generation by the actions of this mob. I would like to say here and now that this administration, our administration, and the people of Chicago have never condoned brutality at any time, but they will never permit a lawless group of terrorists to menace the lives of millions of people, destroy the purpose of the convention, and take over the streets of Chicago."

The mayor had played it consistently to the end, even though the week had left a chancre in his heart, even though, having accepted the tragic role, he would now step back in brooding anger, hesitating where he had never before doubted, putting off programs he would once have pushed through, pulling his cloak more tightly about him as he contemplated only one thing, the reclaiming of the good name of Daley and of Chicago.

"This is my statement, gentlemen," he said. "It speaks for itself."

[17]

Grand Things

"Ah, Frank," he said softly, "you've done
grand things. Grand, grand things."
"Among others," Skeffington said.
 —Edwin O'Connor, *The Last Hurrah*

"You've got a good job. You've got a nice family," Richard J.
Daley said softly to a protégé who had just received a new federal appointment. "Now don't get greedy."

The old chieftain could still draw from the deep pools of
tribal wisdom that had always lain in his soul so quiet and
clear. But the waters had been roiled and clouded ever since
the sieges and battles of the convention, and while he was the
same man he was also a different man, an angrier man whose
surest weapon, self-control, seemed less dependable than it had
once been; a leader who was still loved by his people, a man, in
fact, who could now sense hardly any distinction between
himself and his land and his followers and who spat out the
bitter dregs of the disgrace and misunderstanding that had en-
veloped them all in 1968.

Daley was acting more instinctively, more from the viewpoint of his Bridgeport neighborhood than from his arduously
acquired lawyer's education. Indeed, the great years of planning and programs that had won such praise for him and Chicago, the enormous achievements in municipal development
and public services, the sound financial condition of the city
and the booming construction that was freshly vesting his

bride of a city—these had won praise from other mayors, like Detroit's Jerome P. Cavanagh, who had said, "All of us—Lindsay, Stokes, myself—have picked up ideas and even copied social programs that Daley initiated"; yes, and the unanimous support of all the Chicago papers, as well as comments he might frame, such as that from the *Los Angeles Times,* which, in August 1968, had said that Daley "has done a heroic job of restructuring and cleaning up Chicago's governmental system which, only 20 years ago, was unquestionably the most corrupt big city in the nation and which is now less corrupt than most and better governed than any."

But there was a shadow across the willingness of his heart; he resembled a sovereign who might let his scrolls be furled by the wind as he stalked through his castle and pondered the fate that had struck him. Daley, the most noble and hardworking of leaders, as he saw it, regarded recent events with a sense of betrayal and misinterpretation which he could neither understand nor shake off. He was more convinced than ever that the media were at fault; the media with their never-ending curiosity and their brash and insulting versions of his every motive and deed; the media, with most of their reporters sympathetic to the liberal do-gooders he despised; these were the Lilliputians who had tied him down while his city was delivered to the wolves of shame. And if he could never please them, neither could he seem to do enough for the blacks or for the Spanish-speaking, never enough for these groups who were so different and seemingly so demanding. He would, in a press conference late in 1969, put into words some of his frustration with the world which had changed so much. He had pledged to guarantee protection for Puerto Ricans in a plan of construction opportunities for minorities, only to learn that the Puerto Ricans were still disappointed. "Everyone is disappointed these days," he said, with a mixture of irritation and disgust. "I'm going to get a big sign that says, 'I'm happy. Are you?' "

Daley was testy that day and a little tired as well, his patience worn as thin as a beggar's shoe. How would he respond, a reporter wished to know, to the charge made by Cook County Sheriff Joseph Woods that George Dunne, president of the Cook County Board, was his "tool"?

"Would I respond to it?" Daley answered derisively. "I'd laugh a little about it." Then he laughed deliberately as he went on to speak of the man whom millions of Americans had seen sitting next to Daley as the mayor had jeered Senator Ribicoff at the 1968 Democratic Convention. "George Dunne stands on his own feet. . . . As to a tool, what would I ask Dunne to do? For fifteen years I have been mayor of Chicago, and I will match that record against that of any keyhole-peeker or transom-looker on a ladder, any time. What is wrong with Daley? I do not interfere. . . . This has been the policy of the Democratic party and the policy of Daley."

Well, then, what about the report of a congressional committee that some networks had slanted their coverage during the 1968 Democratic Convention?

Such questions seemed as if they would never go away. He would answer again, trailing out the complaints he had been making for over a year about the media. "We knew this all along," he said in the tones of a man who cannot fathom why others cannot see the truth as plainly as he. "They were doing a hatchet job on Chicago because we wouldn't succumb to their program of bringing both political conventions to Miami Beach."

How long would he have to live with this tarnished image, with this faint sense that, even though he, almost by himself, had cleansed Chicago of the Capone-and-corruption stereotype, the city had been unfairly displayed as prejudiced, if no longer wanton, as medieval and fascistic, if it was no longer filled with booze and gangsters? It was enough to make a man irritable and evasive, more than enough to make it seem that a certain staleness had invaded the office that was once filled with ideas and action all the time.

"Wait until after the next election," was the typical comment through which the once eager mayor explained his reluctance to press forward with programs for which plans were being developed in various departments of the administration. He seemed preoccupied with the need to re-establish himself as a respected national figure and to recapture the sense of greatness which, in his every pore, he felt to be Chicago's destiny. He had heard of the reform efforts in the national Democratic party after the narrow victory of Richard Nixon in November of 1968, but he had little sympathy and no liking at all for such amateur crusaders who, as he viewed them, neither appreciated nor made a full commitment of themselves to the day-to-day work of government. Elections would still be delivered by basic organizational operations, through the special ministry of precinct captains and the effective management of patronage workers. He did not pay much attention, for example, when, in March, a young lawyer named William Singer forced a runoff in Paddy Bauler's old ward under the banners of an anti-Daley candidacy. The reporters, at the post-election news conference, asked if the Singer victory was a defeat for the organization.

"None whatsoever," Daley responded, adding that "local issues control aldermanic elections," and that he never interfered in them and that the organization candidate, James Gaughan, would win the April 8 runoff election.

But Singer, an aggressive and ambitious young man whose piping voice added to the impression of his playing David to the organization's Goliath, was elected and Daley would hear a lot from and about him in the next few years. It would be Singer who, in the general shambles of the Democratic Convention of 1972, would deny Daley his delegate's seat. There would be trouble enough before that, however. In October 1969 the Weathermen faction of the Students for a Democratic Society visited a "Day of Wrath" on the near North Side of the city, breaking windows and defacing property. Party loyalist Richard Elrod, son of an old West Side politician, was severely injured when he tried to tackle one of the demonstrators; he would walk stiffly on canes after his recovery, and Daley would slate him for sheriff in the election in 1970. He would also send Adlai Stevenson III, dogged, but unblessed with his father's charm, to the United States Senate as successor to Everett Dirksen, who had died in September 1969.

In December the state's attorney, Edward Hanrahan, an organization man with features as keen-edged as a scythe and a personality that was compounded of charm, quirkiness, and high explosives, authorized a predawn raid on an apartment in which Black Panther leaders Mark Clark and Fred Hampton were shot to death. The circumstances of the attack and the awkward efforts to prove that it had been a gun battle rather than a massacre would be discussed for years; the misery of it all was just what Daley neither wanted nor needed and, although he defended the police as usual, he seemed somewhat resigned when he was interviewed by a local television commentator at year's end. Perhaps it was just the strain of all the previous months; perhaps it was the conflict he experienced within himself as he continued out of an old-fashioned sense of duty to defend the war in Vietnam which he had inwardly opposed for so long.

Daley even defended long hair and beards as, sipping water from a coffee cup, he spoke in the soft tones which he used when he was either very mad or in the presence of a friendly interrogator. Local news commentator Fahey Flynn, bow-tied, with wavy graying hair and the face of the first curate at the cathedral, put the questions gently, almost reverentially, to the mayor.

"You look at pictures of Christ, Abraham Lincoln," Daley said, "you see them with wigs and beards." He spoke of young people. "We should understand their problems, living in a time of war and uncertainty. This idealism they have is a good thing for all of us; it will make for a better society. I think we should be a lot more patient, and not try to impose our ideas on them."

Well, if he was sympathetic to youth, what of the convention protestors who were now on trial in a federal court in Chicago?

"People came with the idea of disrupting the convention and they did," the mayor replied. "It was a disgrace." He blamed their behavior on the Vietnam war and, in solemn, almost weary tones, he added, "I hope to God we never see a nineteen sixty-eight period again. There was so much bitterness in this war. There was so much hatred of President Johnson. The divisions were so intense. I hope to God the war will terminate." He turned then to the Democratic Convention that would be held in 1972, expressing his wish that young people would attend, "not with the idea of fighting the Establishment, but with constructive suggestions. I hope there will be more young delegates."

By 1972 he might have had second thoughts about all that when a commission chaired by Senator George McGovern had come up with selection formulas to guarantee that there would be more women, minority-group members, and young delegates. By the time the state-wide election of convention delegates was held in March 1972, Daley had won yet another massive victory in his 1971 mayoral campaign against a young Republican named Richard Friedman.

"What about nineteen seventy-five?" a reporter asked on election night.

"Nineteen seventy-five," Daley responded, "will take care of itself."

And things seemed to take care of themselves in the 1972 primaries, in which 59 of the Illinois delegation of 170 were Daley's candidates. What legal grounds could justify the charges made by Alderman Singer, joined now by black leader Jesse Jackson, that the rules of the McGovern Commission had not been observed? Daley's questions made no difference to Singer or to Jackson; their motivation was not merely to have a voice in the supposedly reformed convention process but to gain attention and power in the mayor's own kingdom in Chicago. Insouciance was grafted to steady nerves as Singer held caucuses throughout the city, some with only a handful of people in attendance, to elect a fresh slate of delegates. It was a move of almost comic daring, like a mouse dragging away the lion's dinner or a novice burglar who leans against the strong-room door and finds that it falls open.

It seemed incredible to Daley and to his associates that this group of insurgents would get away with ousting him and the other delegates, who, however handpicked, had been elected according to state laws in the traditional manner. But Daley was a realist and he understood the essentially political nature of Singer's strategy. If Singer got to the convention, he might also elect his own people to the Democratic National Committee; he might, in fact, come home with far more power than he had when he left. It seemed clear that what Singer and Jackson wanted was recognition from Daley in Chicago far more than they wanted a total victory in the July gathering at Miami Beach. Even if they had to compromise with Daley, that would put them in a new relationship with him; a piece of the power base would be delivered to them through any willingness on his part to do business with them.

The same held for the independent Democrat, Daniel Walker, who had genuinely surprised the Daley organization by defeating its candidate and securing the Democratic nomination to run for governor of Illinois in 1972. Walker, former counsel for the Montgomery Ward company, had written the report on the 1968 convention disorders; in it he had accused the police of rioting against the demonstrators. It was not only poisonous to the stomach for Daley to watch Walker gain attention by walking the length of the state and obtaining the nomination, but it was the most ancient of dangers to have a man like Walker, who regularly denounced Daley when he spoke to downstate voters, establish an independent Democratic power base in Illinois. It did not matter that Walker, ruggedly if self-consciously handsome, had his eyes on the White House; it did not even matter if Walker felt, like a young gunslinger, that he could increase his reputation most by taking on the toughest and strongest man in town; no, what mattered—the only thing that ever mattered—was that he posed a threat to the power of the Cook County Democratic organization.

That was an area that Daley had guarded jealously even against old friends like Sargent Shriver and Robert Kennedy when, in previous years, they had tried to bring federal programs of one kind or another into Chicago. He had fought them as he might have fought a dragon, because they intended to give the power to run their programs and to dispense their funds to persons other than Richard J. Daley. In his politician's heart there was no hospitality for such moves, even on the part of men who had been on his side in previous battles; Daley would offer no light or comfort to such well-intentioned pilgrims when they crossed the Cook County line. The power to dispense belonged to him alone; he allowed nobody else to exercise it on even the slightest matter in Chicago; he had not gained it so carefully and totally in order to give it away mindlessly to those who asked for it; that was charity for the dispensers of broth at the monastery gate, and this was real life. This was the simplest secret of political power: If you have it, you keep it all.

So Daley was in no mood to compromise with Singer and Jackson as they fought their way through the courts, inching ever closer to the July convention at Miami Beach even though the judges ruled against them in Illinois. It seemed astounding that the question would get as far as the convention credentials committee in Washington a week before the Miami Beach nominations were to begin. The committee was pro-McGovern, and it was made clear in advance that the vote would go to the Daley delegates if Daley himself would commit himself to McGovern before the convention.

But here, too, the powdered arsenic had been cooked deeply into the proffered side of beef. Daley was not that hungry; he would not go for McGovern, whose chances, despite his primary successes, seemed minimal to the mayor, who would not violate his lifelong instincts by issuing a premature endorsement. If nominated, McGovern would need Daley and his organization far more than he would need Singer and his romantic followers.

Still, on the day the credentials committee was to convene, Daley met with reporters and praised McGovern's group as "the greatest political organization that has ever been put together in the country." Then he added, somewhat puckishly, "Some people call it something else."

What, the reporters asked, would he call this organization?

"You are the ones that call it . . ." Daley responded.

"Machine?" a reporter suggested.

"No, just a vehicle," Daley said with a smile.

There were more questions and finally one about the fact that the month before, in this campaign in which the war was still a major issue, Daley had broken with Nixon's policies and assailed him for waging a war without the consent of Congress. Daley had strongly opposed Nixon's orders to blockade North Vietnam. He still opposed that, he said, even though he had recently endorsed the President's offer of military withdrawal after a cease-fire and the release of U.S. prisoners of war. Vietnam was still sticking in the throats of the people and the party; it was the curse of the generation. Nobody asked him what he thought of the arrest, only the week before, of a group of burglars in the offices of the Democratic Committee in a Washington building complex known as Watergate.

In Miami Beach, the credentials committee, with twelve abstentions, voted 71 to 61 to unseat the Daley delegates and to award the places to the Singer-Jackson group. Singer stepped off the plane when he returned to Chicago with the look of the boy-hero in a fairy tale who has been to the giant's castle and returned home safe. "We," he announced, "are the delegates now."

Daley had been accused by the credentials committee of failing to follow party guidelines because he had used a slating process which they judged not to be open, of employing party apparatus to do this, and of not working aggressively enough to assure delegation balance by age, ethnic group, and sex. The mayor was not pleased when he commented on this report at his Tuesday news conference. He rejected the report's reasoning, clipping off arguments for his own side: "Nine hundred thousand people participated in the election. There's no reference to that in the report. There's no reference that, although there were six to eight delegates elected in every district affected, there were fifteen to thirty-six candidates." The quota system, he added, was "typically, in my opinion, un-American."

"What about a compromise with the challengers?" he was asked.

"Compromise on what?" he responded hotly. "On quotas? How do you compromise? Give half your seats to someone else?" The mayor, however, indicated that he would speak to McGovern's campaign manager, Frank Mankiewicz, "or with anyone," about the situation.

What, the reporters asked, would he do if he were kept out of the convention? Would he sit out the campaign or give his support to President Nixon?

"You know they wouldn't do that to me," he said, like a man discounting the power of termites to destroy his house even as the beams creaked ominously above his head. "I'm a Democrat. I was raised in the cradle of the Democratic party in the stockyard area and I think the Democratic party will have an outstanding candidate."

But they did do it to him, with the joy of revolutionaries who have just burned down the capital but are not quite sure of what they will do next. Even though Judge Daniel A. Covelli ruled in Chicago against Singer and his group and issued an order against their taking their seats at the convention, the young alderman, savoring the publicity of his extraordinary triumph, flew to Florida with his delegates and received the proper credentials through Convention Chairman Lawrence O'Brien, an old Daley cohort who, as party chairman, felt that he had to follow the guidelines of the Democratic reform movement. As a matter of fact, Daley had placed a call to O'Brien on the weekend before the convention was to open. "He was very understanding," O'Brien later recalled, but he had given Chairman O'Brien a clear signal.

"I realize," Daley had told him, "that this isn't your role as chairman. I wanted to let you know that there is some interest in having discussions with the McGovern people." Daley was calling from his lakeside home in Grand Beach, Michigan, where, in that rainy summer, the waters had begun to rise swiftly and to swallow large chunks of the shoreline. It was a bad omen for what was taking place on the ocean-washed island of Miami Beach.

O'Brien relayed the message to McGovern and devoted himself to a careful study of the parliamentary decisions that he would have to make in view of the complications of the Illinois delegation and others, among them California. He conferred with aides Joseph Califano, the party counsel, and a small group, including Lew Deschler, the parliamentarian of the House of Representatives. His intention was to preserve the power of the chair to rule effectively at the convention. Back in the Midwest, Daley, chafing at the delays and the seeming injustice of the situation, looked at the convention from another viewpoint. He could hardly believe that the party which he had revered, to which, indeed, he felt he had dedicated his life with as many seals and promises as a monk to his abbey, that this party would now reject and publicly embarrass him. His delegates were already in Miami Beach at the Diplomat Hotel; there would still be an effort to seat them, but Daley would remain at a distance while the play was acted out. While the reporters and editors swallowed hourly rumors about Daley's imminent arrival at the convention, Daley looked out at the lake and, speaking of the McGovern forces, said simply, "My mother used to say that if you don't expect much from people, you won't often be disappointed."

Aghast at what he felt to be the amateurism of the convention proceedings, Daley was sure about two things. He would never make a compromise with McGovern about the delegates, because such an arrangement in Miami Beach would force him to make compromises with Singer and Jackson back in Chicago. That was out of the question on the most basic grounds of professional politics; he would outlast the convention and he would catch up with William Singer, but he would not make the mistake of offering a compromise just to preserve his seat at the convention. Second, he felt, as he had so often before, that the convention officials, including people like O'Brien and Califano, were influenced far too much by newspapers and television as they made their decisions. Daley felt that the media created an artificial environment that was not the same as the real world in which politics had to live. What he wanted to convey to O'Brien was that the party guidelines were only guidelines and that a convention makes up its own rules on its own terms. Throw Singer and his crowd out, he wanted McGovern and others to know, and then he would come and work with them. But below his beachside windows, Lake Michigan rose steadily and clots of dune continued to fall into the swirling waters. The lake would, in fact, rise in a fearsome storm on Election Night in November, causing so much damage that the whole county in which Daley's estate lay would be declared a disaster area.

He was angry, as the convention, like a swaying sea animal that lives out of ordinary time and space, rejected his delegates while it accepted the California delegates—all of whom were for McGovern because California followed the unit rule. The new convention rules, however, clearly and unequivocally prohibited the use of the unit rule. To Daley this seemed damned contradictory. It was, at last, a celebration of new politics and a vigil service for old bosses, among whom Daley, in the eyes of the enthusiastic delegates, was thought to be the most ancient and unreformed. The dragon had been penned, if not killed, and the party was now in the hands of a new and, as they styled themselves, freer and more loving generation.

Singer's victory on the floor was to be the high point in his arc of triumph. Caught up like revelers drunk on power, Singer's faction began, in the caucus of the Illinois delegation, to splinter and fall apart. It was not just their arguments about whether the lettuce in the delegates' lunchboxes was picked by the members of Cesar Chavez's Farm Workers Union; it was something more fundamental in their fatal innocence about power and its exercise. Present as delegates were some *ex-officio* members, like Michael Howlett and Illinois State Democratic Chairman John Touhy. The latter, in constant telephone contact with Daley, would give Singer and his group a bitter lesson—more painful than a schoolmaster's caning—in the art of political maneuver, Chicago style.

While a Daley delegate like Twenty-fifth Ward Alderman Vito Marzullo, enraged at his exile from the convention, stormed out of the Diplomat Hotel shouting, "These sons of bitches have treated me like a goddamn dog," Touhy watched as Singer fell into the trap of procedural moves which he had spread under him. The meeting dragged on, tempers flared, and the enthusiasm that had accompanied the triumph over Daley began to sour a little. Singer's people began to disagree among themselves on how to proceed while the clock moved toward dawn and they continued to fail at the task which, in the economy of party power, was now most essential for them: the election of their own candidates to the Democratic National Committee. That was the important move; the convention would last but a few days but the Committee would continue to function and hold the purse and the power.

But Singer could not get his group to follow through, nor could he deal successfully with the intricate motions and modifications which Touhy continued to propose. First light had spread above the green ocean when, in a bone-weary shambles, the delegates accepted Touhy's motion to put off the election until a later time back in Chicago. The day may have been lost, but the long night had been won. Touhy called Daley and said, "Everything is under control again."

"We all know," Daley said softly into the bank of microphones, "everybody knows Dan Walker will make a great governor." It was Election Night, November 7, 1972, and the grim scenario of the summer had played itself out in the windy rain of the day. Walker, dedicated to carving off a large slice of the mayor's power, had beaten the incumbent, Richard Ogilvie, by almost 80,000 votes. A Republican state's attorney, Bernard Carey, had been elected in Nixon's overwhelming sweep of the country. McGovern had lost Illinois, along with 48 other states, but Daley, the rejected boss of the July convention, had delivered Cook County for him. It was not, however, the happiest of nights as Daley turned away from the glaring lights and headed back to the comfort of his family in Bridgeport. Where else could a chieftain recover his strength if not with his wife and children back on South Lowe Avenue where the last yellow leaves of autumn clustered in wet heaps along the curb?

There was nothing more sacred to Daley than his family and, even though he may have drained them as much as he nourished them emotionally, he would permit nobody, on any pretext, to invade their privacy. For years the media had followed them, just as they pursued him, anxious for a story. Finally, the mayor himself provided the story when, at the turn of the year, he gave instructions to City Controller David Stahl to transfer large segments of insurance business, principally, that which had formerly gone to the company of the recently dead Democratic leader Joseph Gill, to Heil and Heil, whose offices were in Evanston, a city just over the northern boundary of Chicago. It was the company which Daley's next-to-youngest son, John, 25, had just joined.

Earl Bush, Daley's veteran public relations director, got word that the newspapers were investigating the shift of business to Heil and Heil and went and asked Daley about it. The mayor exploded at the very idea of such an investigation, claiming defiantly that there was nothing illegal in what had taken place, nothing wrong with giving some business to the firm for which his son now worked.

Bush, wary of the public relations impact of any revelations on the subject, told Daley that, despite its legality, giving $200,-000 in insurance commissions to Heil and Heil might, because his son worked there, be interpreted as Daley's giving the money to himself. Daley was both furious and adamant; could not the chieftain distribute gifts to his own? Was this not a tribal right, the duty, in fact, of any real father to care for his sons? He gave no ground.

On February 8 the story broke in the *Chicago Daily News,* and Daley was questioned about it outside his offices. The mayor, trying now to slam the stable door after the horse was gone, made public a statement which he said had been drawn up a week before. It stated that all city insurance business would be sent out for bid. "We talked about it six months ago," Daley said, "and then two months ago." (It was, in fact, the same month in which Richard Nixon was having some conversations that would finally prove embarrassing to him about the Watergate affair.) Daley was just trying to run the story to ground, to keep the reporters from digging further at him and his family.

But it was to be a month of revelations. Controller David Stahl would carefully say that Daley himself had "suggested" the shift of business to Heil and Heil; Stahl would resign the next month for a job in Washington. Jay McMullen of the *Chicago Daily News* would obtain a copy of a memorandum prepared by Earl Bush several weeks previously that had argued against the insurance transfer and reprint it for the public to read. It was the beginning of the end for Bush, who would shortly be demoted to speechwriter and be replaced as public relations director by Frank Sullivan. His memo, after all, could be construed as showing that Daley had known beforehand the possible consequences of what he was doing. The memorandum in the newspapers was like an ax plunged into the family crest.

It was the week before this, however, when Daley threw aside his control as though it were ill-fitting armor that hindered his fighting; it was then that fumes of rage poured up out of his gut as fierce and black as those from the steel mills at the end of Lake Michigan. He was walking from City Hall to a meeting of the Cook County Democratic Committee, whose headquarters were now in the LaSalle Hotel, when he suddenly saw another banner headline with new charges, this time against his sons Richard and Michael, both lawyers, who had received what were described as "lucrative" court appointments in custodianship cases. If there was not much substance to the story, there was poison in the headline itself, and Daley, walking swiftly, his long dislike of the media coagulated now into an ultimate, lavalike rage in his innards, decided that he had suffered enough. He would let them know just how he felt, and the Cook County Democratic committeemen would be the first to hear about it.

Daley, his face livid, wasted no time in getting to the point. There was only one white-hot focus for his anger at what he experienced as violations of the territory where no stranger was welcome, his home and family. He would never apologize for using his influence to help his sons. "If I can't help my sons," he stormed to the audience that was numbed into silence by his bristling presence, "then they can kiss my ass." There was no sound but that of his own fiery breathing. "I make no apologies to anyone. There are many men in this room whose fathers helped them, and they went on to become fine public officials."

It was a talk that would be long remembered. Daley turned to other subjects, such as President Nixon's slashing of federal funds for cities, and complaints about the Chicago Transit Authority. He used the phrase "God damn" six times before he was through, a measure of his rage better than any other, for Daley never spoke that way in public, and rarely in private. But he was mostly the outraged head of the clan, proud of his bloodlines and committed to helping his own no matter what others thought; he seemed more the king than the elected official, for in his anger the distinctions between him and the city and his treasured family all blurred and then dissolved completely.

It was not a famous day for him but it was a day on which all the misery of the last few years exploded like a planet giving birth to an angry red moon, a blood-red moon that would circle him for the rest of his days. Committeemen would soon be on their feet to try to reassure him, to tell him that they also believed in fathers helping their sons. But now he glared at them in the room where no chair squeaked nor foot shifted.

"If a man can't put his arms around his sons, then what kind of a world are we living in?"

[18]

Survivors

The mayor and the chairman of the City Council Finance Committee, Alderman Thomas E. Keane of the Thirty-first Ward, were in Daley's office checking over the expense accounts of some officials who had traveled overseas on municipal business.

"Look at this," Keane said indignantly as he pointed out an entry to Daley, who leaned forward for a better look. The traveler had entered a $4.00 item as a "club membership" and both the mayor and Keane exploded in anger.

Let us hold them in focus just as they are, gesturing and scowling in well-kindled wrath at the audacity of the man's using city money in such fashion. For here sit two warlords, with hides as coarse as sisal cord, full of scars and triumphs, two men with long memories and harsh looks who had worked together for many years in governing the city of Chicago. They had long ago taken each other's measure, and there was no need to pretend to the deepest sentiments of friendship; they were comrades in arms, authentic professionals who found a sinewy bond in their lack of trust in each other, in the fact that they kept their armor on in each other's presence, for the vulnerability of affection was not a gift they ever exchanged.

Keane had been Daley's closest ally and supporter for almost two decades, but that did not mean that he would not seize every advantage, that did not mean that he would not press the mayor, as, indeed, the mayor pressed him ruthlessly on any occasion; they were not men to turn their backs on each other. But, witnesses to the raising and spending of millions, they enjoyed outrage at a minor expense account item.

Keane, descendant of an old political family, had been with Daley as a state senator in Springfield; he had resigned in 1945, at the request of Mayor Edward Kelly, in order to run for his late father's seat in the City Council. There was little that Keane, a sturdy man with the pinched face of a squire who traveled the length of his land every morning regardless of weather, peering through eyes that had been narrowed against glaring sun or windy rain in order to deliver to himself the satisfaction of seeing all his fences again, there was, in fact, nothing that Keane did not understand about city government and finance. He was another kind of Irish warrior, the brilliant tactician whose Catholic piety, like a full stomach, nuzzled comfortably against his conqueror's heart. And yet, powerful as he was, he could never usurp the chieftain's place, perhaps because he had stopped to pick up so many trophies of war along the way, or perhaps because he had become a millionaire through his many business interests and had not, like Daley, given his complete concentration to the acquisition and preservation of power alone. This may be the difference between a king and a crown prince; it certainly was in Chicago, where these two remarkable men, harsh and decisive, as unsentimental about political moves as surgeons surveying a pan of gallstones, as wise as elders about programs and financing, labored in tandem through most of Daley's years in office. But we must look at them now, at the height of their power and beyond summons or question, two strong men who display for us the essence of the political personality—the crafty, utterly pragmatic capacity to deal with a world that was afflicted with something very like Original Sin.

Perhaps this is why nobody was particularly surprised at

Keane's toughness when, on May 2, 1974, he was indicted on seventeen counts of mail fraud and one count of conspiracy in connection with having assembled and sold off 1900 parcels of tax-delinquent land to various public agencies with enormous financial profits to himself. He was not the first political figure to be pursued by the youthful, John Wayne–sized United States attorney, James R. Thompson.

A Nixon appointee, Thompson had brought down Federal Judge Otto Kerner, former Illinois governor, in the previous year for bribery, conspiracy, mail fraud, income tax evasion, and perjury in connection with a raceway stock scandal. He had also won a conviction of the snowy-haired county clerk, Edward Barrett, for accepting $180,000 in bribes from a voting machine company. Thompson was winning acclaim, and the headlines that would help him become the governor of Illinois in 1976, through his vigorous prosecution of men who had been close to Richard J. Daley. Keane, contemptuous of Thompson, felt that he was being made a prisoner to the U.S. attorney's own political ambitions; he would not surrender the mantle of his own self-assuredness in the face of such charges; no, he would stare icily at reporters and at the public as the media exploded in headlines and special reports about his dilemma.

On the day of Keane's indictment, Daley was holding a summit meeting on criminal justice in his City Hall office. He looked soberly at the newsmen, holding his expression as though posing for an old-fashioned photograph. "I have great confidence," Daley said, "in Thomas Keane as one of the finest leaders in the City Council. I've known him for many, many years, and I think he represents one of the finest family men that I've met. And I know him," Daley continued (neglecting to add just how well he knew him), "and I know his fine wife. I surely am shocked, stunned, to see anything like this happen."

Was this, the reporters wanted to know, part of what the mayor had characterized the month before as a political "vendetta" on the part of Attorney Thompson?

Daley did not alter his expression as he said, in soft tones that did not completely mask his irritation, "It speaks for itself."

The last year had been stressful even for such an agile and proven survivor as Daley himself. It had begun with the attack on his sons, and it had escalated through the convictions of Otto Kerner and of old Eddie Barrett in February and March of 1973. They had tried to get Keane that May on conflict of interest charges, but a bench trial had cleared him and another Democratic alderman of the charges. It seemed as if the agents of every federal bureau had been investigating many of his aides ever since then; they had, Daley knew, found little, but they had used another technique very effectively.

The federal attorney granted immunity to nonpolitical figures involved in cases like Kerner's and Keane's in exchange for their testimony. It was, as Daley saw it, a deceitful and treacherous tactic, but the media had applauded Thompson, while practically convicting every accused Democrat in the headlines. It was enough to make the mayor's already simmering insides boil over in anger. "Where is the justice in this?" he would ask in aggrieved tones.

He was a man still in control but it was hard to be near him without feeling the tension generated by the rasping engines of his self-restraint. He knew very well that all of the investigations—perhaps, a paranoid banner read, the wish of a Republican President?—were aimed finally at him. They were like the exploding shells of an artillery gunner who has not quite got the range yet. Well, the old chieftain was tough, and he would deny knowing anything about these money-making activities of so many of his assistants. They could find no money in his bank account that had come from corrupt sources; he took pride in that. He seemed to many businessmen woefully underpaid, in view of his responsibilities, and yet Daley never took money for himself. Once, when an investment counselor had written to offer his advice on Daley's stock portfolio, the letter had been handed on for answering by an assistant with a notation from Daley's personal secretary, "Confidentially, the mayor has no portfolio."

The year 1973 had ended with the next to the last act in the tragic life of Matthew Danaher, the slender 46-year-old circuit court clerk whose mother, an Eleventh Ward neighbor, had asked Daley to get her son a job back in 1948. Daley had done so, making Danaher his driver, and taking him on as his administrative assistant when he became state revenue director in the Stevenson cabinet. Danaher had been like a son—or perhaps the younger brother he never had—to Daley, who took him along to City Hall when he became mayor in 1955. Danaher was given the job that went to only the most trusted of assistants; he was placed in charge of patronage for Daley. He went everywhere with the mayor; he married and settled down in a new colonial-style house just half a block away from the Daley home on South Lowe. He was everything Daley needed: reasonably bright, willing, and—requisite of requisites—completely loyal to Daley.

And yet there was tragedy just a step away; Danaher had the look of the fellow who gets killed at the end of the movie, the look of faulted innocence which seems to invite doom on every level. Danaher had moved on to become alderman of the Eleventh Ward—there were those who spoke of him as Daley's eventual successor—and later to become a popular vote-getter in the office of circuit court clerk.

Yet the rising curve of his career snapped suddenly in a blind and cruel event, in a night with a curse on it, in the horror of his son's death in Danaher's own arms after he had been struck by a car while going to the store for his parents. He had come home safely once, but he had brought macaroni instead of spaghetti and so he hurried back, a small child at the intersection of South Lowe and 35th Street just by the police station and the fire house; was there a safer place? And so he died in his father's arms and neither Danaher nor his wife nor their life together was the same after that. It was the prelude to an orchestration of disasters that finally destroyed Danaher completely.

He began to drink, the very thing Daley warned his aides about all the time. The mayor was always giving advice about not drinking at lunch; he had, in fact, even called aides who were drinking in bars and told them to get home to their families. He had given strong support to the establishment of the Chicago Alcoholic Treatment Center soon after he had become mayor, and this had become a model institution. Daley was famous for telling politicians the ground rules about giving after-dinner speeches: "Don't talk more than ten minutes. Don't tell off-color stories. If you've had something to drink, stay home."

He would serve drinks to guests and he drank moderately himself. But he had gazed into some wild part of the Irish soul, perhaps in saloon-filled Bridgeport; he had seen crying women waiting for their husbands on payday; he had seen Irish good looks washed away by drink. It was not, he felt, a small weakness.

And now, of all things, Matt Danaher had begun to drink and to stay out late, frequently at piano bars downtown. The mayor's own bodyguard detail would seek him out and sometimes roll him out on his own front lawn at an early hour of the morning. Matt Danaher was lost in Irish melancholy, and it was beginning to show in his work and in his face; he was a wasted man in his forties with a puffy look to his skin and dark circles under his eyes.

Daley was disturbed, but he did not seem to be able to reach his aide. If there was heartache in this, there was also the alarm bell of self-concern, because as the reports came in about Danaher's behavior, Daley began to worry about himself as well as his former star protégé. "Danaher's around in bars talkin' a lot," he said one day, and then added, the real source of his concern finally emerging, "and he's talkin' about *me!*"

The mayor had not survived by being worried about the fate of others. In the long run, the chieftain kept the kingdom together by being concerned finally only for his family and for himself. Let anything else happen, let men hang themselves in their own cruel ways or even let them be drowning an oar's length away; that was the time when self-concern was not to be confused with charity. So it was with Danaher; Daley might know the makings of his fate but, if he could not successfully intervene, he would not be pulled down by the death grip of a collapsing friend. Everyone was a foe in such a moment, everyone who was not part of the clan.

Still, it was bad news when an investigation sponsored by the *Chicago Sun-Times* and the Better Government Association disclosed that Danaher had shared in some $300,000 in payoffs from two Chicago builders who needed zoning changes and private financing in order to build two subdivisions. The disclosure came on December 20, 1973; Danaher had been with Daley on that day just nineteen years before when Daley had first accepted the Democratic slating for the office of mayor, and the memory of this and the closeness of Christmas made it all seem even sadder. Daley seemed more subdued and serious than on previous occasions when reporters had asked him about charges against other Democrats. He had been suffering from a cold, and he spoke hoarsely outside his City Hall office.

"I don't know the facts. If the facts are as alleged, it's a shocking and stunning thing to me."

The next day Daley did not come to work at all. Danaher was not available for comment, but it was announced a week later that he and his wife, who had been separated for six months, were filing for divorce.

Daley was not surprised by Danaher's eventual indictment on federal conspiracy and income tax charges on April 10. Alderman Paul Wigoda, a Democrat from the North Side, who had been sponsored by Thomas Keane, had been indicted on income tax charges in connection with an alleged $50,000 bribe just five days before. In February, Daley's former public relations director, Earl Bush, had been indicted on charges connected with his interest in the advertising firm that held the contracts for O'Hare Field.

The year had held grief enough for the mayor, who, as each

case broke, stolidly denied knowledge of the activities of any of these associates. But everyone in Chicago understood that, under Daley's one-man rule, there had never been any delegation of power, there had never been any activity, of any nature, that could have been carried on without his knowledge. To think otherwise was to be naive; it was a wish for nonexistent virtue in the mayor, whose instincts insisted that power should never be sliced into sections, nor given over, even in molecular amounts, for someone else's use. The Daley kingdom made room for no pretenders to the throne and, if it was true that he had no connection with any of these enterprises, it was also fair speculation that he knew about them, because everything in Chicago finally had to be cleared with him.

And so the pressure on the boiler plates of his soul increased as the indictments, like the knives of a circus artist, thudded closer to his own head. The charges against Keane moved *Chicago Sun-Times* political analyst Jerome Watson to write on Sunday, May 5, 1974, "So important is the indictment that some political sources have speculated that if Keane is convicted, it might dissuade Mayor Daley from seeking re-election in 1975. . . . U.S. Atty. James R. Thompson, whose string of big indictments in city scandals has made him something of a national figure, well could be in a position to send Daley hurtling to the canvas, KOd into a bitter, humiliating Last Hurrah."

The next day, Daley, now in his twentieth year as mayor, went through his regular routine until midmorning, when he began to feel ill; there was a numbness in his leg and his speech was slurred. He asked his secretary to arrange an appointment with his doctor, Thomas Coogan, and, staring straight ahead, surrounded by his police detail, he walked to the elevator, ignoring the greetings of others, and rode down to his limousine.

Daley walked into the doctor's office as, indeed, he would into Presbyterian-St. Luke's Hospital a short time later. Then a veil of secrecy was drawn across the incident. He had suffered a slight stroke. Daley was down, for the first time in his career, while Chicago reacted with shock and disbelief. He would not be seen again in public until after Labor Day; he would undergo surgery to increase the blood flow to his brain through the artery on the left side of his neck. He would talk to his family, and he would even speak to his wife about things as grim as his possible wake and funeral.

And, in a strange way, in a way that nobody could remember, there was a great silence and stillness in the heart of City Hall. He would recuperate at his place in Michigan while the nation went through the last agonies of Watergate and President Nixon's resignation. If there was speculation about his health or his return to office, if there was talk about a possible successor, it was in the most muted tones, for who knew when the king might rise out of the sea and cross the waters to take charge of his battered kingdom once more?

"Hi-ya, gentlemen and friends," Daley said into the glare of television lights; it was September 3, three months after his neck surgery, and the mayor, twenty-five pounds lighter, had returned once more to his kingdom. "It's great to be back," he said in a voice that was reedier and less powerful, as though not all the pipes had yet begun to function.

He seemed subdued and less at the mercy of his roiled stomach, even though the reporters threw questions at him about all the sensitive issues over which he had exploded so fiercely in the spring. This was not a chieftain at bay as much as a man with a new note of peacefulness, of jagged edges having settled into place inside him; he was the same and yet he was a shade different as well. He declined to comment about the roster of political allies scheduled for trial, spoke of bringing the Republican and Democratic conventions to Chicago in 1976, and said that he would give his top priority to work on the 1975 budget.

Was there any medical reason that he should not run again?

"Absolutely none," he replied in thin but certain tones.

"If you were strong enough," a reporter asked, "then you would?"

"Right," the mayor said, adding a moment later, "The state of my health is very good, but the mayor's job is an arduous job. I'll try it and let you know a little later."

After a quarter of an hour, Daley moved slightly away from the rostrum and, as he had a thousand times before, hung a pennant of challenge in the air. "Any more questions?" Then, as the assembled journalists watched him closely for the slightest sign of a limp or a sway, the mayor moved steadily and swiftly, the sovereign back in stride, across the outer room and into his office. As one reporter noted, all that was needed was a band to play "Chicago."

Later in the fall he would seem less sure of his intention to run again. "The wish isn't always there," he said to a newsman's question, but this, despite the accumulating charges, was a thought more like a distraction at prayer than a serious hesitation; merely mentioning it caused it to fade away, a twitch of consciousness never to be experienced again. Daley never wanted any other job; he had, in fact, rejected all offers of cabinet posts or nominations for higher office. His soul was coextensive with the city and, having moved out of the shadow of the stroke and the surgery, he was back in the position that fulfilled him, the office in which, despite crises and setbacks, he was supremely happy.

One of his oldest foes had speculated even before Daley's stroke about the reasons that might keep him from running again. Fifth Ward Alderman Leo Despres, writing in a local newspaper, charged that men "whom Daley has publicly praised, elevated, and protected for years" had been pillaging the city. He also cited the "insurance premiums and lush appointments" given to members of Daley's own family and added that "when he discharged Earl Bush as public relations man . . . he made a grave error of judgment." Despres charged that Daley had "abandoned the skillful Bush policy of 'Bend to the wind, and spring back later.' The present policy seems to be: 'Let the wind blow.' "

He had once told a friend, in reply to the purest of hypothetical questions, that if he had had to choose between being mayor and being Cook County Democratic chairman, he would have taken the latter position. The question—like the answer—was academic. Daley had both positions, and he intended to keep them both tightly in his own grasp.

The fall offered little comfort except at the very end when, in December, he would travel to Kansas City for the mini-convention of the Democrats, at which he would be received warmly as a party leader by the delegates from around the country. The good name of Daley and the honor of the city of Chicago were being made whole; the long forced march from the wreckage of 1968 had led into fresh uplands at last. The king would return to Chicago certain of his decision about the 1975 campaign, which he now envisioned as the next rather than the last hurrah. December was the traditional slate-making month; it was filled with sweet memories of political challenges accepted against the background of the first snowfall and the bells and lights of Christmas. Daley would enter the hotel meeting room; why, it would be like old times with the cheers and applause that are acclaim enough for any ruler, and in a moment, as predictable and yet as touching as a sunrise, a necessary ritual moment, the chieftain would proclaim his willingness to continue his rule. Against the slide and snap of cameras, he would announce that he would join once again in the great good work of the Democratic party in Chicago. The rest would be lost in cheers and applause, in the relief of many and the stifled regrets of a few that the old warrior was ready for another campaign.

But October had been filled with woe as guilty verdicts came in the same week against Aldermen Paul Wigoda and Thomas Keane and former Public Relations Director Earl Bush. Daley had agreed to testify at the trial of Bush, who had been acquitted of a number of the original charges at a previous trial. At that time, because of his illness, Daley had given a deposition in which he had denied any knowledge of Bush's ownership of the Dell Advertising Company, which won the contracts for the work at O'Hare Field. The trial had come down finally to one point: Bush had filed a statement with the city clerk in which he stated his ownership of Dell, but he had omitted this fact in the statement copy filed in Daley's office. Was it illegal for a man to deceive his boss? Was it unethical? And how much did Daley really know anyway? The government, as it had done in the case against Keane, invoked mail fraud as a charge, on the grounds that Bush had received his dividends by letter through the postal system. What would Daley say?

As it turned out, it was not so much. He praised Bush for his loyalty and his work; he had been, the mayor said softly in the twenty-third–floor courtroom of the Federal Building, a "very fine employee." It was a low key performance as Daley said that if Bush had recommended that a certain agency be considered, he would have acted as he always did, and sought more information, inviting the interested parties to make a presentation to William Downs, the commissioner of aviation. It was gentle testimony and quiet support, if anything, for his old assistant. As Daley left the courtroom, he was confronted by reporters with the news of Keane's conviction that very afternoon. The mayor's bodyguards pushed the reporters aside as Daley, without a word, entered an elevator to the basement, where his limousine waited to take him home to Bridgeport.

So it had been a hard year and yet, as the shopping days before Christmas dwindled, Daley had set his face, which home cooking had begun to restore to its fullness, toward the future. He would run again, for there was a score to settle with William Singer, the independent Democrat who had stolen his convention place in 1972 and who was now going to challenge him, along with former State's Attorney Edward Hanrahan and black hopeful Richard Newhouse, in the February primary. It was Sunday, December 15, when Daley received a phone call to tell him that Matt Danaher, Matt, the once-favored prince, had been found dead in his room at the Ambassador West Hotel, where he had been living for six months since his separation from his wife. Matt, the high liver who had hired the Shannon Rovers to play at his political meetings, died in the quiet loneliness, in the melancholy exile of the nearby North Side hotel.

Daley and his wife expressed their sympathy and the mayor, with the gravest of expressions, served as a pallbearer when Danaher's body was brought down the steps from the Nativity of Our Lord Church in Bridgeport. It had been a tortured year but, if many had fallen, Daley himself was still erect, for one did not survive by looking back.

There is a limit to sentiment in political survivors; they may feel sorry for others but their main preoccupation has to do with preserving their own skin. Tom Keane has done it in the Federal Correctional Institute in Lexington, Kentucky, in the great red-brick compound set among the white-fenced horse farms, where the bulletin board in the lobby, like that in a convention motel, announces that the warden is having a staff meeting in the Sulky Room at 1:00 P.M. It is nonetheless a prison, despite its modernistic logo on the glass front door, and Keane, every spirit of Chicago politics still sparking in the narrow eyes beneath the wiry white brows, is not surrendering to it. The toughness, so like Daley's that they could have exchanged skin grafts, is still there, as is the certainty that he has been unjustly deprived of his liberty by an excessively ambitious federal attorney.

"Don't give them any idea I'm doing penance down here," he says simply, and one feels in the company of legions of Chicago politicians, past and present, who have never surrendered an inch of their self-righteousness.

Keane, in his seventies, is playing the only game in town, surviving, the great contest which, for much higher stakes, he has played all his life. He had even threatened the prison with a lawsuit for denying him basic privileges during his first months there.

"They kept a key in the door," he says, looking as lined now as the aged Adenauer.

He talks of the great programs that he and Daley got

through the City Council, and of his wife, now holding his seat in the council, and his twenty-three grandchildren.

"I admired Daley and Truman," he says, "because they both knew government so thoroughly and they were both so decisive."

Here is the essence of political self-assuredness, the seed and flower of the strain, made hardier by jail as some organisms are by penicillin; of Irish big city power; of the stuff, coarse but vital, of the captains and kings, the Keanes and Daleys, the survivors of the Democratic wars. For Keane speaks also of piety and the need for religious education for the proper emotional formation of the child. And he talks of his spiritual reading, of *Saul of Tarsus*, his favorite book, and of how he kneels down to say his prayers every night and of his sadness that his roommates—bankers and financiers—don't follow his good example. He speaks too of the downfall of modern civilization, brought on by sexual license and gambling, the latter made worse by state approval. He looks and speaks like a bishop.

Keane, in whose breath one senses something of the many whispered conferences with the mayor, in whose eyes one can still see the glance, hard and full of light as a diamond, that locked so often with the even harder eyes of Richard J. Daley, has turned finally to writing. He would like to do a book on proper planning and financing, a manual to explain how Chicago kept its fiscal balance while New York and other places fell apart.

"But the offers I get are not for books like that. They all want me to write a Watergate-style book."

And (humorless, one is sure) Keane smiles—a knowing and contented smile—and asks a question for which he wants and needs no answer. "What do they want me to do," he says, "put everybody in the penitentiary?"

[19]

The Last Hurrahs

> It is not a public chore, to be got over with.
> It is a way of life. It is the life of a domes-
> ticated political and social creature who is
> born with a love for public life, with a de-
> sire for honor, with a feeling for his fel-
> lows; and it lasts as long as needs be.
> —Plutarch

"You're supposed to be down to City Hall," Daley said with mock seriousness into the telephone. "You're scheduled to be second in line."

"Second in line for what?" responded the bewildered Father Gilbert Graham, who was just preparing to go to St. Patrick's Church to offer the mass of its patron saint on March 17, 1975.

"To have your behind painted green!" Daley responded with an explosion of laughter. "My mother always told us that she had to go to City Hall on St. Patrick's Day in order to have that done!"

Daley was enjoying himself on the feast which, in Chicago, had come to celebrate him as much as St. Patrick. It was a day, as he had told reporters at his news conference the previous Friday, "to forget your gloom and doom, to have a little humor, a little food, a little drink."

And Richard J. Daley was ready for a celebration. On February 25 he had faced off in the Democratic primary against William Singer, the dragon-killer of the 1972 convention, and had crushed him along with challengers Edward Hanrahan and Richard Newhouse. Daley's victory, despite opposition from some of the newspapers, had been massive and reassuring; he could replace his sword in his scabbard, for he had settled a score and healed a wound. His facial expression did not change, of course, and to look at him one would hardly know whether he had rejoiced or, perhaps more likely, had merely made a mental note of a scalp taken and a debt paid off, and passed on to other things.

He arrived like a patriarch at old St. Patrick's Church for mass. The kilted Shannon Rovers, their eyes sparkling above their puffing cheeks, were arrayed on either side of the church entrance as the black limousine with its outriding police escort rounded the corner and nudged its way into the large crowd. A bulky man in a tweed coat whispered, in the manner of a child first spotting Santa Claus, "It's himself!"

The door of the Cadillac opened and Richard J. Daley, wearing a bright green snap-brim hat and holding a shillelagh thick as a drainpipe in one hand, stepped into the sunshine to the open-throttled piping and the applause of the men and women who had waited to see him. The mayor leaned back to assist his wife out of the car and swept the crowd with his impassive glance; he looked as healthy as Khrushchev waiting at the plane steps for the welcoming girls to hand him a bouquet. His left eye seemed clouded for just an instant as he gathered his children and grandchildren about him for a family procession up the church steps, but, except for an almost invisible, talcum-powdered scar that rose an inch or two above his collar toward his left ear, there was no sign of the effects of the stroke or the surgery of the previous year.

The primary campaign had not been without its problems, and Daley had, on occasion, lost his temper, especially over the twin devils of his later years, the problem of racial discrimination and charges against the Chicago Police Department, to which he was tied by so many bonds of kinship and loyalty. He had been angry at the decision of Federal Judge Prentice Marshall which had denied $76,000,000 in funds to the city on the grounds that the Police Department had not been sufficiently integrated. Daley had been convinced that the case was filled with hypocrisy, with the desire of a Republican administration to harass him as it had done in the prosecution of so many of his aides. The Chicago Police Department had a good record of integration, far better than most cities, and he had stormed over the problem for months.

Shortly before the primary he had disclosed that the city had been forced to borrow $55,000,000 from Chicago banks to tide it over until the revenue-sharing funds, frozen by Judge Marshall, were released. The judge, Daley said hotly, was "a disgrace to the federal judiciary," and he went on to claim that the city was in compliance with all the court orders in the case. "There's never been a more flagrant abuse of power of a federal judge than happened in this case," the mayor said, as he assured the citizens of Chicago's financial solvency.

He had been equally upset a few weeks previously when he charged that the media had distorted the remarks of his fire commissioner, fellow Bridgeporter Robert Quinn, on the subject of integration in his department. It had been reported that in a 1973 deposition, Quinn had tossed off a question about the investigation of discrimination with the answer "Why should I? I am more concerned with other stuff than that."

Daley, clearly irritated at inquiries about the matter, had made a frontal assault on the assembled reporters, as he hurled back what may have been his favorite question for rebuttal, "Did you read all the testimony? Don't believe everything you read in the papers. I thought it was proper, if you're not reporting for political purposes, to report all the questions and answers, and not take things out of context. That's what was done to Quinn."

Yes, Daley was feisty again. He had, in fact, quietly retained Earl Bush to write his speeches and aid in campaign planning through 1975 and 1976. It seemed like old times and, despite his savage frame of mind toward the press, he was winning, in some strange alchemical way, the affection and respect of many of the reporters even as he attacked them head-on. "What kind of fairness are you people trying to portray?" he asked, not pausing but shifting into tones of ridicule. "Fortunately the people doubt your credibility, so I'm not worried about it." He gazed stonily at the journalists. "Tomorrow they will say, 'With a flash of anger, Daley said these things. He reddened up. They thought he was going to have another stroke.' "

But he had not suffered another stroke; he had won another victory and, as he gazed from the State Street reviewing stand at the first of the 156 units of the parade, he beamed, in anticipation both of the day's celebrations and of the sixth term in office which he would claim two weeks later in a race against John Hoellen, the lonely Republican who had opposed Daley so long in the City Council. Daley would take 78 percent of the vote that night and even see that Hoellen, scapegoat and sacrificial lamb wrapped into one anguished and harried candidate, lost his aldermanic seat as well.

The election would find Daley campaigning on a highly reduced schedule, but it would be one last great seal on his reinstated influence and power. Perhaps its best symbol would lie in the fact that Hoellen was not even able to get President Gerald Ford to do more than shake his hand in a White House corridor. It would be an Election Night to suit every whim of the recovered warrior, who would once again promise in almost inaudible tones on that evening to embrace mercy and walk humbly with his God. The city of neighborhoods would embrace him in his great victory and he would feel clear of the terrible years through which he had just passed, the dark years of shame and embarrassment, of charges and indictments against family and old friends, of visits by the angels of illness and death; yes, he could wipe them away as one brushes away the sour-tasting veil of a spider's web in the dark. Chicago loved him as much as had the policeman's grandmother who, laid out in her best dress, her rosary twined in her fingers, wore a "Daley in '75" badge like a corsage on the night of her wake.

"Your Eminence," Daley said, turning to Cardinal John Cody and pinning a shamrock on his collar, "here's some green for the parade."

Daley looked pleased as labor leaders began to climb up from the street to give him their greetings. "Say hello to the Cardinal," Daley said, as he turned each one toward Cody, who, although younger than Daley, looked gray and lifeless next to him. The stand was as busy as an anthill all through the afternoon as political allies, business supporters, and persons of varying degrees of celebrity were brought to wish Daley a happy St. Patrick's Day.

"Say hello to the Cardinal," he bade each one, like a faithful son fearful that an aged parent might be ignored at a party. It was a grand day, as the afternoon sun kept the cool shadows of March at bay. It might have been a time for remembrance, for all the twenty years, come now and gone, of his tenure in City Hall.

There was the time back in his first term when a labor leader from New York had come to apply pressure on Daley, who was then mediating a taxi strike. The burly man, unaware of the moods or humors of Chicago, had entered the mayor's office while the cab company officials were meeting in a room down the corridor. He would show Daley some Eastern toughness.

"Look out at LaSalle Street," he said, not even addressing Daley by name or title. "Not a cab there." He gestured toward the street as Daley watched him without even a hint of reaction. "That's our power!" the union leader stated, "and that's where we start from. There's no bargaining for us. We have nothing to lose, and the owners ought to understand it. It's our terms or no terms."

The mayor rose and walked to the window, glanced out, and then, turning back to the union leader, he began to speak—danger sign of danger signs—very softly and deliberately. "Yes, I admit you are right. There are no cabs out there." He took a step toward the union man and looked directly at him. "But now let me tell you something. These drivers have about enough money to last until tonight. Tomorrow, a few of them will be out on the street. And the day after that, more of them will be out. And the next day the street will be filled with cabs." Daley paused; he was moving in without blinking, as steady as a cannon adjusting its trajectory. "Now, listen to this. You don't come in here and try to threaten me. You don't come in here and say you won't negotiate." It was very quiet now for, although the mayor and the union boss were a foot apart, they were locked in combat. "And if your men try to do anything to any of those drivers, ten thousand Chicago policemen will treat your people the way they would any lawbreaker." Daley paused. "Now, let's get this settled right now." He sounded as though he were ready for any contest—arm-wrestling, a bare-knuckle brawl, or pistols at twenty paces. "We're here to talk. Those men down the hallway are here in good faith. Do you want to talk or not?" Daley's presence had curled, like a wave gathering energy, and had broken in a great shudder of white water over the man, as he added, his simplest words being the most ominous, "You aren't scaring any of us."

The labor leader, glad to be standing even though he was now sopping wet, replied quietly, "I get what you're saying. I think we'd better talk."

Men were nothing if not controlled in his presence, even when he was telling a story or trying to make a joke. Daley did not exchange even humor on the same level with other men; his was a chaffing, one-step-up kind of merriment, a shouldering exercise in steering the conversation his way, in keeping it in his own hands. His laugh, a shaking eruption of teasing giggles and hurricane-force laughter, drew those nearby with him, even when their will was set not to be amused. They were drawn by something that attracted and bewildered them at the same time, for his laugh was almost a phenomenon in itself, the symbol of his own satisfaction in or relishing of a situation, a judgment he handed down that displayed his amusement and stated that it would stand whether anybody else agreed or not; it was the laughter of a man who saw the world as a king might, from the perspective of a throne, the laughter of a man whose jolliness was almost a declaration of independence, the laughter that said he was at the center of his own good times and if you did not join in, you might be left standing alone.

Daley's charm lay at least partially in the way he supplied a universe of meaning for others, who, in exchange for their loyalty, were encouraged and rewarded, not merely with jobs or contracts, but with some sense of well-being about themselves. Such endowments were not given cheaply, and those who served Daley found themselves in a difficult position because they needed him and loved him and yet they recognized their profound dependence on him and became uneasy and hostile about it. Once they had signed on, they were given over for life to his service, to unquestioning support and devotion; if it made their lives, it also extracted something from them, something like the price people pay who are nice to rich and imperious relatives in whom they invest their best hopes.

At the far end of the stand Governor Daniel Walker, the independent Democrat who had supported Singer against the mayor in the primary, had stood bareheaded all through the parade. Daley had not even glanced in his direction. Walker, with the handsomeness of a man in a cigarette ad, checked his watch and, somewhat edgily, began to move toward Daley to say a formal good-bye. Walker touched Daley's arm and the mayor seemed startled, as though he had no idea that Walker had even been there until that moment. In the surprised tones of a man implying that he would surely have killed the fatted calf had he known Walker would be there, Daley said, "Oh, hello, Gov'ner."

Walker began to whisper a sentence about leaving early, but Daley had already taken his arm and begun to move him down toward Chicago's Archbishop.

"Say hello to the Cardinal," Daley said, as he turned back to see a float commemorating his mother. "Lillian Dunne Daley Was a Feminist," the banner read, and Daley good-naturedly called, "Sure she was!" into the roar of the crowd.

But Daley had thoughts about Walker, who was, after all, fumbling for the keys to the mayor's own kingdom. Even if he

was a Democrat, he was obviously dangerous and would have
to be eliminated.

Several years before, Daley had sent an aide to a meeting of
some police officers who had become irritated with Superintendent O. W. Wilson's efforts to assert greater authority over
them. The mayor's assistant had been roughed up and thrown
out of St. Jude's Meeting Hall. A few weeks later, one of the
policemen who had organized the meeting came to City Hall
with the assistant's hat, which had been cleaned and reblocked;
he had also brought photographers to get some publicity out of
this gesture. Daley became furious when he heard about the
incident. "Why the hell did you let him pull a stunt like that on
you?" he asked. Daley then instructed him for future reference.
"Listen to your stomach. Your first reaction is always better.
He's a no-good son of a bitch and you resented his bringing
your hat back. You should have trusted your resentment and
said, 'Get out of here. I've got no meeting with you.' "
But Daley's stomach had not proved to be infallible. It had
not helped him a few years earlier when black Congressman
Ralph Metcalfe, a one-time Olympic athlete and former party
loyalist, raised a question about the problem of police brutality. That, as had so many questions about the police, infuriated
Daley, who nevertheless agreed to hold a meeting on the subject. He called Earl Bush and gave him a list of people to whom
telegrams of invitation should be sent. Metcalfe's name had
been purposely omitted, a stroke of the pen whose energies had
been pumped up from the deepest well of Daley's bile. Bush
returned to the mayor's office to suggest that Metcalfe be invited and the mayor, flashing into a rage, rose from his desk
and physically chased Bush out of the room. A short time later
Daley calmed down and notified his secretary to send Metcalfe
an invitation. By one of those quirks of fate, however, the delay
proved to be crucial, and Congressman Metcalfe did not receive his telegram in time. He broke openly with Daley after
that, donning the mantle of a hero in the press and causing
Daley more inner grief.

But, despite the occasional misjudgments and miscalcula-
tions of his stomach, Daley continued to operate instinctively
to the very end of his days.

Daley enjoyed the parade, which lasted until late in the afternoon. It had nourished his sense of himself and of his Irish
heritage. Even better, it had been an occasion to honor his
wife, Eleanor Daley; she and the widow of the old plumber,
Steve Bailey, had been the Grand Marshals.

We cannot understand Daley unless we understand the love
story, simple and old-fashioned, at the heart of his life. Eleanor
Daley was not a person who complemented Richard Daley;
she matched him almost exactly in conviction, devotion, and
toughness. It was a relationship into which we cannot look too
deeply; it was one whose strength was best measured in small
gestures, in the ease of their intimacy when they were together,
in the quality of their fidelity, and in their fierce commitment
to the values of Bridgeport. It was a relationship that gave him
life and fixed him in a certain cultural setting at the same time;
it was elixir and cement for the mayor, who, if he understood
the sexual weakness of men, allowed no breath of it to be connected with his own life. Eleanor kept things going while
Daley led his triumphant and infinitely busy political life; she
maintained the home, raised the children, and kept in touch, in
a way that defies the understanding of many modern wives,
with the man she loved. It is an old-fashioned story but Daley,
the modernizer of cities, the innovator in governmental programs, lived an old-fashioned life.

After this St. Patrick's Day, the mayor could look across the
coming year to the Presidential primary campaigns, to the
visits by all the Democratic hopefuls to his City Hall office; he
could see himself restored at last to the great councils of the
Democratic party. And, so indeed, he was, when in July 1976
he traveled to New York for the convention in Madison
Square Garden. When he was in New York, Daley always remarked, "I get the feelin' that nobody's in charge here."

But he was sought out by interviewers from all over the world as he sat on the aisle in the Illinois delegation, a respected and much-honored elder statesman. Perhaps there was a small moment of revenge for him when, as Senator George McGovern got up to speak, he left his own seat, saying, "I've got to go get a sandwich."

In September, Daley would stage a torchlight parade for Jimmy Carter, and, on emerging from his home on Election Day, he would glance at the lowering skies and say, "It will be a great Democratic victory."

But it was not so in the Illinois governor's race, in which Michael Howlett, who portrayed himself as independent of Daley during the campaign, went down to defeat, and the Republican state's attorney was re-elected, despite strenuous Democratic efforts to unseat him. There were commentators who said that Daley had been the big loser in the election, but he did not believe what he read in the papers, and he did not feel in the least shaken about his domination of the city of Chicago. He began, in fact, to talk actively again about programs for Chicago. The long climb back from the disgrace of 1968 had been completed and he could turn his full attention once more to municipal affairs.

At the same time he began to speak in public of things which he had seldom mentioned before. He referred, for example, to the fact that he sometimes made grammatical errors, something that had previously been a keenly sensitive subject. He spoke, in a way that few could understand, about the fact that many men had tried to corrupt him in his life, but none had succeeded. He seemed to deal with bits and pieces of his soul that were snagged or snarled; if we pulled on the thread, what would we discover in his unconscious as December began in icy rain and snow? Do we sense some misgiving, some slight hint of his efforts to deal with issues or events that had supposedly been dealt with long before?

To everybody he would seem the same, still energetic, still in control, even as autumn drifted slowly down to its last few days. It was the season with which so many memories had been associated, the days before Christmas in which he had managed his own first slating as a mayoral candidate and during which he had repledged it so many times, the sweet season of Christmas, in which, with the help of his smallest grandchildren, he lighted a Christmas tree in the Civic Center Plaza "for all the children of Chicago who don't have one." He joined in the singing of the Christmas carols and, as one passed beyond the Picasso statue, his would be the ruddiest face against the cold dark evening.

Something was being worked out in the last days before Christmas; cycles were intersecting, and clocks and seasons moved steadily in an ever more exact and mysterious synchronization.

Bob Hope came to his office and cracked a stream of jokes about Chicago and about the Catholic School–Public School Football Championship Game that was to be played on December 18. "You people don't fool around here, do you?" Hope said, as though giving a TV monologue. "You put it right on the billboards, Catholic against Public," and Daley enjoyed the joke immensely.

It was a full week, with time to attend the luncheon of the Irish Fellowship Club at which Leon Uris, author of *Trinity,* a novel sympathetic to the Catholic Irish, was the speaker. Uris told of discussing his book at a press conference in London. "And now I am held in the same esteem the press used to reserve for Frank Sinatra and Mayor Daley."

The mayor laughed loudly.

He went to businessman Pat O'Malley's annual party on Friday night and to the benefit for St. Ignatius High School on Saturday. Sunday was the Christmas feast at the mayor's house and all the children and grandchildren were there; Father Graham offered a home mass and presents were exchanged.

It was bitter cold on Monday morning, and his wife urged him to see the doctor right away since he had felt some discomfort during the weekend. No, he said, he had appointments to keep; he would see Dr. Coogan that afternoon. Besides, they had to go to the department heads' breakfast, and they would talk later of their plans to visit Ireland. There was a mood of fullness in his life in this last month of 1976; he seemed more settled and he took to quoting a line from Robert Bolt's *A Man for All Seasons:* "If you can't make it all right, make it as little wrong as possible." But, what were the invisible forces that inhabited this day? What was this date anyway?

The weekend had been, day for day, like that weekend twenty-two years before, when he had told the Democratic Central Committee that he had to talk over his slating for mayor with his family; he would let them know on Monday, yes, Monday the twentieth, at about two o'clock. And now the revolving hands on all the clocks would meet; they were aligned almost exactly as Dr. Coogan explained to Daley that he thought he should be hospitalized for further tests. The last seconds were marked off stiffly as the mayor called his son and replaced the phone. It was just after 2:00 P.M. and twenty-two years—almost to the minute—from the time Daley had taken up the challenge of becoming Chicago's mayor.

Now from some level deep in the recesses of his chieftain's awareness, in the caverns from which arose his incredible powers of control over self and city, he laid it down for good.

Index